DATE DUE

RACE, AMERICAN LITERATURE AND TRANSNATIONAL MODERNISMS

Modern poetry crossed racial and national boundaries. The emergence of poetic modernism in the Americas was profoundly shaped by transatlantic contexts of empire-building and migration. In this ambitious book, Anita Patterson examines cross-currents of influence among a range of American, African-American and Caribbean authors. Works by Whitman, Poe, Eliot, Pound and their avant-garde contemporaries served as a heritage for black poets in the USA and elsewhere in the New World. In tracing these connections, Patterson argues for a renewed focus on intercultural and transnational dialogue in modernist studies. This bold and imaginative work of transnational literary and historical criticism sets canonical American figures in fascinating new contexts and opens up new readings of Langston Hughes, Derek Walcott and Aimé Césaire. This book will be of interest to scholars of American and African-American literature, modernism, postcolonial studies and Caribbean literature.

ANITA PATTERSON is Associate Professor of English and American Studies at Boston University.

CAMBRIDGE STUDIES IN AMERICAN LITERATURE AND CULTURE

Editor
Ross Posnock, *Columbia University*

Founding Editor
Albert Gelpi, *Stanford University*

Advisory Board
Alfred Bendixen, *Texas A&M University*
Sacvan Bercovitch, *Harvard University*
Ronald Bush, *St. John's College, University of Oxford*
Wai Chee Dimock, *Yale University*
Albert Gelpi, *Stanford University*
Gordon Hutner, *University of Illinois, Urbana–Champaign*
Walter Benn Michaels, *University of Illinois, Chicago*
Kenneth Warren, *University of Chicago*

Recent books in this series

RACE, AMERICAN LITERATURE AND TRANSNATIONAL MODERNISMS

ANITA PATTERSON

CAMBRIDGE
UNIVERSITY PRESS

CAMBRIDGE UNIVERSITY PRESS
Cambridge, New York, Melbourne, Madrid, Cape Town, Singapore, São Paulo, Delhi

Cambridge University Press
The Edinburgh Building, Cambridge CB2 8RU, UK

Published in the United States of America by Cambridge University Press, New York

www.cambridge.org
Information on this title: www.cambridge.org/9780521884051

First published 2008

Printed in the United Kingdom at the University Press, Cambridge

A catalogue record for this publication is available from the British Library

ISBN 978-0-521-88405-1 hardback

Contents

Acknowledgments

I am grateful to the many people who made this book possible. Thanks first to Christopher Ricks, Werner Sollors, Bonnie Costello, John Paul Riquelme, Larry Breiner, and Jahan Ramazani, as well as Ronald Bush, Larry Buell, Cristanne Miller, Susan Mizruchi, Maurice Lee and James Winn who generously offered responses to chapter drafts. The translations, and any errors in them or anywhere else in these pages, are my own. I am also grateful to Derek Walcott for granting me an interview, and to my fellow Americanists and other colleagues at Boston University for their inspiration, advice, and friendship. In addition I would like to thank my students at Boston University for their questions and insight, and the Humanities Foundation for funding that brought the project to fruition. Thanks also to Ray Ryan at Cambridge University Press for taking interest in the book, to series editor Ross Posnock for his continual support, to Joanna Breeze and Maartje Scheltens for help through all phases of production, to Leigh Mueller for her meticulous copy-editing, and to my anonymous readers, whose superb suggestions fundamentally reshaped my argument. Sections of the book were presented at the Modernist Studies Association, the International American Studies Association, and at the American Studies Program at Doshisha University in Kyoto. I am indebted to all who contributed to these collegial occasions. Part of chapter 4 appeared in different from in *The Journal of Commonwealth Literature*, and is reproduced by permission of Sage Publications Ltd.

I dedicate this book to my husband Orlando, whose love I will always cherish, and to our daughter Kaia, born in the midst of my revisions, who has brought such everlasting joy and hope.

Introduction
Towards a comparative American poetics

"Those countries," says T. S. Eliot, "which share the most history, are the most important to each other, with respect to their future literature."[1] The purpose of this book is to examine how shared history – of colonial settlement, empire-building, slavery, cultural hybridity and diasporic cosmopolitanism – informed the emergence, and revisionary adaptation, of modernist idioms in the Americas.

James Clifford reminds us that the global practice of migration is very old and widespread.[2] Still, critics such as Amy Kaplan, Betsy Erkkila and John Carlos Rowe have suggested that the formation of American literature should be examined in light of the diasporic consequences and multilingual contexts of imperialism.[3] Sensitive to the constructed nature of national myths, Americanists are ever more alert to the need for analytical perspectives that situate United States cultures in a transnational framework.

Within sociology, the term "transnationalism" has, since the mid-1990s, been used to denote social processes involved in the movement of migrant populations from one nation-state to another, processes that call into question the geographical delineation of national boundaries.[4] In 1993, Paul Gilroy noted how attention to "transnational structures of circulation and intercultural exchange" brought about by diasporic history could help diminish the "tragic popularity of ideas about the integrity and purity of cultures."[5] Seven years later, Amritjit Singh and Peter Schmidt announced the arrival of a "transnational moment" in literary scholarship, where the analytical frameworks of postcolonial and ethnic studies are being productively confronted with one another. The revelation of shared histories, they insist, calls for new comparative studies of diasporic identities across national boundaries.[6]

Such renewed interest in comparative methodologies has already contributed a great deal to American Studies, helping critics uncover hidden nationalist agendas and move beyond regional ethnocentrism.[7] I want to push this argument further, though, by studying how transnationalism informs our understanding not just of "black," "postcolonial" or "ethnic" writers, but of American modernism more generally. Certainly, as Homi Bhabha contends, we should bear in mind crucial discrepancies among various manifestations of cosmopolitanism, and the suffering of those who were forced to migrate to the New World.[8] But Rowe is also right to suggest that many people, not just slaves and exploited migrants, were dislocated by imperialism; to forget this, he argues, would occlude the densely interwoven and variegated histories out of which these new global phenomena arose.[9]

With regard to the United States, the story of these historic uprootings has been told many times before.[10] The Great Migration of 1630, the accelerating advance of the western frontier, and the arrival of 35 million transatlantic European immigrants during the nineteenth and early twentieth centuries present a vivid backdrop for the sustained, paradoxically fruitful confrontation of disparate national cultures, relations tortuously inscribed in the contradictory poetics of self-identification on both sides of the Atlantic ever since the colonial period. Between 1880 and 1930 alone, 27 million people, mostly from Southern and Eastern Europe, came to America in the hope of escaping starvation, at the same time that many Americans were migrating internally to urban areas, especially in the northeast and midwest.

Why did migration remain so consequential for American literature in the twentieth century? The estrangement, alienating aesthetics and cultural self-reflexivity of literary modernism involve, as Anthony Giddens has observed, an oscillation between local and global points of view that was brought on by enhanced mobility.[11] Raymond Williams surmises that, because so many artists were immigrants, and experienced their role as "stranger" in such fundamentally new ways, migration served as an important catalyst of modernist and avant-garde movements.[12] Wondering at the vast scale and consequences of New World diasporic history, and only hinting at its possible effect on the oddly measured cadences of American verse, Henry James ambivalently questioned the very meaning and possibility of nationhood: "Who and what is an alien, when it comes to that, in a country peopled from the first under the jealous eye of history? – peopled, that is, by migrations at once extremely recent, perfectly traceable and urgently required . . . Which is the American, by these scant measures?"[13]

The opening chapters of this book lay a foundation for those which follow by establishing a context for Eliot's transnational self-conception as a New World poet. Tracing a line of development from Poe and Whitman, to Jules Laforgue (who was born in Uruguay), to Eliot and the Guadeloupean

Creole poet St.-John Perse, I show how the reciprocal exchange of influences between Eliot and Perse helped to nourish the germination of modernist forms in Francophone Caribbean poetry. A. James Arnold has persuasively shown how early poetry by Aimé Césaire was inspired by modernism in Europe, and Michael Dash has argued for modernism's role in shaping the political and literary cultures of Haiti and Martinique.[14] But neither of these scholars examines how Eliot and Perse aided the growth of poetic modernism in Francophone regions. Reconfiguring the preconceived boundaries of American literature, and reconciling historiographic methods with formal analysis and postcolonial theory, I uncover a dense matrix of hemispheric and transatlantic convergences.

Chapter 1 demonstrates that the transnational implications of Poe's landscapes and style exerted a far greater and more direct influence on Eliot's work than critics have previously maintained. Adapting topographical methods from Poe, Eliot creates richly ambiguous geographical idioms that deepen his poetry's ties to history and express his transnational predicament by evoking contrasts between the Old World and the New. Exploring Eliot's progressive engagement with Perse, I show how a common attraction to Poe as a New World antecedent made fruitful, intercultural relations possible, and laid the foundation for the flourishing of modernist styles in the Americas.

There has been a growing interest in the problem of Eliot's anti-Semitism, but we have still to learn more about the related question of how his poems instantiate his awareness of hybridity on the American frontier.[15] Chapter 2 examines neglected but essential sources of hybridity in Whitman's poetry that explain why Whitman exerted such a strong, inescapable influence on Laforgue, Eliot and Perse. The first of these is the colonial settlement of the New World by the French, Spanish and British, a legacy indelibly etched in New World landscapes. The second involves Amerindian place names that recall the practice of "regeneration through violence" as a constitutive feature of the frontier.[16] These recollections, and the fact that Eliot's early encounter with Whitman happened indirectly through Laforgue, are powerfully brought to bear on Eliot's choice of French as the primary medium in which to sculpt a hybrid idiom. Situated within the Whitmanian contexts elaborated over the course of my argument, the importance of Eliot's translation of Perse's *Anabase*, and Eliot's gradual recognition of the cultural New World dilemmas he shared with Perse, will be brought to light. The painful obliquity of Eliot's reference to the frontier in early poems is, I argue, comparable to what Edouard Glissant refers to as Perse's "dilemma of the White Creole," since both poets embody the contradictions of a New

World settler culture that simultaneously defined itself as colonizer and colonized.[17] The collaboration with Perse warrants closer attention than it has so far received, given that it addresses the concerns of recent Americanist critics by situating both Whitman's frontier and Eliot's modernism within the hemispheric, comparative contexts of migration and empire-building.

Here and throughout I contend that Eliot's historical sense intimately informs his modernism, enforcing his minutest stylistic decisions. But the intertwining diasporic histories associated with New World imperialism extend well beyond Poe's topographies, Whitman's hybrid poetics and the transnationalism of Eliot, Laforgue and Perse. They also involve the Middle Passage, and the movement of African-Americans from southern provinces to urban areas up north. Historians have shown that, when the First World War broke out, the rising number of job opportunities created by war industries combined with hard times and terrifying exploitation in the South, led to another Great Migration, with many African-Americans traveling to cities like Chicago, New York and Detroit.[18] In addition to drawing black migrants in search of jobs, cosmopolitan centers such as Harlem also attracted leading writers and artists; and, with the growing popularity of jazz, blues and African-American dance during the 1920s, the literary arts movement known as the Harlem Renaissance was born.

Chapter 3 begins by examining Hughes's close affinities with Eliot's transnational modernism, affinities that help explain Hughes's contribution to the rise of black internationalism and the hybridity of the Harlem Renaissance, as well as the volatile interplay of influences between that Renaissance and other avant-garde movements in the USA, Europe and the Caribbean. The deceptive simplicity of Hughes's early lyrics obscures a concern with craft and stylistic innovation he shared with his modernist contemporaries, and his engagement with the European avant-gardes, and poets such as Laforgue and especially Baudelaire, was deeper and more extensive than has previously been shown. Like Eliot, whose attraction to vaudeville and jazz is now becoming better understood, Hughes was vitally concerned with the relations between poetry and music and the creation of a modern poetics he described as "Jazz . . . putting itself into words."[19] Like Eliot's poetry, Hughes's work crosses the divide between "high" and "low" culture.

Finally, and most important for the larger argument of this book, Hughes's influence, like Eliot's, extends to the Caribbean – not just through Aimé Césaire but also through Jacques Roumain, a Haitian poet and novelist whose works Hughes translated and who played a central role in the Haitian Renaissance during the 1920s. Hughes's relations with Roumain established a cross-current of New World influences that, like Eliot's relations with Perse, would foster the cultivation of modernism and *Négritude* in the Francophone Caribbean. My emphasis on reciprocal influences across racial boundaries resonates with works by George Hutchinson, Michael North, Ross Posnock, Werner Sollors and others, who have attempted to halt the petty division of literature into niches according to each writer's "authentic," socially marked identity.[20]

My final two chapters document responses to modernism in the Anglophone Caribbean. Drawing on the work of Wilson Harris and Derek Walcott, two of the most self-conscious Caribbean modernists who came of age during the decade leading up to independence, I explain how and why they creatively revised the experimental techniques of poets such as Whitman, Eliot, Pound and Crane. Once again, as in my discussion of Hughes's poetry, I explore differences as well as similarities. I present Walcott and Harris within a complex historical contention: at the same time that these Caribbean poets drew on resources that would help them resist assimilation of their distinct local cultures to a modernist project, the internationalist ethos and varied formal repertoire of modernists in the USA helped them to reconceive their roles as New World poets.

As a result, they recovered and realized an unwritten history of migratory cosmopolitanism in the region. Nearly four centuries after African slaves were first brought to the New World, over half a century after indentured laborers arrived from India and China to work on Caribbean estates in the post-emancipation era, and a decade before the onset of the Great Migration of African-Americans in the USA, the pull of large, labor-intensive projects such as the Panama Canal and the growth of sugar industries in Cuba stimulated an early wave of external migration from the Anglophone Caribbean at the turn of the century.[21] During the late 1950s and early 1960s, rapid industrialization in developing countries such as Jamaica, Trinidad, Guyana and Barbados prompted internal migrations to urban areas; external migrations of colonial subjects, present and former, into London as the imperial center; and, since the mid-'60s, a more or less constant movement to and from the eastern USA.[22] The consequences of this diasporic history for emergent Anglophone writers were formative and far-reaching. "What religion is not a mélange?" asks Walcott; "What culture is not a mélange? . . . And that to me is very 'New World.'"[23]

Given the shared history and fertile crossing of cultures throughout the New World, it is surprising that the link between US modernism and the development of poetry in other parts of the Americas has been a relatively neglected area of research – although, thanks to the efforts of critics such as Dash, Simon Gikandi, Jahan Ramazani and Charles Pollard, the tide of criticism has begun to turn.[24] The omission is all the more striking when we realize that Harris and Walcott have repeatedly stressed the affinity, in sensibility and style, among modernists in the USA and writers from other regions in the Americas.

One plausible cause of such neglect is that the importance of modernism in the Caribbean has been obscured by theoretical rubrics such as "postmodernism" and "postcolonialism." There is also an insidious tendency among critics to use the terms "modernist" and "modern" synonymously, ignoring Stephen Spender's useful contention that not all modern artists consciously elected the mannerisms of modernist style.[25] Adding to this confusion is the unhelpful temptation to generalize about a uniform condition of "modernity," in the Black Atlantic and elsewhere. And because any consensus regarding the meaning of "postmodernism" is riding on the claim that Euro-American culture has by now made a radical break from modernism, the "modern" has, in its turn, been personified, often melodramatically, as a force threatening to destroy whole literatures and societies in the non-Western world.[26]

Another cause for neglect has been the charge of elitist absolutism raised against Eliot by multiculturalists who regard him as a provincial, rigid apologist for a racially circumscribed canon of classic Western literature. As a result, far too little has been said about how Eliot's poems instantiate his awareness of hybridity, an awareness reflecting his own close knowledge of the frontier. We may well disagree with Eliot's hierarchical valuing of cultures, his conviction that hybridity was, as he put it, an "insoluble problem," or the nature of his political commitments. But the fact remains that Eliot's work was of signal importance to subsequent generations of black poets in the Americas, and it is well worth asking why.

Finally, the application of global contexts and perspectives to Caribbean literature is a source of anxiety to scholars who fear this will efface national, regional and ethnic distinctions that are a source of cherished cultural uniqueness. Thus, it is understandable that Silvio Torres-Saillant, in *Caribbean Poetics*, warns against the dangers of a hemispheric approach to Caribbean literatures that "aim[s] to unveil global truths about writing in the archipelago" but ends up "underestimating the validity of the knowledge produced by Caribbean minds."[27]

It is true, as Torres-Saillant demonstrates, that the Caribbean has produced a metadiscourse that explains its own literature. Such a metadiscourse has been and will continue to be invaluably illuminating, as my own reference to writings by Walcott, Harris and various Caribbean critics will confirm.[28] But it would be erroneous to conclude from this that we know all there is to know about the history of Caribbean poetics without considering the roles of Eliot, Pound, Hughes, Crane and Perse in the historical emergence of modernism in the region. Despite its limitations, as one possible conceptual configuration among many, my hemispheric, comparative, transnational approach offers a salutary corrective to Torres-Saillant's "internal logic" and "centripetal vision," because it reveals cross-currents of influence that are obscured by his study.[29] Continuing with earlier attempts by scholars to resist separatist oversimplification and restore historical linkages between modernism and the colonial and postcolonial archives, I define the skeptical reassessment of modernism as a crucial aspect of Caribbean discourse. The influences I document are openly acknowledged by the writers themselves, and are essential to a comprehensive account of modernism in the region.

Simply put, this book explains how the transnational modernism of Eliot and his avant-garde contemporaries served as a heritage for black poets – not just in the USA but elsewhere in the American hemisphere – and why shared New World history would have made a difference in bringing this about. Although recognizing these intertextual relations is vital, the account I give in the pages that follow is not intended in any way to be exhaustive. My purpose is more general – to reveal the contours of "lyric history" in America, where history inheres in the meaningful articulation of poetic form.[30] Robert Pinsky warns against the dubious supposition that American poetry is somehow bereft of historical memory; the uniqueness of any poet's voice, he maintains, has to do with the poem's embeddedness within cultural reality.[31] And, years ago, Paul de Man offered a powerful admonishment against the ahistoricism of New Critics in the United States:

> In evaluating what American criticism stood to gain from a closer contact with Europe, one would have stressed the balance achieved in some of the best European works between historical knowledge and a genuine feeling for literary form. For reasons that are themselves part of history, the same synthesis was rarely achieved in America . . . The predominant influence, that of the New Criticism, was never able to overcome the anti-historical bias that presided over its beginnings.[32]

Surely, to correct against the anti-historical bias of formalist criticism, it is better to strive for a balanced synthesis of historical knowledge and literary form than to abjure formal analysis altogether.

Therefore, in addition to showing how each poet's intimately regional perspective is defamiliarized within a labyrinth of transnational convergence, this book also defends a corollary claim about the mutual entailments of history and modernist poetics. I wish, for example, to consider how a collective, hemispheric memory of dislocation might encourage a creative practice of allusion, where black poets in the Americas could find expressive freedom by looking to their modernist precursors as an idiomatic resource. Each of the chapters demonstrates how poets from very different cultures and regions arrived at singularly local lyric standpoints, not by casting off modernist techniques as anxiety-provoking vestiges of an earlier era, but by "signifying," in Henry Louis Gates's sense, on modernist forms that encrypted, in a highly condensed fashion, the experience of diasporic estrangement.[33] Attending to specific questions of language and poetic method, I hope not so much to emphasize the assimilation of regional differences as to demonstrate the remarkably various and unique ways in which every idiom evokes the fact of transnational mobility and, in so doing, works against racial and national separatism.

Adopting a comparative approach that brings history back into modernist forms, but retains insights won by theory and stylistic analysis, I hope to contribute both to the critique of exceptionalism in American Studies and to the historicist reconsideration of Eliot's modernism begun in recent years.[34] I extend the work of Americanists such as Kaplan, Erkkila and Rowe by taking poetics as an enriching, essential correlative to history and politics, and my account of Eliot's abiding, fraught relationship to Whitman and Poe, as well as Symbolists such as Baudelaire, Laforgue and Perse, confirms Albert Gelpi's pathbreaking reassessment of modernism's subtle continuities with Romanticism.[35] And though I am ever mindful of local cultures, I consistently question polemical paradigms that have pitted a vastly oversimplified caricature of hegemonic "white" modernism against the subversive tendencies unleashed by black poetry.[36] Hybridity, cosmopolitanism, cross-culturation: these are not the special province of any nation, race or -*ism*. The territorial divide between "modernism" on the one hand, and "postmodernism," "postcolonialism" and "black," "mass" and "folk" culture on the other, may have served, for a time, to create necessary critical distance from an era too close, and too complexly diverse, for comfort. But given that such abstractions have become more of a hindrance than a help, the historicity of poetic forms should now be brought more deliberately to bear on their use.

CHAPTER I

Transnational topographies in Poe, Eliot and St.-John Perse

ELIOT, POE AND THE ENIGMA OF NATIONALITY

Weighing the importance of Poe's style for his own coming of age as a poet, in a 1948 lecture Eliot presented Poe as something of an enigma. "One cannot be sure that one's own writing has *not* been influenced by Poe," he said; "I can name positively certain poets whose work has influenced me, I can name others whose work, I am sure, has not; there may be still others of whose influence I am unaware, but whose influence I might be brought to acknowledge; but about Poe I shall never be sure."[1] Contrasting with this perceptible uncertainty in "From Poe to Valéry," in a previously aired BBC broadcast Eliot remarked upon Poe's enduring power in terms that were far more unequivocal. "Poe chooses to appear, not as a man inspired to utter at white-heat, and not as having any ethical or intellectual purpose, but as the craftsman," he observed; "His poetry is original . . . ; he has the integrity not to attempt . . . to do anything that any other poet has already done. And . . . his poetry is significant: it alters the Romantic Movement, and looks forward to a later phase of it. Once his poems have become part of your experience, they are never dislodged."[2]

There are many reasons Poe's body of work would have had a persistent but ambiguous appeal for Eliot over the course of his lifetime. First, and most often discussed, is the point raised by Eliot in the radio broadcast, and by F. O. Matthiessen two years earlier in *American Renaissance*, regarding Poe's emphasis on craftsmanship and advocacy of an impersonal poetics.[3] Second, and closely related to this, is Poe's connection to the Romantic Movement. Matthiessen proposed that Poe's significance inhered in his declaration that lyric practice must not be separate from the theory that includes it, as well as Poe's "strict if brittle" adherence to principles of art that would liberate Baudelaire and the French Symbolists from the "effluvia" of Romanticism.[4] In a 1927 review of Hervey Allen's *Israfel*, Eliot suggests that Poe was actually far more closely aligned with the Romantics than

Matthiessen implied. For Eliot, it was Poe's ability to inherit and explain Romanticism that proved to be so liberating to his successors; by calling attention to Poe's transmutation of the Romantic legacy through Byron's poetics, he shrewdly addressed a conspicuous omission in Poe's own copious writings on this subject.[5]

Evidently, Eliot was drawn also to Poe's isolation and originality – two aspects of Poe's condition as an American writer that gain significance in the context of Eliot's effort to come to terms with his own isolation during the emotionally volatile years leading up to *The Waste Land*. "The great figures of American literature are peculiarly isolated," he contended in another early review,

and their isolation is an element, if not of their greatness, certainly of their originality . . . Hawthorne, Poe and Whitman are none of them so great as they might
have been. But the lack of intelligent literary society is not responsible for their
shortcomings; it is much more certainly responsible for some of their merits. The
originality, if not the full mental capability, of these men was brought out, forced
out, by the starved environment. This originality gives them a distinction which
some heavier-weight authors do not obtain.[6]

Finally, well before he publicly celebrated Poe's literary merits or concern with craft, Eliot extolled Poe's embrace of what Poe himself described as the ideal of "a criticism self-sustained" – his advocacy and practice of impartial independence as a critic.[7] In the same 1919 review, Eliot praised Poe as "the directest, the least pedantic, the least pedagogical of the critics writing in his time in either America or England."[8] This insistence upon Poe's achieve-
ments as a critic, combined with his emphasis on Poe's originality, helped to promulgate a robust tradition in biographical and literary scholarship – a tradition that began with James Russell Lowell's influential account of Poe's criticism as "fearless" and "without the heat of partisanship" – that depicted Poe as one of the rare poet-critics in nineteenth-century America who managed to maintain a principled opposition to the nationalist bias and cliquish favoritism that pervaded the literary marketplace during his era.[9]

Eliot's view of Poe is restricted and idealized. As a reviewer, and as editor of the *Southern Literary Messenger* and the *Broadway Journal*, Poe wrote criticism that was often shaped by the institutional pressures of literary nationalism and a national literary marketplace in ways Eliot would have condemned.[10] But, to his credit, Poe made no secret of his antipathy towards the nationalist sentiment flaunted by critics and politicians in his day. An 1845 letter in the *Broadway Journal* roundly castigated editors for their "indiscriminate laudation of American books – a system which, more than any other one thing in the world, [has] tended to the depression of that 'American Literature' whose elevation it was designed to effect." Three years earlier, in *Graham's Magazine*, Poe lamented the fact that, having given up the stance of farcical subservience to the cultural authority of Great Britain, the extremity of this reaction had led to an even greater folly: "[T]he watchword now was, 'a national literature!' – as if any true literature *could be* 'national' – as if the world at large were not the only proper stage for the literary *histrio*. We became, suddenly, the merest and maddest *partizans* in letters." Even in his ardent defense of international copyright, Poe drew a distinction between the dangers of nationalism as it pertained to the writing of literature, and the importance of nurturing American writers by protecting their intellectual property through international copyright.[11] Taken in their entirety, Poe's writings question the very possibility of cultural originality and nationhood insofar as his conception of authorship was for the most part reactive and dialogic.[12]

Given Poe's hostility to nationalist bias in criticism, it is surprising and paradoxical that, as a result of his entanglements in the public sphere, Poe was nonetheless gradually transformed into an icon of literary nationalism. Rather than isolating Poe from the marketplace conditions of his time, his stance of critical impartiality was the primary reason his public image became increasingly enmeshed within the rhetoric of literary nationalism, facilitating his rise as a spokesperson for the literary and political agenda of the Young Americans, an influential group of nationalist intellectuals.[13]

To what extent was Eliot aware of Poe's paradoxical significance as an internationalist national icon? Did Eliot regard Poe as a modernist precursor solely for his exilic sensibility and concern with craft, or was he also drawn to Poe's Americanness – Poe's complex regional affiliations with Boston, New York, Baltimore and Richmond, for example, or the fact that Poe, like the young Eliot, spoke with a slight Southern drawl? Both Poe and Eliot were attracted to Dickens's literary delineation of local Cockney dialect, and both tried consciously to reproduce the rhythms of conversation in lyric poetry. Henry James, with his strong ties to New York and the northeast corridor, and comparatively little exposure to the South, was not American at all, according to Eliot, "in that sense."[14] But what about Poe?

We know that Eliot's first encounters with Poe occurred at a formative, early period. John Soldo reminds us that, after discovering Poe's work in a dentist's office, Eliot procured a copy of *The Poems of Edgar Allan Poe* in 1906, the same year he graduated from Milton Academy and entered Harvard College.[15] In 1922, the year of *The Waste Land*, Poe was evidently on Eliot's mind as a figure embodying his own cosmopolitan aspirations. In "The Three Provincialities," an essay published in the second issue of the *Tyro*, Eliot endorsed Poe as "one of the greatest and least local" of authors, and an exemplary critic of provincial nationalism in the USA, Ireland and England.[16]

Despite his early, strong admiration for Poe's internationalism, however, Eliot would also constantly revisit, and attempt to define, Poe's enigmatically local qualities. Whereas, in the years leading up to *The Waste Land*, Eliot would champion Poe as a staunch critic of the pedantic provincialism that prevailed among the literati of Boston and New York, by the late 1940s and early 1950s Eliot modified his view to acknowledge, and value, Poe's identifiably local attributes. In 1919, Eliot vividly portrayed Poe's literary emergence in America's starved environment, drawing on imagery that anticipated the sterile landscapes of *The Waste Land*.[17] By 1948, this thesis had developed into a more subtle view, reconfiguring the opposition between locality and universality into terms that were reciprocally implicated and dialectical. Again, in 1953, Eliot had revised his description of Poe's isolation from his surroundings so as to emphasize that Poe had not altogether transcended his provinciality. He contends that Poe's provinciality – his profound familiarity with the places he knew best – was in itself an invaluable source of universality, and Poe's puzzlingly local quality, not his cosmopolitanism, was a vital source of his universal appeal:

It is very puzzling; but then Poe remains an enigma, a stumbling-block for the critic. Perhaps Poe's local quality is due simply to the fact that he never had the opportunity to travel, and that when he wrote about Europe, it was a Europe with which he had no direct acquaintance. A cosmopolitan experience might have done Poe more harm than good; for cosmopolitanism can be the enemy of universality – it may dissipate attention in superficial familiarity with the streets, the cafés and some of the local dialect of a number of foreign capitals; whereas universality can never come except through writing about what one knows thoroughly . . . Perhaps all that one can say of Poe is that his was a type of imagination that created its own dream world; that anyone's dream world is conditioned by the world in which he lives; and that the real world behind Poe's fancy was the world of the Baltimore and Richmond and Philadelphia that he knew.[18]

Eliot concludes that the shaping consequences of nationality and history in the rendering of Poe's favorite settings presented a lasting enigma to literary critics, but much the same could be said of Eliot's own poems. As we shall see in this chapter, the transnational implications of Poe's lyric practice exerted a far greater and more direct influence on Eliot than critics have previously maintained. Eliot's firm grasp of the dense, reciprocal entailments of Poe's cosmopolitanism and nationalism, combined with his abiding, if ambivalent, attraction to the form of Poe's poetry, help to explain Poe's presence in both "Gerontion" and *The Waste Land*. In "Gerontion," as I hope to show, Eliot adapts Poe's topographical methods, creating a richly ambiguous geographical idiom that deepens the poem's ties to history and expresses Eliot's own transnational predicament by evoking contrasts between the Old World and the New. In doing so, he brings about a transatlantic hybridization of French and American Symbolist influences that allowed him to mitigate and contravene the limiting deficiencies of each. In *The Waste Land*, too, there is ample evidence that Eliot had in mind a very early, ambitiously long poem by Poe called *Al Aaraaf.* This suggests Eliot's attraction to the sheer range and variety of sources that went into the making of Poe's lyric, as well as Poe's principled stance – a stance exemplified by his formal approach to poetry, and capably expressed in lucid critical prose – against the insidious distortions of nationalist ideology.

The main point of this chapter, and an important aim in this book as a whole, is to place Eliot's modernism within a New World context – a context where, it turns out, Poe's writings played a surprisingly large role in the emergence of Francophone Caribbean modernism. Exploring the affinity with Poe shared by Eliot and the Guadeloupean Creole poet St.-John Perse, I will conclude by showing how Eliot's bold and productive commingling of French and American influences, his growing involvement with French periodicals such as the *Nouvelle Revue Française* and *Commerce*, and especially his encounter with Perse contributed to the development of Eliot's style during the important transitional period when he was writing "The Hollow Men" and *Ash-Wednesday*. Tracing Eliot's progressive engagement with Perse as a Symbolist contemporary, I shall examine how a common attraction to Poe as a New World antecedent made such fruitful commerce possible, and laid the foundation for the flourishing of modernist styles in the Americas.

POE, BAUDELAIRE AND THE TRANSATLANTIC CROSSING OF
NUANCES IN "GERONTION"

In 1953, Eliot recalled that, viewed in the context of their nineteenth-century milieu, Poe and Whitman "stand out as solitary international figures."[19] Eliot would have come to this realization very early, since Poe's transatlantic influence on French Symbolist poetry is mentioned in Arthur Symons's *The Symbolist Movement in Literature*, which Eliot read shortly after it appeared in 1908.[20] The subject of Poe's impact on French poetry is one Eliot would repeatedly return to, but his position remained essentially unchanged. Eliot consistently distinguished between Poe's poetry, and his concern with the rationale or aesthetic theory of poetry, in his discussion of his effect on the Symbolist movement in France. For Eliot, Poe's theory – and especially his fascination with the act of composition – was the primary aspect of his work to be taken up by Baudelaire and the Symbolists. In a foreword to Joseph Chiari's 1956 study, *Symbolisme from Poe to Mallarmé*, he surmises:

A book about Mallarmé must also be a book about Poe and about Baudelaire, and must not ignore Mallarmé's most illustrious disciple, Paul Valéry . . . It is difficult for us to see how three French poets, all men of exceptional intellectual gifts, could have taken Poe so seriously as a philosopher – for it is Poe's theories about poetry, rather than his poems, that meant most to them.[21]

In what would become his best-known commentary on Poe and the French Symbolist movement, "From Poe to Valéry," Eliot dwells at length on three of Poe's ideas that had the greatest significance for his transatlantic influence. First is the notion raised in Poe's "The Poetic Principle," that a poem should have nothing in view but itself, a claim Baudelaire elaborated in an 1856 essay introducing Poe to French readers.[22] Second, Valéry's contention that the act of composition is more interesting than the poem itself recalls Poe's interest in conscious and deliberate composition. Finally, Eliot draws on Poe's example to clarify the meaning of *la poésie pure*, a concept Valéry developed in his account of Poe's influence on Mallarmé.[23] Tracking Poe's influence on Symbolist poetics in "The Dry Salvages," Eliot alludes to a line from Mallarmé's sonnet on Poe that refers to the ideal of purity in poetry: "Donné un sens plus pur aux mots de la tribu."[24] But in contrast to Valéry, Eliot's essay distinguishes between Poe's "impure" language and the self-reflexive emphasis on treatment Eliot defines as *la poésie pure*. "In the sense in which we speak of 'purity of language' Poe's poetry is very far from pure, for I have commented upon Poe's carelessness and unscrupulousness in the use of words," he observes; "But in the sense of *la poésie pure*, that kind of purity came easily to Poe. The subject is little, the treatment is everything."[25]

Critics have rigorously studied Baudelaire's interest in Poe, and evidently he was attracted to aspects of Poe's work that Eliot does not mention in his essay.[26] Like Eliot, Baudelaire was fascinated by the American conditions of Poe's emergence, his exceptionally solitary mind, his revisionary encounter with Romantic convention and his emphasis on meticulous craftsmanship.[27] But, as an American, Poe also appealed to Baudelaire's love of the exotic; and though Eliot would probably concur with Baudelaire's approval of Poe's love of impeccable form, he did not go so far as Baudelaire in heartily endorsing Poe's exaltation of the sensations, concern with irresistible perversity, and love of the grotesque.[28] Eliot says next to nothing about Baudelaire's practice as a translator of Poe's poems: why, for example, Baudelaire chose to render one of Poe's favorite archaisms, "throng," as "multitude" in "The Conqueror Worm"; or why he considered Poe's "The Bells" untranslatable.[29]

Certainly, in "From Poe to Valéry," Eliot gives passing consideration to Baudelaire's translations, remarking that Baudelaire improved significantly upon Poe's language.[30] But he refrains from giving any account of Baudelaire's initial encounter with Poe when, in 1846 or 1847, Baudelaire's interest had been sparked by two translations of Poe ("Le Chat Noir" and "Crimes de la rue Morgue") rendered by Mrs. Isabelle Meunier, a woman born in England who was married to a French publisher.[31] Nor does Eliot point out that Poe's transatlantic influence was, in its earliest phase, fostered by Baudelaire's shocked identification with his American precursor. In a letter, Baudelaire once described the uncanny experience of translating Poe, whose subject matter and phrases felt as if they were Baudelaire's own.[32] The act of translation entailed a willful remaking of Poe, in Baudelaire's image.[33]

There is also a distinguished tradition of scholarship, beginning with studies by Edmund Wilson and F. O. Matthiessen, that shows how Eliot's encounter with Poe was mediated by his encounter with Baudelaire.[34] More recently, Edward Cutler has contended that "The question of Poe's considerable presence among Baudelaire and other new writers and painters in later-nineteenth-century France . . . necessitates a transatlantic consideration of emerging forms of modernism."[35] This makes sense when we recall that Eliot first obtained a copy of Poe's poems just two years before he would have read Symons's account of Baudelaire's discovery of Poe in *The Symbolist Movement in Literature*.

But although Poe may well have exerted an influence mediated by Baudelaire, in "Gerontion" critics have uncovered evidence of influence that is far more direct. Discussions of Eliot's creative dialogue with Poe in "Gerontion" have tended to focus on Poe's influence on Eliot's development of an ironic, ventriloquizing and self-dramatizing style in his dramatic monologues. Grover Smith, for example, asserts that, in "Gerontion" and elsewhere, Eliot's speaker exhibits a Poe-like stance that has been further modified by the influence of Laforgue.[36] In a much earlier study, Hugh Kenner subtly compared Poe's adoption of the "detachable procedures" associated with incantation and imprecision to the historically embedded technique of "ventriloquial pastiche" Eliot discovered in "Gerontion." Although both poets cultivated ambiguity, its effect in "Ulalume" is to evade history altogether, whereas the "controlled ambiguity" in "Gerontion" deliberately exhibits the historical range of every word. "Though we can trace *Ulalume's* derivation from English romanticism," Kenner contends, "it has the air of a complete poetic method invented out of nothing and then exhausted, leaving no more for a successor to do . . . Eliot's dealings with such methods were more knowing and subtle than Poe's, founded on close analysis, a quickened historical sense (Poe's past is a collective yesterday, not a process), and considerable careful apprenticeship."[37]

Kenner's account of the differing effects of ambiguity in Poe and Eliot is illuminating, especially when we consider their respective evocations of locality and reference to place names. In "Gerontion," Eliot's diction alters appropriately, not only to mark shifts in time, as David Moody has suggested, pointing to Gerontion's entrapment in his illusory vision of history's chaotic randomness and complexity.[38] It also indicates the poem's shifting, dizzyingly particularized topographical perspectives. The word "estaminet," for example, was not only brought back to London from France by the troops in the First World War, it also recalls "Anvers," a poem by André Salmon that is entirely about an estaminet, a poem that Christopher Ricks says is "as attentive to national and international *mélange* as is 'Gerontion.'"[39] Gerontion's self-dramatized stance inheres in his declared existence "here," but is the poem set in postwar London, and how would we know this to be the case? Eliot opens with nothing more than a series of dislocating negations, followed by details of a domestic environment in a rented house and the "windy spaces" of a sensibility that could be just about anywhere.[40] Even the names of places and nationalities do not serve to anchor us in a concrete locality, adding instead to proliferating, thickly layered ambiguities:

> Here I am, an old man in a dry month,
> Being read to by a boy, waiting for rain.
> I was neither at the hot gates
> Nor fought in the warm rain
> Nor knee deep in the salt marsh, heaving a cutlass,
> Bitten by flies, fought.
> My house is a decayed house,
> And the jew squats on the window sill, the owner,
> Spawned in some estaminet of Antwerp,
> Blistered in Brussels, patched and peeled in London.
> The goat coughs at night in the field overhead;

Rocks, moss, stonecrop, iron, merds.
The woman keeps the kitchen, makes tea,
Sneezes at evening, poking the peevish gutter.
                              I an old man,
A dull head among windy spaces.[41]

Despite this ambiguity, however, Eliot's practice of allusion, and rendering of Gerontion's upwelling thoughts of strange figures from exotic places install poem, poet and speaker in a vast historical panorama. Gerontion's account of cosmopolitan conspirators, or tourists, self-consciously performing empty rites of communion suggests that the dissolution of European civilization, like his own spiritual torpor, is an inevitable consequence of past events.

Consider, as well, the following lines, where Eliot's evocation of place presents a transnational enigma that only deepens his poem's ties to history:

In depraved May, dogwood and chestnut, flowering judas,
To be eaten, to be divided, to be drunk
Among whispers . . .[42]

Matthiessen was the first to recognize the opening paragraph of *The Education of Henry Adams*, which Eliot reviewed for the *Athenaeum* while he was composing "Gerontion," as one source of Eliot's suggestive imagery:

The old New Englander was apt to be a solitary animal, but the young New Englander was sometimes human. Judge Hoar brought his son Sam to Washington, and Sam Hoar loved largely and well. He taught Adams the charm of Washington spring. Education for education, none ever compared with the delight of this. The Potomac and its tributaries squandered beauty. Rock Creek was as wild as the Rocky Mountains. Here and there a negro log-cabin alone disturbed the *dogwood* and the *judas-tree*, the azalea and the laurel. The tulip and the *chestnut* gave no sense of struggle against a stingy nature. The soft, full outlines of the landscape carried no hidden horror of glaciers in its bosom. The brooding heat of the profligate vegetation; the cool charm of the running water; the terrific splendor of the June thunder-gust in the deep and solitary woods, were all sensual, animal, elemental. *No European spring had shown him the same intermixture of delicate grace and passionate depravity that marked the Maryland May.* He loved it too much, as though it were Greek and half human. (emphasis added)[43]

Like the *Education*, "Gerontion" offers what Eliot describes in his review as a "fragment" of the American mind. The passage from Adams memorably contrasts the lush, elemental, New World landscape with landscapes encountered in Europe and suggests that even the most unwilling nostalgic receptivity to springtime in the South would pose an obstacle to the New England expatriate's complete assimilation to ways of life in the Old

World. Both Adams and Gerontion "could believe in nothing"; both are "eager" and well read but "unsensuous" intellectuals; both live, by choice, imprisoned in "egotism"; both are unaware that education is, in Eliot's phrase, "a by-product" of passionate absorption with a real world outside the self.[44] Like Gerontion, and like Eliot himself, Adams is intensely aware of the "tainting" effects of interregional and international migration, noting elsewhere in the *Education* that "he was not of pure New England stock, but half exotic. As a child of Quincy he was not a true Bostonian, but even as a child of Quincy he inherited a quarter taint of Maryland blood."[45]

Gerontion's reference to Antwerp is another telling recollection of the *Education* – the moment when Adams, en route to Berlin in the late 1850s, crossed the English Channel and first discovered the continent:

He crossed to Antwerp . . . The taste of the town was thick, rich, ripe, like a sweet wine; it was one of the strongest and fullest flavors that ever touched the young man's palate; but he might as well have drunk out his excitement in old Malmsey, for all the education he got from it. Even in art, one can hardly begin with Antwerp Cathedral and the Descent from the Cross. He merely got drunk on his emotions, and then had to get sober as he best could. He was terribly sober when he saw Antwerp half a century afterwards. One lesson he did learn without suspecting that he must immediately lose it. He felt his middle ages and the sixteenth century alive. He was young enough, and the towns were dirty enough – unimproved, unrestored, untouristed – to retain the sense of reality. As a taste or a smell, it was education, especially because it lasted barely ten years longer; but it was education only sensual. He never dreamed of trying to educate himself to the Descent of the Cross. He was only too happy to feel himself kneeling at the foot of the Cross; he learned only to loathe the sordid necessity of getting up again, and going about his stupid business.[46]

Here, as in his Maryland sojourn, Adams finds himself mired, like Gerontion, without guide or direction, in an education that is not sensuous but "only sensual." The wealthy American tourist's first encounter with local culture – having the "taste of the town" touch his palate like wine in a failed ritual of the Eucharist; kneeling at the foot of the Cross, but not "trying to educate himself" to it; the "stupid business" of merely getting drunk on emotion – suggests that his is an alien, desecrating presence, like that of the Jewish landlord from Antwerp in "Gerontion."

In Adams, as in Eliot, there is also guilt and endless rationalization. Adams, concluding his beautifully phrased, ambiguous and self-justifying reflections about the American South, says he loves the region's grace and passionate depravity "too much," though he never explains why; Gerontion speaks obscurely of "such knowledge" and, after that, "what forgiveness?" In his review, Eliot observed that the corrosive counterforce of Adams's skepticism rendered his conscience "ineffectual," and the same holds true for Gerontion: if nothing is believed in, no heroic action can ever be performed.

Gerontion is guilty, in part, because he isolates and protects himself, while others die in battle, defending a cause. But there is another possible source of guilt, vaguely referred to in an extraordinarily difficult last section of the poem, where Eliot's litany of place names obliquely traces the route followed by slave merchants driven by the Trades:

> . . . Gull against the wind, in the windy straits
> Of Belle Isle, or running on the Horn,
> White feathers in the snow, the Gulf claims,
> And an old man driven by the Trades
> To a sleepy corner.[47]

Although the most obvious topographical referents in "Gerontion" are to European cities and the First World War, it is significant that Eliot employs a Southern frontierism, "squats," a usage that first appeared in the 1800 *Mississippi Territorial Archives* to denote "settlement upon new, uncultivated, unoccupied land without any legal title and without the payment of rent."[48] Gerontion also implies that the failed Eucharist partaken by his fellow boarders is cannibalistic, a common nineteenth-century metaphor used by abolitionists to depict the moral and economic effects of slavery.[49] In contrast to Adams, who never explains why the presence of a "negro log-cabin alone disturbed the dogwood and the judas-tree," in "Gerontion" Eliot reveals his awareness that, as both a Southerner and an American, he cannot escape the devastating moral, socioeconomic and cultural consequences of slavery and the Civil War. Eliot once said that the Civil War and its aftermath corroded the moral community of New England, even before it ruined the South; it was, he professed, "certainly the greatest disaster in the whole of American history."[50]

The topographical intimations of Adams's springtime in Maryland in "Gerontion" would also help to explain Poe's presence in the poem. Eliot would, memorably, employ glass container imagery to describe both writers and the different, but equally burdensome, conditions of their emergence. Poe, like a bulb "in a glass bottle," could only exhaust what was in it, and Adams possessed "wings of a beautiful but ineffectual conscience beating vainly in a vacuum jar."[51] Like Adams, Poe was closely associated in Eliot's mind with Maryland and the South, and Poe's own repeated self-identification as a Southern writer may well have been at the back of Eliot's mind during a time when he was confronting the effects of his geographical separation from his family and the distinctive Mississippi landscape of his youth.

What Eliot found so appealing about Poe was that his most cosmopolitan and universal qualities were shaped by deeply local causes, and nowhere is this reciprocal entailment more evident than in Poe's treatment of landscape. Consider Poe's largely overlooked transnational topographies in "Ulalume – A Ballad" and "The Valley Nis." Poe's settings in these poems raise topographical quandaries, and contain elements that ambiguously refer to a variety of regions and national cultures. The sequence of end-rhymes in the opening stanzas of Poe's "Ulalume," for example, anticipates the first word uttered in the second stanza, the deictic "Here." As in Eliot's "Gerontion," in "Ulalume" the word calls our attention to the speaker's hauntingly dubious assertion of place:

> The skies they were ashen and sober;
> > The leaves they were crispéd and sere –
> > The leaves they were withering and sere:
> It was night, in the lonesome October
> > Of my most immemorial year:
> It was hard by the dim lake of Auber,
> > In the misty mid region of Weir: –
> It was down by the dank tarn of Auber,
> > In the ghoul-haunted woodland of Weir.
>
> Here once, through an alley Titanic,
> > Of cypress, I roamed with my Soul –
> > Of cypress, with Psyche, my Soul.
> These were days when my heart was volcanic
> > As the scoriac rivers that roll –
> > As the lavas that restlessly roll
> Their sulphurous currents down Yaanek,
> > In the ultimate climes of the Pole –
> That groan as they roll down Mount Yaanek,
> > In the realms of the Boreal Pole.[52]

Much ink has been spilled over the ambiguity of place names – Auber, Weir and Mount Yaanek – in "Ulalume." T. O. Mabbott posits that Auber could be a reference to a French composer, Daniel-François-Esprit Auber, whose ballet was presented in New York at about the time Poe wrote the poem, and that Poe's "rhyme with 'October' agrees with the unusual pronunciation of the surname when it is borne by Americans." Another theory is that Poe is referring to the small river Awber, on the east boundary of Derbyshire, described by Charles Cotton in his continuation of Izaak Walton's *Compleat Angler*.[53] During the 1940s, both Mabbott and Lewis Leary worked to identify real and existing referents in the poem's imaginary setting – proposing, for example, that "Weir" referred to Robert Walter Weir, a member of the Hudson River School of painting, and "Yaanek" to the only active volcano in the Antartic, Mount Erebus, which was discovered in 1840.[54] "But why Poe called it so is a crux to which no quite satisfactory answer, as yet, is forthcoming," Mabbott cautions; "The double vowel suggests that Poe had something Arabic in mind."[55] Poe's habitual obscuring of particular references to actual places has led many critics, including James Miller, to argue that names such as "Weir" were entirely made-up, and chosen solely on the basis of their mellifluous sounds, not sense.[56]

Mabbott's uncertainty about the exact location of Mount Yaanek, and the fact that scholars such as Miller have persuasively asserted that Poe was using made-up names in this poem, point to a crucial difference between Eliot and Poe. Whereas in Eliot's transnational topography place names such as Antwerp, Brussels and London illuminate and deepen ties to history in "Gerontion," Poe's gorgeous incantation of place names has the opposite effect of gradually emptying names of all significance. The poem grounds itself in history, only to dramatize a flight from concrete fact.[57] This is in keeping with Poe's belief that "distant subjects" are the most desirable, and "The true poet is less affected by the absolute contemplation than the imagination of a great landscape."[58]

"The Valley Nis" is another poem by Poe that offers a revealing comparison with Eliot's transnational topography in "Gerontion." Here, again, Poe raises the question of locality, but in more explicit terms than he did in "Ulalume," which first appeared in 1847, almost two decades after "The Valley Nis" was published in Poe's 1831 volume *Poems*. In the earliest version of this poem, the opening stanzas offer no clear indication of where the valley is located, but only what its name refers to in approximate terms, "at best." The sound of Poe's incantation works formally against the lyric's fragmented syntactical distortions, giving an immediate effect of coherence, and stirring, as Eliot says, a deep feeling of nostalgia and loss. We are lulled into accepting the speaker's inability or unwillingness to gratify our desire for "sense" in the poem, including any substantive details regarding the time, exact location or history of the setting:

> Far away – far away –
> Far away – as far at least
> Lies that valley as the day
> Down within the golden east –
> All things lovely – are not they
> Far away – far away?
>
> It is called the valley Nis.
> And a Syriac tale there is
> Thereabout which Time hath said
> Shall not be interpreted.
> Something about Satan's dart –
> Something about angel wings –
> Much about a broken heart –
> All about unhappy things:
> But "the valley Nis" at best
> Means "the valley of unrest."[59]

Like the place names in "Ulalume," the richly ambiguous name "Nis" has generated a number of speculative inferences among critics eager to explain its etymology and fixed geographical referent. Some have suggested that the obsolete word "nis," meaning "is not," is familiar from Chaucer and Spenser: this would in turn confirm a reading of Poe's landscape as being entirely imaginary, and of the poem as an allegory of a world full of illusions. Killis Campbell notes that "Nis" may be related to "ha nâs," a phrase that occurs in some ancient texts of Jeremiah 48:44, and means "those who flee," while others have noticed that "Nis" is "Sin" backwards.[60]

But although both of Poe's poems evoke a puzzlingly commingled geography to suggest an imaginative landscape that is tenuously related to historical reality, there is, nonetheless, a salient point of difference between them. In every variant of "The Valley Nis," Poe refers to one indisputably real place, the Scottish Hebrides:

> *Now* the *unhappy* shall confess
> Nothing there is motionless:
> Helen, like thy human eye
> There th'uneasy violets lie –
> There the reedy grass doth wave
> Over the old forgotten grave –
> One by one from the tree top
> There the eternal dews do drop –
> There the vague and dreamy trees
> Do roll like seas in northern breeze
> Around the stormy Hebrides . . .[61]

R. M. Hogg has argued that this crucial and historical aspect of Poe's topography is based on memories of a short visit to Irvine he took with his foster parents in 1815.[62] The "old forgotten grave" – a topos that also recurs in all the variants but was significantly changed from forgotten to "nameless" in the final version published in 1845 – was a well-known local historical site that tourists regularly stopped at on the old road from Glasgow to Edinburgh. Poe journeyed past this legendary gravesite with the Allan family during their brief stay in Scotland. We also know the grave was near a place called Boston Cottage.[63]

Do these topographical elements have any bearing on the way we read "The Valley Nis"? If so, what do they imply? The persistent allusion to Scotland in "The Valley Nis" brings out an essential similarity between Poe's poem and Eliot's "Gerontion": namely, that both employ topographical techniques to pose a question about national origins and, in so doing, underline a longstanding history of empire-building, transatlantic resettlement and migratory cosmopolitanism in the Americas.

In "Gerontion," Eliot's allusion to Henry Adams obliquely contrasts American and European landscapes, suggesting the fertile, discomfiting ambiguity of an identity suspended between national cultures. It is equally difficult to ascertain the exact localities and nationalities depicted in Poe's "The Valley Nis"; in Poe, too, we are invited to share the speaker's restless, transnational stance, and to confront a quintessentially American question about hybrid and unknown origins. Poe's mother was of English descent; his father was the son of an Irish-born Revolutionary War patriot; and his foster father, John Allan, was born in Scotland. Poe deftly intertwines and inscribes all three of these identities in the literary and linguistic associations borne by his poem's landscape. He alludes, for example, to earlier images of the Scottish Hebrides in works of English literature, ranging from Milton's "stormy Hebrides" in *Lycidas*, to Wordsworth's "farthest Hebrides" in "The Solitary Reaper," to the "Syriac tale" about the Isle of Skye narrated in Boswell's *Journal of a Tour to the Hebrides*. Hogg theorized that "Nis" was the way Poe wrongly pronounced "innis," the Gaelic word for island, and Mabbott added that Poe's decision to omit the name in 1845 when he changed the title to "The Valley of Unrest" would confirm such a view, since the omission indicated that Poe was aware of his error.[64] That the nameless grave in the poem was associated with a real place called Boston Cottage gives Poe's topography an added symbolic resonance, since the name "Boston" evokes a history of transnational migration and settlement, not just with reference to England and Scotland, but also to colonies in the New World and the city of Poe's birth.

If Eliot had Poe in mind when he was writing "Gerontion," he was more consciously aware of Baudelaire.[65] Eliot readily acknowledged Baudelaire as a poet who taught him not just to see possibilities in a new stock of contemporary urban imagery, but to elevate that imagery to the first intensity as a liberating mode of universal expression and release. "From Baudelaire," he stated in 1950:

> I learned . . . that the sort of material that I had, the sort of experience that an adolescent had had, in an industrial city in America, could be the material for poetry; and that the source of new poetry might be found in what had been regarded hitherto as the impossible, the sterile, the intractably unpoetic . . . It may be that I am indebted to Baudelaire chiefly for half a dozen lines out of the whole of *Fleurs du Mal*; and that his significance for me is summed up in the lines: "Fourmillante Cité, cité pleine de rêves, / Où le spectre en plein jour raccroche le passant . . ." [Swarming City, city full of dreams, / where the spector confronts the passer-by in broad daylight . . .] I knew what that meant, because I had lived it before I knew that I wanted to turn it into verse on my own account.[66]

Equally significant, in Eliot's view, was Baudelaire's active involvement in a fecund transatlantic exchange of idioms, a poet who "gave to French poets as generously as he borrowed from English and American poets."[67]

One poem that unmistakably points up Baudelaire's transatlantic poetics is *Le Voyage*, which Baudelaire added in 1861 to the very end of *Les Fleurs du Mal*. Fowlie, who was the first to single out *Le Voyage* as a textual antecedent to "Gerontion," noted that the two poems not only share a wide range of motifs (for example, motifs of time and consciousness of evil), and speakers possessed of a similar worldview, they also exhibit comparable ambiguities in chronology and space.[68] The poem's urban landscape is surprisingly similar to Poe's setting in "The City in the Sea."

Given the ample body of scholarship showing that Eliot's encounter with Poe was mediated by Baudelaire, it is entirely possible that Eliot would have been struck by Baudelaire's apparent recollection of Poe in section four of *Le Voyage*, where the speaker's gaze takes in imagined cityscapes beautifully lit by the setting sun and reflected in a violet sea. His yearning for the impossible converges with an impishly perverse death wish, again reminiscent of Poe, as Baudelaire formally implies the ambivalence of this desire by constraining powerful feeling within the rational order of rhymed quatrains.

> La gloire du soleil sur la mer violette,
> La gloire des cités dans le soleil couchant,
> Allumaient dans nos coeurs une ardeur inquiète
> De plonger dans un ciel au reflet alléchant.[69]

[The glorious sun on the violet sea, / The glorious cities in the setting sun, / inspire in our hearts a restless desire / To plunge into the alluring reflection in the sky.]

Similarly, in Poe, the turrets and walls of the city are lit from below, as the sun shines out of the sea, and there is also mention of violet:

> No rays from the holy heaven come down
> On the long night-time of that town;
> But light from out the lurid sea
> Streams up the turrets silently –
> . . .
> Up many and many a marvellous shrine
> Whose wreathéd friezes intertwine
> The viol, the violet, and the vine.[70]

Eliot may have also been drawn to *Le Voyage* because the New World figures so prominently in the poem's second section, which depicts a voyage to the Americas from the relentlessly self-parodying perspective of a disillusioned imperialist. The passage acquires an even greater transnational significance in this context when we consider Jacques Salvan's contention that Baudelaire must have been thinking of Poe when he was writing *Le Voyage*, because he began to translate Poe's work just a few months after he composed the poem; and, furthermore, that the first two stanzas in the second section of *Le Voyage* echo Poe's *Eureka*.[71] Baudelaire's European speaker is tormented by curiosity and driven by a nostalgic yearning to escape the metropolis and discover a saving utopian paradise. His compulsion to pursue goals that "se déplacent," false and ever-receding romantic ideals such as love, glory and happiness, is a source of endless disappointment. Like an old drunk who is perpetually inventing "Americas," the Eldorado he envisions inevitably turns out to be "un écueil," just a rock:

> Singulière fortune où le but se déplace,
> Et n'étant nulle part, peut être n'import où!
> Où l'Homme, dont jamais l'espérance n'est lasse,
> Pour trouver le repos court toujours comme un fou!
> Notre âme est un trois-mâts cherchant son Icarie
> Une voix retentit sur le pont: "Ouvre l'oeil!"
> Une voix de la hune, ardent et folle, crie:
> 'Amour . . . gloire . . . bonheur!' Enfer! C'est un écueil!
>
> Chaque îlot signalé par l'homme de vigie
> Est un Eldorado promis par le Destin;
> L'Imagination qui dresse son orgie
> Ne trouve qu'un récif aux clarets du matin.

Ô le pauvre amoureux des pays chimériques!
Faut-il le mettre aux fers, le jeter à la mer,
Ce matelot ivrogne, inventeur d'Ameriques
Dont le mirage rend le gouffre plus amer?[72]

[Strange fortune to chase an ever-receding goal, / A goal that's nowhere, and perhaps it makes no difference where! / Where Man, whose hope springs eternal, / Runs endlessly, like a fool, searching for repose! // Our soul is a ship searching for Icarie / A voice on deck says: "Open your eyes!" / A voice from the crow's nest, wild with desire, cries: / "Love . . . glory . . . happiness!" Hell! It's just a rock! // Each island spied by the man in the lookout / Is an Eldorado mandated by Destiny; / The Imagination dreaming of an orgy / Never finds more than a reef in the light of dawn. / Oh poor lover of chimerical countries! / Must he be put in chains, thrown into the sea, / This drunken mariner, inventor of Americas / Whose illusions only make the gulf more bitter?]

Since the Straits of Belle Isle are situated near the Atlantic entrance to the Gulf of the St. Lawrence river, Eliot's geography in "Gerontion" closely correlates with Baudelaire's in *Le Voyage*: the tiny rock island, Belle Isle, would be the first land sighted by ships from Europe traveling to the New World. Another poem by Baudelaire, *Un voyage à Cythère*, may also have been a source for Eliot's oblique reference to this gateway to the Americas. Like Salmon's "Anvers," Baudelaire's *Un voyage à Cythère* (which is known to have influenced an earlier poem by Eliot, "Embarquement pour Cythère") figures in the transnational topography of "Gerontion" because it, too, contains a veiled but marked reference to the New World. Salmon's poem hints at the French and Dutch military presence in "les Antilles," and in Baudelaire we encounter a "belle île," another Eldorado that turns out to be rocky, deserted and barren:

Belle île aux myrtes verts, pleine de fleurs écloses,
Vénérée à jamais par toute nation,
Où les soupirs des coeurs en adoration
Roulent comme l'encens sur un jardin de roses

Ou le roucoulement éternel d'un ramier!
– Cythère n'était plus qu'un terrain des plus maigres,
Un désert rocailleux troublé par des cris aigres.[73]

[Lovely isle of green myrtle and blooming flowers, / Worshiped forever in every land, / Where the sighs of adoring hearts / Roll like incense on a garden of roses // or the eternal cooing of a turtle-dove! / Cythère was no more than barren terrain, / a deserted rock unsettled by shrill cries.]

Baudelaire's lyric of idealistic yearning and disillusionment, written after Watteau's *Embarquement pour l'Île de Cythère*, is ostensibly about mythic Cythera, near the birthplace of Venus, the island of love for which pilgrims embark but never arrive. But the reference to "belle île" also commemorates the historical settlement of New France: embarking for America from Saint-Malo on April 20, 1534, Jacques Cartier reached the eastern coast of Newfoundland, entered the Straits of Belle Isle and, touching the coast of Labrador, formally took possession of the country in the name of his king by planting a cross and hanging upon it the arms of France.

Eliot's "Gerontion" not only implicitly recalls Baudelaire's reference to the presence of French imperial interests. The poem also represents a formative moment in Eliot's own emerging self-conception as a New World poet insofar as, turning to France for influences, Eliot deepened his historical understanding and sense of place in the broader Americas. Like "Gerontion," Baudelaire's poems present a point of view that is associated with the decline of European empire and civilization in the first decades of the twentieth century. Both "Gerontion" and *Le Voyage* dramatize the rootless inner life of a vagabond and "vieillard" who mentally withdraws from a sordidly filthy setting, both suggest his inability to escape the chaotic detritus of contemporary history, and both refer to the failure of a Diasporic Chosen People to enter their Promised Land as an allegory of the exilic condition in the twilight of European civilization and the wake of World War.

Finally, both Baudelaire and Eliot make ample use of topographical allusions. But Baudelaire's topographical idiom resembles Poe's more than Eliot's, insofar as it tends towards the mythic. In *Le Voyage* an old man dreams of paradise, and in *Un voyage à Cythère* the gorgeously idealized frontier landscape obscures France's historical settlement of the New World. By contrast, Eliot's topography, though ambiguous, emphasizes its historicity, including the transatlantic triangle of trade associated with slavery, and a legendary scene of imperial conquest in the New World. Eliot's "Horn" could be either the Horn of Africa or Cape Horn, at the Southern tip of South America; the "Gulf" suggests both the Gulf of Mexico en route to the Caribbean and the Gulf of St. Lawrence en route to Canada; and the Straits of Belle Isle is the gateway to the New World as approached from Europe, between the island of Newfoundland and Labrador-Ungava peninsula, Canada.

Kenner once observed that Eliot's "interbreeding of nuances" from Laforgue and later Elizabethan drama – a hybridization of influences drawn from two completely different national cultures – allowed him to mitigate and contravene the limiting deficiencies of each.[74] In "Gerontion," Eliot attempts a similar transnational crossing of influences, and his enigmatic landscapes intimate a formative experience of transnational in-betweenness also present in Poe and Baudelaire. It is understandable that Eliot would have been attracted to both of these poets, given their respective developments in the direction of Symbolism, cosmopolitan aspirations, and skepticism towards nationalist discourse. But the practice of topographical ambiguity has distinctive effects, and the differences between these poets should be considered along with any similarities. Whereas Eliot's diction and geographical references in "Gerontion" ultimately work to illuminate and deepen the poem's ties to history, Poe and Baudelaire historically ground their poetics so as to dramatize a flight from concrete fact.

TRANSNATIONALISM, *AL AARAAF* AND ELIOT'S *THE WASTE LAND*

There is substantial evidence of Poe's influence on Eliot's urban landscapes in *The Waste Land*. We know, for example, that Poe's portrayal of the big-city crowd, an essential condition confronting the modern imagination, conditioned Eliot's rendering of the frightening incomprehensibility and oppressive heterogeneity of the London crowd.[75] Conrad Aiken and, more recently, Lee Oser have examined Poe's "The City in the Sea" as an antecedent to Eliot's apocalyptic vision of the falling city towers in "What the Thunder Said."[76] One reason Eliot may have recalled Poe's lyric in this context is that Poe's topography closely resembles Eliot's in *The Waste Land*. Poe's cityscape, like Eliot's London, recalls the City of Dis in the sixth circle of Hell in Dante's *Inferno*.[77] Both poems evoke a frontier setting: Poe's city, we are told, is "far down within the dim West"; and, in *The Waste Land* (v), Eliot traces an eastward journey into a desert with endless plains.[78] Finally, both poems refer to biblical, Middle Eastern locales: Eliot hints at the destruction of Jerusalem, and Poe's lyric draws on legends about the famed ruins of "Cities of the Plain" that sank in the Dead Sea.[79]

There is yet another compelling reason for Eliot's allusion to Poe's "The City in the Sea" – namely, that the first version of Poe's poem, "The Doomed City," which appeared in his 1831 volume *Poems*, was actually a fragment taken from this passage describing a temple on a mountain, in a long poem called *Al Aaraaf*.[80]

Uprear'd upon such height arose a pile
Of gorgeous columns on th'unburthen'd air.
. . .

A dome, by linkéd light from Heaven let down,
Sat gently on these columns as a crown –
A window of one circular diamond, there,
Look'd out above into the purple air,
And rays from God shot down that meteor chain
And hallow'd all the beauty twice again,
Save when, between th'Empyrean and that ring,
Some eager spirit flapp'd his dusky wing.
But on the pillars Seraph eyes have seen
The dimness of this world: that grayish green
That nature loves the best for Beauty's grave
Lurk'd in each cornice, round each architrave –
And every sculptur'd cherub thereabout
That from his marble dwelling peeréd out,
Seemed earthly in the shadow of his niche –
Achaian statues in a world so rich?
Friezes from Tadmor and Persepolis –
From Balbec, and the stilly, clear abyss
Of beautiful Gomorrah! O, the wave
Is now upon thee – but too late to save!
Far down within the crystal of the lake
Thy swollen pillars tremble – and so quake
The hearts of many wanderers who look in
Thy luridness of beauty – and of sin.[81]

The parallels between Poe's *Al Aaraaf* and Eliot's *The Waste Land* are numerous and striking. Both poems evoke an apocalyptic atmosphere by drawing heavily from the Book of Isaiah and Revelation; both employ the Ganges river as a central image; and Eliot's "hyacinth girl" recalls the heroine of Poe's poem, who is named Ianthe, or Hyacinth. Both poems are centrally concerned with the destruction and forgotten fragments of civilizations throughout human history. In *Al Aaraaf* the temple's sumptuous magnificence raises comparisons with four other historic and now ruined cities: Tadmor, which was built by Solomon and destroyed by the Roman Emperor Aurelian in AD 272; Persepolis, the capital of ancient Persia, which was burned to the ground by Alexander the Great in 330 BC; Ba'albek, an ancient city called Heliopolis by the Greeks and colonized by the Romans, whose buildings were largely destroyed by an earthquake in 1759; and Gomorrah, one of the five legendary Cities of the Plain that sank into the Dead Sea.

Perhaps even more significant is the range and variety of transnational sources that went into the making of both poems. Like *The Waste Land*, *Al Aaraaf* encompasses a vast array of references to literature, historic sites and events, and religious cultures from around the globe, from the account in the Koran of a limbo-like place between heaven and hell (and for which Poe's poem is named); to the writings of the Persian poet Saadi; to French and British travelogues such as Chateaubriand's *Itinéraire* and Joseph Pitton de Tournefort's *A Voyage into the Levant*; to works by Dante, Byron, Thomas Moore, Goethe, Shakespeare, Marlowe and others. Both poems also exhibit a wide-ranging, dense and often shrewdly parodic apparatus of scholarly footnotes. And, as in *The Waste Land*, Poe's footnotes ask to be read as part of the poem and are, at times, a significant distraction from the verses they accompany.[82]

Consider, as well, these lines from "A Game of Chess," for which Poe's description of the temple in *Al Aaraaf* may have been a significant, and previously overlooked, source:

> The Chair she sat in, like a burnished throne,
> Glowed on the marble, where the glass
> Held up by standards wrought with fruited vines
> From which a golden Cupidon peeped out
> (Another hid his eyes behind his wing)
> Doubled the flames of the sevenbranched candelabra
> Reflecting light upon the table as
> The glitter of her jewels rose to meet it,
> From satin cases poured in rich profusion.[83]

Poe's growing importance to Eliot during the years leading up to the First World War is suggested by his renewed study of Poe in 1914. The opulent imagery of this passage was very likely inspired by Poe's fiction, especially "The Murders in the Rue Morgue," "The Assignation" and "Shadow in a Parable," which Eliot mentioned in an essay on "Prose and Verse" published a year before *The Waste Land*.[84]

But there are also significant similarities in setting, imagery, style and diction in "A Game of Chess" and Poe's *Al Aaraaf*. Poe's setting anticipates the exotic, theatrical qualities of Eliot's perfumed interior; both passages foreground the presence of marble and the wealth of empire; and Poe's "peering" cherubs bear a striking resemblance to Eliot's "peeping" Cupidon. Despite the fact that the ecclesiastical qualities of these settings imply a possibility of transcendence through divine love and faith, both dramatize an utter failure to believe or disengage from the burdensome guilt of historical memory. Poe's rich, beautiful world, we are told, is lurid, sinful and dim, a place where even the sculptured cherubs peer in ways that are "earthly."

In Eliot, the cherubim and "burnished throne" in the wife's boudoir conjoin the wealth, exotic beauty and romance associated with empire, as evoked by Cleopatra's appearance on the ceremonial barge in *Antony and Cleopatra*, with recollections of the golden "mercy seat" in the Temple of Jerusalem from Exodus (25:17–21, 26–27). But here, too, the Orientalist rendering of an exotic otherworld is suffused with dismal reminders of life's sordid, inescapable reality: Eliot's allusions serve only to reveal how faithless materialism has ruined this marriage, turning it into a tedious, violent bondage, and this personal tragedy of failed marital communion figures, in its turn, as part of *The Waste Land*'s panoramic history of decaying empires and the conflict of nations leading to World War.

It is certainly true, as Betsy Erkkila and John Carlos Rowe have argued, that Poe's transnational poetics was shaped by discourses of Orientalism, imperial conquest and racial nationalism that pervaded nineteenth-century American culture. But from what we have seen it is also clear that Poe's *Al Aaraaf* does not present a safe haven from historical memory, a "space of beauty . . . [,] pure poetry, [and] aesthetic experience."[85] Here, as in his other poems, Poe grounds his setting historically in order to dramatize a yearning for transcendence: the action in *Al Aaraaf* takes place on a star that was discovered by Tycho Brahe in 1572 and disappeared two years later. What may have attracted Eliot to the poem in the first place was the way Poe's dream world in *Al Aaraaf* was profoundly conditioned by the world in which he lived. Like Gerontion, and like Eliot's speaker in *The Waste Land*, Poe's speaker is trapped in time, plagued by horror and foreboding, intensely aware of the impending, cataclysmic consequences of racial nationalism and imperial conquest that are unspecified, but nonetheless historical and real.

NEW WORLD MODERNISMS: ELIOT, POE AND ST.-JOHN PERSE

Ronald Bush has written, "The path to the *Quartets* was one in which Eliot followed his symbolist inclinations to their conclusion . . . In his last major critical essay, 'From Poe to Valéry' (1948), Eliot by implication locates himself at the end of the symbolist tradition."[86] The difficulties in Eliot's *rapprochement* with his Symbolist heritage stem, in part, from his ambivalence towards his own propensities towards incantation, a procedure he dismissed, in his 1948 remarks on Poe, as a negligent privileging of sound over sense.[87] Despite this ambivalence, from the mid-1920s Eliot was increasingly drawn towards the incantatory poetics of the Symbolists, bringing him into the orbit of St.-John Perse.[88]

Studying Eliot's encounter with Perse leads to a crucial juncture in this analysis, not least because it laid important ground for the flourishing of modernist idioms in Francophone and Anglophone Caribbean regions, as discussed in the latter half of this book. There are many striking similarities between Eliot and Perse that would help explain the ease, and force, of their reciprocal, formative influence. Both men, for example, were New World poets with ties to the American South and tropical landscapes: Eliot in St. Louis, Perse in Saint-Leger-les-Feuilles, a tiny Guadeloupean islet owned by his father's family, where he was born in 1887 and reared until adolescence. Archibald MacLeish writes that Perse's ancestors "moved to New Orleans during the war in the Dominican Republic and [had] given three sons and three ships to the Confederacy," and in a 1928 preface to Edgar Answel Mowrer's *This American World*, Eliot recalled how, when he was young and vacationing in New England, he missed Missouri's "long dark river, the ailanthus trees, the flaming cardinal birds, the high limestone bluffs where we searched for fossil shell-fish."[89]

Both Eliot and Perse spent crucial years in London before the First World War; both frequented Sylvia Beach's bookstore, Shakespeare and Company, in Paris during the 1920s; both changed their handwriting at a formative moment in their coming of age as poets; both were strongly attracted to Hinduism, Buddhism and the Orient; both were admirers of Joyce and Edward Lear.[90] Both were acutely self-conscious about their regional accents. Elsewhere in the same 1928 preface, Eliot described the regional impurity of a Southern accent that he eventually dropped or, as he puts it, "lost":

My family were New Englanders, who had been settled – my branch of it – for two generations in the South West – which was, in my own time, rapidly becoming merely the Middle West. The family guarded jealously its connexions with New England; but it was not until years of maturity that I perceived that I myself had always been a New Englander in the South West, and a South Westerner in New England; when I was sent to school in New England I lost my southern accent without ever acquiring the accent of the native Bostonian.[91]

Perse, according to one biographer, wondered "how his own speech would be received [in France] and felt a mixture of reticence and defiance as he considered his status that of a stranger in this land."[92] Like Eliot, Perse was, from very early, drawn to Baudelaire, because his work illuminated the poetic possibilities of a sterile, intractably unpoetic industrial New World setting: Pointe-à-Pitre of the 1890s in Guadeloupe occurs in Perse's *Éloges*, and Arthur Knodel has shown how "the very intensity of light, heat, and filth gives a certain beauty to this town 'jaune de rancune.'"[93]

Finally, and most important of all for the purposes of this argument, Perse, like Eliot, absorbed the shaping influence of Poe, and even acquired his first copy of Poe's *Poems and Essays* in 1906, the exact same year Eliot did. Perse possessed many other editions, in French and English, including an 1897 edition of the well-known translation by Mallarmé. During his youth, Perse owned a photograph of Poe which he kept on his writing desk, and he even went so far as to imitate Poe's gestures when his own portrait was taken in 1906. Later in life, when he was living in Georgetown, he hung a picture of Poe near his front door so that it was the very first thing any visitor would see upon entering. His first words on meeting Paul Valéry in 1912 are reported to have been "Edgar Poe and you, the two men I have most desired to meet," and his correspondence is full of references to Poe, often expressing a wish that he were still alive.[94] Writing to Jacques Rivière in 1909, for example, Perse mentions the recent publication of Florent Schmitt's symphonic poem, *Étude symphonique pour le "Palais enchanté" d'Edgar Poë*, and, in a 1949 letter to Allen Tate, Perse wrote, "You know that in spite of Eliot's opposition, I keep my affection for Poe, because of the possibility he represents."[95]

Perse's role in the development of turn-of-the-century Caribbean modernism has been pointed out, in different ways, by Edouard Glissant and Derek Walcott. In both accounts, Perse's experimental poetics is fraught with contradiction. Tracing the contours of a formal and thematic paradox engrained in Perse's poetry, Walcott observes that his "revolutionary . . . vision is as deeply rooted as the patrician syntax." Perse's French is, as Walcott says, "classic," his tone majestic; the "strict . . . armature" of his poems formally attests to his inheritance of "the tradition of the metropolitan language."[96] In this respect, Perse's poetry may be regarded as a figurative dramatization and celebration of the cultural benefits of colonialism: Glissant suggests as much when he comments that Perse "[justifies] the ravages of conquerors, by having regard for their work as synthesizers."[97]

Perse's resolute emphasis on metropolitan tradition also helps to explain why he never used any French creole words in his Antillean poems. In the first printed version of the early poem *Pour fêter une enfance*, he used the creole word for mosquito, "pieds-gris," but, significantly, replaced the creole word with the more familiar word for mosquito ("moustique") in the book-version of the poem.[98] In his scrupulous avoidance of creole, Perse resembles Poe: Mallarmé's tribute to Poe notwithstanding, Eliot would explicitly praise a fellow Missourian with a lifelong interest in the possibilities of dialect – Mark Twain, not Poe – for having brought the American language "up to date, and in so doing, 'purified the dialect of the tribe.'"[99]

At the same time that Perse strongly affirms his metropolitan heritage, however, his highly experimental style also marks what Michael Dash describes as "an imaginative and epistemological rupture within the tradition of tropical exoticism in the French Caribbean."[100] Both aspects of Perse's idiom are equally vital to the creation of his art: in Glissant's view, Perse's yearning for "stabilization," manifested in the patently traditional aspects of his form, provides a necessary, shaping counterforce to the "explosive" potential of Caribbean experience. By bringing the clarifying vocabulary of poetic form to bear on the exigencies of New World individuality, Perse immeasurably enriched the cross-cultural poetics of modernism. "Beyond all this," Gissant concludes, "Saint-John Perse is still vital to everyone, and this is the most deserving tribute to be made to the poet."[101]

The affinity between Perse and Eliot – an affinity that would prove essential to the first stirrings of poetic modernism in the Caribbean – is clearly illustrated by their shared admiration for their New World precedessor, Poe. *Images à Crusoé*, a lyric sequence Perse dated 1904 but which was probably composed two years later, carried an English epigraph from Poe's "A Dream Within A Dream" when, in 1909, the poem first appeared in the *Nouvelle Revue Française*.

> O God! Can I not grasp
> Them with a tighter clasp?
> O God! can I not save
> *One* from the pitiless wave?[102]

In a note to his translation of Poe's "A Dream Within a Dream," Mallarmé cited the work of a critic who asserted Poe's whole life was summed up in the stanza Perse drew from in his epigraph.[103] Despite Perse's omission of the epigraph when *Images à Crusoé* was published in the 1911 collection *Éloges*, Poe's poem evidently meant a great deal to him: in his copy of Poe's poetry, Perse annotated "A Dream Within A Dream" with diacritical marks, so as to indicate the correct English pronunciation.[104]

Like Poe's lyric speaker in "A Dream within a Dream," in *Images à Crusoé* Perse's speaker elaborates, and complicates, the theme of dreaming. Adapting and extending Poe's water imagery ("le flux," "s'épancher," "les brisants," "les rives," "les ondes," "la mer"), in the opening lines of "The Bells" – the opening lyric in the Crusoe sequence – Perse's speaker imagines Crusoe as a castaway stranded once again, but this time despoiled ("dépouillé") by civilized London, an old man with empty, naked hands ("aux mains nues"), weeping when the sad tolling of the Abbey bells makes him dream of his lost desert island paradise:

> *Vieil homme aux mains nues,*
> *remis entre les hommes, Crusoé!*
> *tu pleurais, j'imagine, quand des tours de l'Abbaye,*
> *comme un flux, s'épanchait le sanglot des cloches sur*
> *la Ville . . .*
> *Ô Dépouillé!*
> *Tu pleurais de songer aux brisants sous la lune; aux*
> *sifflements de rives plus lointaines; aux musiques*
> *étranges qui naissent et s'assourdissent sous l'aile close*
> *de la nuit,*
> *pareilles aux circles enchaînés que sont les ondes d'une*
> *conque, à l'amplification de clameurs sous la mer . . .*[105]

[Old man with naked hands, returned to men once again, Crusoe! You wept, I imagine, when from the towers of the Abbey, like a flood, the sob of the bells poured out over the city . . . Oh Despoiled! You wept to recall the moonlit waves; the hissings of more distant shores; the strange melodies that are born and self-muffled under the folded wing of the night, like the linked circles that are the waves of a conch, the amplification of clamors under the sea.]

The reliance on synesthesia is reminiscent of Poe but, unlike Poe, Perse subordinates prosody to imagery and often employs densely compounded metaphors.[106] And whereas Poe's incantatory style, as we have seen, tends to effect a flight of the imagination from concrete fact, Perse's style combines incantatory musical aspects with scientifically accurate descriptions of the Caribbean setting. On the one hand, with the repetition of words and phrases, we experience the dominance of psalm-like rhythm and feeling. On the other hand, Perse's close, vividly accurate description in *Images à Crusoé* of fleshy mangroves, plants with long pods full of a black substance, and the salt of the trade winds evinces his commitment to scientific realism:

> *Et tu songes aux nuées pures sur ton île, quand l'aube*
> *verte s'élucide au sein des eaux mystérieuses.*
> *. . . C'est la sueur des sèves en exil, le suint amer des*
> *plantes à siliques, l'âcre insinuation des mangliers charnus*
> *et l'acide bonheur d'une substance noire dans les gousses.*
> *C'est le miel fauve des fourmis dans les galeries de*
> *l'arbre mort.*
> *C'est un goût de fruit vert, dont surit l'aube que tu*
> *bois; l'air laiteux enrichi du sel des alizés . . .*[107]

[And you dream of pure clouds on your island, when the green dawn sheds light on the breast of mysterious waters . . . It is the sweat of saps in exile, bitter oozing of plants with long pods, the acrid insinuation of fleshy mangroves, and the acidic bliss of a black substance in the pods. It is the wild honey of ants in the galleries of the dead tree. It is the taste of a souring green fruit in the dawn which you drink; milky air enriched by the salt of trade winds.]

One of Perse's most formative influences was that of Father Düss, a botanist-priest whom he met as a young boy, and who compiled manuals on Antillean flora that became standard works in their field. "The love of the scientifically exact term," writes Knodel, "explains in a large measure Perse's whole vast and recondite vocabulary. Alongside the purely scientific terms there are the technical terms from the trades, specialized crafts, and professions."[108]

Finally, Perse sustains a tension between repetitive, incantatory elements and the poem's more progressive formal aspects, such as the progressive elaboration and complication of metaphor. This tension self-reflexively dramatizes the tension between stasis, nostalgia and old age on the one hand and, on the other, the imagery of birth and amplification described in the poem's opening lines. The tension between echoes of the past and movement into the future is also affirmed by the way Perse reconciles tradition and individual talent in *Images à Crusoé*. "The Bells," for example, represents a gathering together of voices from the past, but the poem is also self-consciously presented as a tidal advance of the language. The poem recalls Baudelaire's sonnet "The Cracked Bell," Laforgue's "Complaint of Bells" and especially Poe's "The Bells," another poem Eliot comments on in his 1948 overview of Poe's work, and a poem to which both Laforgue and Baudelaire were indebted.[109]

The idealized dream of a childhood paradise threatened by imminent destruction surfaces throughout Perse's Antillean poems. Régis Antoine explains Perse's characteristic lyric stance of detachment as an implicit recognition of death and decay at the heart of the luxuriant tropical setting.[110] Far less explicitly than Poe's tale of Gothic horror "The Fall of the House of Usher," Perse's *Pour fêter une enfance* depicts a garden landscape bearing historic traces of hidden horrors, a garden so lush it is partly rotten, where trees (and family trees) are "too tall" and "weary" of their own, elaborate obscurity ("trop grands, las d'un obscur dessein") – a dreamed-of island Eden where the family cemetery is a haunting reminder of violent death in the last terrace of the garden ("le dernier étage du jardin").[111]

Walcott has written that:

The great poetry of the New World does not pretend to . . . innocence, its vision is not naïve. Rather, like its fruits, its savour is a mixture of the acid and the sweet, the apples of its second Eden have the tartness of experience. In such poetry there is a bitter memory and it is the bitterness that dries last on the tongue.[112]

Despite its incantatory, other-worldly qualities, Perse's poetry is suffused with a sense of New World history: as one critic puts it, the poet exalts order, "but only in order to place us on the threshold of great upheavals."[113] We know that Perse did considerable research into the history of colonial settlement in the Americas. Régis Antoine comments that, throughout his readings in New World history, Perse underlined passages that described scenes involving the arrival and founding of European settlers.[114]

Perse's concern with history brings his work closer to Eliot's than to Poe's. The topographical ambiguity of poems such as *Pour fêter*, where Perse employs the only fictitious place name in all his poetry – "King Light's Settlements" – is not intended to sever connections with the real world. Rather, it expresses the shared history and cultural hybridity that are the legacy of slavery and empire-building in Francophone and Anglophone regions in the Americas. Though the details of the poem suggest a Francophone locale such as Guadeloupe, the name could also be taken as a reference to an imagined British colony – Barbados, for instance, or Massachusetts Bay.

Given the depth of Perse's historical sense, it is a serious misreading of his work to say that it blindly celebrates the consequences of imperial expansion in the Americas. Though his poetry is written from the standpoint of power, of the privileged Creole elite in Guadeloupe, it is in no way self-deluded or illusory about the upheavals to which his island civilization was already subject in the late nineteenth century, or the "precariousness" of the caste he represented.[115] A skeptical ambivalence subtly contravenes the incantatory praises in *Pour fêter* and *Éloges*. Although Perse, adapting the poetics of psalms and odes, employs a parallelistic device that is similar to what biblical prosodists call the "envelope," these chanted expressions of praise are implicitly qualified by the use of disruptive line breaks (as in *Pour fêter* (II): "Ô / clartés! Ô faveurs!" [Oh / brightness! Oh favors!]), or else they are set against images and expressions intimating loss, mourning, doubt, fear or nostalgia in the stanza's interior.[116] In *Pour fêter* (III), for instance, the speaker's point of view is one of longing for days gone by – before the orderly world of the plantation was diminished, before joy rotted on his lips – and his recollection of whips ("*les fouets*") and the "wounded" sugar-canes at the mill ("*la blessure des cannes au moulin*") hints at the island's violent history of conquest as well as destructive economic forces and the telling presence of technology: "*ici les fouets, et là le cri de l'oiseau Annaô – et là encore la blessure des cannes au moulin.*"[117] [here the whips, and there the cry of the Annaô bird – and there still the wound of the sugar-canes at the mill].

Here, as in his late American epic *Vents*, Perse uses the word "Annaô," the local name for the Lesser Antillean grackle. His lyric speaker maintains a polished surface of praise and esteem for the idealized order of childhood memory, but throughout there is also realist precision, doubt, ambiguity and an undercurrent of internal resistance.[118] Even the paradisal setting and praise of sweet rootedness in *Pour fêter* bring on bitter memories of slavery, as trade winds pierce bitter foliage ("Les souffles alizés . . . / Trouaient l'amer feuillage") and there are ominous hints of a revolutionary Deluge where,

> . . . *dans la crudité d'un soir*
> *au parfum de Déluge,*
>   *les lunes roses et vertes pendaient comme des mangues.*[119]

[. . . in the crudeness of an evening, / with a scent of Deluge, / the moons, rose and green, were hanging like mangoes.]

More explicitly, in *Éloges*, the fragility of the plantation culture's ordered hierarchy is brought to light as the poem progresses towards the somber scene below, the aftermath of an earthquake. Even when viewed from a recollected, childlike perspective, the symbolic order of the funeral procession starkly contrasts with the shocking image of earthquake victims piled in zinc coffins in the marketplace, like "skinned" animals ("des bêtes épluchées"); or, implicitly, like slaves:

Nous avons un clergé, de la chaux.
   Je vois briller les feux d'un campement de Soudeurs . . .
   – Les morts de cataclysme, comme des bêtes épluchées,
   dans ces boîtes de zinc portées par les Notables et qui
reviennent de la Mairie par la grand'rue barée d'eau
verte (ô bannières gaufrées comme des dos de chenilles,
et une enfance en noir pendue à des glands d'or!)
   sont mis en tas, pour un moment, sur la place couverte
du Marché:
   où debout
   et vivant
   et vêtus d'un vieux sac qui fleure bon le riz,
   un nègre dont le poil est de la laine de mouton noir
grandit comme un prophète qui va crier dans une
conque – cependant que le ciel pommelé annonce pour
ce soir
un autre tremblement de terre.[120]

[We have clergymen, and some lime. I see shining fires from a Welders' camp . . . – The victims of cataclysm, like skinned beasts, carried in zinc boxes by the Notables who are returning from the Town Hall along the main street blocked by green water (Oh banners goffered like caterpillars' backs and children in black hanging from golden tassels!) are put in a pile, for a moment, in the covered Marketplace: where standing and alive and wearing an old sack, sweet-scented with rice, a black man with hair like black sheep's wool rises like a prophet about to shout into a conch – while the dappled sky announces another earthquake for this evening.]

Iconically portending cataclysms to come, a black man stands, lives and rises like a prophet about to shout into a conch. With this unforgettable scene, the poem tacitly gestures towards the uncertain future of the region, and Bernabé points out the contradictions Perse knowingly presents with such an image: "The Black man . . . is both enemy and model."[121]

COMMERCE, TRANSLATION AND THE SYMBOLIST LEGACY: "THE HOLLOW MEN" AND *ASH-WEDNESDAY*

According to Richard Abel, Eliot first read Perse's *Éloges* and *Anabase* in 1925, but it is possible that Eliot would have seen *Amitié du Prince* in the summer of 1924, when the poem appeared, along with a translation of fragments from Joyce's *Ulysses*, in the first issue of *Commerce*, a Paris review that took its name from a line in Perse's *Anabase* ("ce pur commerce de mon âme" [this pure commerce of my soul]).[122] *Commerce* was founded by Paul Valéry, Léon-Paul Fargue, Valery Larbaud and one of Eliot's cousins, Princess Marguerite Caetani (whose maiden name was Marguerite Gilbert Chapin), and Eliot became a regular correspondent for it after the second issue appeared in the fall of 1924.[123] Or Eliot may even have read Perse's *Images à Crusoé* or *Éloges* when they first appeared (under the pseudonym Saintleger Leger), respectively, in 1909 and 1910 issues of the *Nouvelle Revue Française*, a periodical Eliot began writing for regularly in 1922.[124]

It is relatively well known that Eliot began work on his translation of Perse's *Anabase* in 1926. It is less well known that, two years prior to that, Perse had published a translation of Eliot's fragment, "We are the hollow men," in *Commerce*. Like Baudelaire's inventive translation of Poe's poems, Perse's translation of Eliot was evidently not intended to be literal. Carol Rigolot has noted that Perse's rendering of Eliot's epigraph "A penny for the Old guy" as "Aumône aux hommes de peu de poids" departs entirely from the sense of the original: "What is, in the original, a reference to Guy Fawkes' Day becomes, in Perse's version, a multitude of human beings defined by their lightness on the scales of social importance."[125] Not exactly a translation nor something completely new and original, entitled "Poème" and parenthetically described as an "Adaptation" in *Commerce*, Perse's work was less ambiguously renamed "En hommage à T. S. Eliot: 'Traduction d'un poème'" in his *Oeuvres complètes*.

Whatever we call it, Perse's "Poème," his only known translation, gains significance when we consider that it was published *en regard* with the original fragment by Eliot, a fragment that marks an important moment of transition in the formation of Eliot's style.[126] Although Eliot was not, at this time, actively working on any translation, he was evidently drawn to the challenge posed by such a project. In his 1924 introduction to Mark Wardle's translation of Valéry's *Le Serpent*, he remarked,

The best stimulus to influence is good translation; the Elizabethan age, as we must not tire of reminding ourselves, was the age in England which produced the most numerous and the most living translations. To translate a poet like Valéry, even into tolerable prose, is extremely difficult: Captain Wardle has succeeded – and success in a translation is no vague commendation – in a task which I should have considered impossible.[127]

Years later, in "American Literature and the American Language," Eliot recalled his desire to absorb and reshape in his own language the wisdom of something said in another language:

Some of my strongest impulse to original development, in early years, has come from thinking: "here is a man who has said something, long ago or in another language, which somehow corresponds to what I want to say now; let me see if I can't do what he has done, in my own language – in the language of my own place and time."[128]

Two lines from Perse's translation of Eliot's fragment, "Ombres sans forme, nuances sans couleur, / Force sans mouvement et geste qui ne bouge . . .," warrant special consideration here, insofar as they embody a dense constellation of influences shared by Eliot and Perse.[129] "Shape without form, shade without colour, / Paralysed force, gesture without motion" echoes "a vision of grayness without form" in Conrad's *Heart of Darkness*, but borrows cadences from Valéry's "Cantique des Colonnes," a poem Eliot quoted in his Introduction to *Le Serpent* to illustrate Valéry's "completion" and "explanation" of the experimental work of Baudelaire, Laforgue and others.[130] Valéry may himself have been recalling lines describing the doomed gamblers in Baudelaire's "Le Jeu," another possible source for the translated couplet.[131]

Perse's 1924 adaptation of Eliot's fragment not only calls attention to an important transition in Eliot's style; it also illuminates how the transnational practice of translation was crucial for the development, and acquisition, of a shared Symbolist heritage.[132] A few years later, in the spring of 1928 and again in the fall of 1929, French translations of Eliot's poems once again appeared *en regard* with the originals in *Commerce*. The first, "Perch' io non spero . . . ," would, two years later, become Part I of *Ash-Wednesday*, and the second, "Al som de l'escalina," would become Part III. Although the poems were translated into French by Jean de Menasce, not Perse, we know that Perse played an important if anonymous role in all aspects of the journal's production.[133]

During this period, Eliot was translating *Anabase* and, as he recalled in a letter published in 1950, this encounter with Perse exerted a definite influence on the rhythm and imagery of his own poetry.[134] Grover Smith has discussed the influence of Perse on "Journey of the Magi," and Richard Abel and Ronald Bush have observed echoes of Perse in the stylized incantatory rhythms of *Ash-Wednesday*.[135] Given what we have already seen with regard to Perse's sustained tension between pained, precise representation of lost childhood and the stylized, incantatory rhythms of praise in *Pour fêter* and *Éloges*, it is possible that Eliot's style in *Ash-Wednesday* was as much influenced by these works as by *Anabase*. It is fitting, furthermore, that the fragments from *Ash-Wednesday* appeared first in *Commerce*, because they exhibit the same close engagement with Symbolist poetics.[136]

Sophie Levie's contention that the syntactical repetitions and Prufrock-ian hesitations of Eliot's *Ash-Wednesday* resemble those found in Perse's *La Gloire des rois* suggests that a reciprocal exchange of influences may have occurred well before their collaborative translation of *Anabase*.[137] In the same, winter 1924 issue of *Commerce* in which Perse's translation of Eliot appeared, Perse published a lyric from this cycle. The lyric, originally enti-tled "Chanson," was, in 1953, retitled "Chanson du Présomptif." Taken together, the similar syntax and provocatively distinct references to pre-sumption in both poems (in contrast to Prufrock's question, "And how should I presume?," Perse's "Présomptif" speaks as an heir apparent) may well imply Perse's deliberate allusion to Eliot's poem. Whether or not this is the case, both poets contend for a place at the end of the Symbolist tradition – as heirs who completed and explained the experimental work of the preceding generation.

CONCLUSION

There are many reasons why Poe's body of work would have a persis-tent and richly ambiguous appeal for Eliot over the course of his lifetime. Eliot was initially attracted to Poe's originality, isolation, cosmopolitanism and reputation as a critic who staunchly resisted nationalist biases in the nineteenth-century literary marketplace. By the late 1940s and early 1950s, however, Eliot's account of Poe had effectively reconfigured the previously opposed concepts of cosmopolitan universality and nationalist locality into reciprocally implicated, dialectical terms. In Eliot's view, Poe's provinciality – his profound familiarity with the places he knew best – was in itself an invaluable source of universality, and Poe's puzzlingly local quality was brought forward as the vital source of his universal appeal.

Eliot's awareness of Poe's significance as an international figure would have stemmed, in part, from the fact that he encountered Poe indirectly, through the work of French Symbolists such as Baudelaire and Perse. But Poe also exerted a direct influence on Eliot's style. During the important transitional period when he was writing "The Hollow Men" and *Ash-Wednesday*, Eliot's growing involvement with Perse's incantatory lyric practice – a style that was, in part, the result of Perse's earlier engagement with Poe – laid an essential foundation for the emergence of Caribbean modernism.

CHAPTER 2

Hybridity and the New World: Laforgue, Eliot and the Whitmanian poetics of the frontier

INTRODUCTION

In 1928, T. S. Eliot distinguished three varieties of *vers libre*: his own, Ezra Pound's and "that of the disciples of Whitman." "I will not say," he wrote:

that subsequently there have not appeared traces of reciprocal influence of several types upon one another, but I am here speaking of origins. My own verse is, so far as I can judge, nearer to the original meaning of *vers libre* than is any of the other types: at least, the form in which I began to write, in 1908 or 1909, was directly drawn from the study of Laforgue together with the later Elizabethan drama; and I do not know anyone who started from exactly that point. I did not read Whitman until much later in life, and had to conquer an aversion to his form, as well as to his matter, in order to do so.

Swiftly dismissing any consideration of the "clap-trap in Whitman's content," Eliot argued that Whitman's claim to originality was "spurious," since what Whitman had heralded as a new form of verse was in fact an instance of great prose.[1]

By 1944, in a lecture on "Walt Whitman and Modern Poetry" at the Churchill Club, Eliot reported that he had conquered at least part of his aversion and had read Whitman, as he put it, "properly." Conceding that he had in fact read Whitman as a youth, Eliot recalled his earliest impression of the poetry as "a matter of lines and passages, and 'O Captain, My Captain.'" Having immersed himself in a more properly systematic study of Whitman resembling his earlier study of Laforgue, Eliot now found Whitman more to his liking:

Whitman is better than he appears on first acquaintance; at first reading, his poems seem to go on and on. When you study and reread them, you find that they cannot be compressed or shortened without mutilation; nor can Whitman's verse be made more rhythmical as poetry. It is perfect, although at first it looks far from it. This singularity is very great and makes Whitman unique in the whole history of literature.[2]

Again, in a 1953 lecture on "American Literature and the American Language" at Washington University in St. Louis, Eliot – having had almost thirty years to reflect critically on the question of Whitman's merits as a poet – praised Whitman as a "remarkable innovator in style." This time, however, instead of faulting Whitman (as he did in 1928) for his lack of poetic method, Eliot argued that Whitman's influence on modern poetry had been exaggerated. Whitman, he said, was like Hopkins: the poet's scope of influence was limited, because his idiom and metric were too idiosyncratic – "perfectly suited for what they had to say; and very doubtfully adaptable to what anyone else has to say."[3]

Here, Eliot would seem to be drawing a deep line in the sand between Whitman's poetic territory and his own. But this is not actually the case. Summing up his position, he declares a strong – albeit equivocal – sense of affiliation with Whitman, a relation of reciprocal intimacy that figuratively verges on the familial:

Having got to this point, let me now suggest that a national literature comes to consciousness at the stage at which any young writer must be aware of several generations of writers generally acknowledged to be great. The importance of this background for the young writer is incalculable. It is not necessary that this background should provide him with models for imitation. The young writer, certainly, should not be consciously bending his talent to conform to any supposed American or other tradition. The writers of the past, especially of the immediate past, in one's own place and language may be valuable to the young writer simply as something definite to rebel against. He will recognize the common ancestry: but he needn't necessarily *like* his relatives.[4]

In this passage, as in most instances, Eliot's gripe against Whitman is more colloquial, vivid, funny and memorable than any of his claims to kinship. This would help to explain why so many scholars, up to the late 1980s, have accepted F. O. Matthiessen's division of modern American poets into the descendants of Whitman and the more craftsmanlike descendants of Poe, or Yvor Winters's castigation of Whitman for his blind faith in progress and lack of skill.[5] As a result, many have played down any tangible effects Whitman may have had on the development of Eliot's style.[6]

To be sure, much of Eliot's poetry is antipodean to Whitman's, and his allusions to Whitman are often cryptic. Like D. H. Lawrence, who once famously compared Whitman to a steam-engine ("They're the only things that seem to me to ache with amorous love"), Eliot decried Whitman's emphatic, facile celebration of material progress.[7] What Eliot called the "ghost of . . . metre," a periodic withdrawal from and return to metrical norms, is altogether lacking in Whitman.[8]

Still, the question of Whitman's influence persists at the sideline of scholarly debate. Since the publication of Sydney Musgrove's *T. S. Eliot and Walt Whitman* in 1952, a growing number of critics have explored Eliot's American antecedents, a study Eliot implicitly encouraged by his own admission, when speaking of the sources of his poetry, that "in its emotional springs, it comes from America."9

The aspect of Whitman's style that has received closest treatment from critics who argue for his influence on Eliot's modernism is Whitman's development of a symbolic method. In *Axel's Castle*, Edmund Wilson suggested that Whitman, like other American writers of his generation, was "developing in the direction of Symbolism"; and, as early as 1945, Matthiessen pointed out that Whitman's technique of isolating the image to the point where it becomes a deliberately maintained symbol – a technique Whitman himself called "indirection" – derived from Emerson.10 But where Matthiessen argued that Eliot's encounter with the Symbolist movement was ultimately rooted, not in the work of Whitman but that of Poe, subsequent commentaries on *When Lilacs Last by the Dooryard Bloom'd* – first by Musgrove and Charles Feidelson, and more recently by Harold Bloom, Gregory Jay, Cleo McNelly Kearns and Lee Oser – have increasingly drawn our attention to Whitman's practice as a Symbolist, especially in this late elegy, as an important and previously overlooked resource for Eliot.11

Thus far, work that has already been done on the connection between Whitman's symbolic method and Eliot's style has been persuasive. There are, however, many other facets of this relationship we have yet to discover. Allen Trachtenberg is right to observe that "The notion of modernism as a foreign import . . . still colors our understanding of the aesthetic movements of the period . . . Tracking [Whitman's] presence and influence can open new routes of investigation into the social history from which artistic modernism sprang."12

In this chapter, I examine two neglected but essential sources of hybridity in Whitman's poetry that explain why Whitman proved, in the end, to be a crucial American antecedent to Eliot's migratory poetics of the frontier. The first of these is the colonial settlement of the New World by the French, Spanish and British, a legacy indelibly etched in the landscapes of Eliot's childhood. The second involves Amerindian place names that recall the practice of "regeneration through violence" as a constitutive feature of the frontier.13 In the previous chapter I showed how Eliot and Perse developed topographical methods that were strongly influenced by Poe and Baudelaire. Here we shall see how Eliot, in "Lune de miel," "Mélange adultère de tout" and his early, suppressed "Ode on Independence Day,

July 4th, 1918," crosses the influences of Whitman and Laforgue, who had been deeply influenced by Whitman's tacit acknowledgment of the hybrid cultural legacy of the American prairies. Whereas Whitman declares that he is absorbing American aboriginal culture into his "chants of the prairies," Eliot is much more troubled by the problem of how to commemorate the violent history of the frontier through the ritualizing power of poetry. The chapter will culminate in an analysis of Eliot's rendering of the frontier in "The Dry Salvages," composed while Eliot was carefully reassessing Whitman's work.

Critics such as Nancy Hargrove and Marshall McLuhan have examined the nineteenth-century British and French antecedents to Eliot's treatment of landscape, but there is still much to be said about the commingled strains of European settler cultures, and the Amerindian legacy of place, that comprise Eliot's poetic heritage in America.[14] By closely examining this small cluster of early, relatively neglected lyrics – all written during the same period and collected in the 1920 volume *Ara Vos Prec* – I will demonstrate how Eliot cultivates formal involution as a way to bear his Whitmanian affiliation, the transformative effects of his global peregrinations and, more generally, his relation to the landscape, literature and history embodied by place names on the frontier.

Although I am primarily concerned to show how Whitman and Laforgue shaped Eliot's self-conception as a New World modernist, I will also discuss his translation of St.-John Perse's *Anabase*, a poem about frontier hybridity and conquest that was significantly indebted to Whitman. Eliot's gradual coming to terms with Whitman's poetics, and his rendering of American landscapes in "The Dry Salvages" and "Cape Ann" were significantly affected by his encounter with Perse's lyric practice.[15] Situated within the Whitmanian contexts elaborated over the course of my argument, the importance of *Anabase* for Eliot's development will be brought to light.

Understanding the roles of Whitman, Laforgue and Perse in the formation of Eliot's frontier poetics will not only clarify the relation between Eliot's modernism and the emergence of colonial and postcolonial literatures elsewhere in the New World. Such an inquiry also enhances our understanding of "hybridity," since the colonial frontier is a "contact zone," a place where cross-cultural encounters and exchanges often happen.[16] In current debates, the concept of hybridity is mainly associated with the work of Homi Bhabha and Jahan Ramazani, though others have also employed analogous theoretical tropes to describe the intercultural consequences of imperialism and migration.[17]

Very little has been said about Eliot's analysis of New World hybridity. Like Homi Bhabha, he defines hybridity in terms that are global and comparative; like Wilson Harris and Edouard Glissant, he closely considers the transformative effects of hybridity on both colonizer and colonized. But whereas contemporary theorists question the hierarchical valuing of cultures, Eliot consistently preserves the distinction between "high" and "low" and, in the late 1930s, New Critics in the American South interpreted this to imply Eliot's sanctioning of a reactionary return to the primitive vitality of Christian religious practice and belief.[18] Subsequently, postcolonialists and others have relied on such sweeping generalizations to dismiss Eliot's poetic experiments in transculturation as part of an authoritarian political agenda.

But Eliot's equivocal stance with regard to Amerindian cultures is not so simple. In "War-paint and Feathers," a review of *An Anthology of Songs and Chants from the Indians of North America* written in the same year he began *The Waste Land*, Eliot's distanced condescension to the primitive is qualified by his admiration for Amerindian art and skeptical questioning of "progress."[19] Ronald Bush has argued that Eliot's affiliation with imperialist practices is not as consistent as it appears, and that by 1919 he had begun to reconsider the foundational hierarchy of values in Victorian primitivism.[20]

Whatever the case, Eliot's writings add considerably to our historical understanding of New World hybridity, in part because his views embody internal contradictions recalling those of a nineteenth-century American settler culture that simultaneously regarded itself as colonizer and colonized.[21] Rather than celebrate the subversive creativity and pleasures of hybridity, Eliot describes it as a troubling source of insoluble "problems."[22] His poems are animated by (and, indeed, unleash animosity against) a condition of New World hybridity he knew first-hand, and this is what drew him to the consciously cultivated hybridity of Whitman and Perse.

LAFORGUE, WHITMAN AND ELIOT'S TRANSCULTURAL *MÉLANGE*

Eliot's debts to Laforgue have been thoroughly examined by Hugh Kenner, Christopher Ricks, Ronald Schuchard and others.[23] Speaking of the "origins" of his *vers libre*, Eliot recalled his study of Laforgue as "the first to teach me the possibilities of my own idiom of speech."[24] Having made such a pregnant discovery, Eliot would also have learned from Symons about Laforgue's New World origins.[25] Born to French immigrant parents in 1860, in the port city of Montevideo – the capital of Uruguay, commonly known as the "Banda Oriental" – Laforgue was taken to Tarbes, France, at the age of six. Considered by many to be a lost paradise, the Banda Oriental was especially popular with Frenchmen from the southwest, seeking a fresh start on the New World frontier.[26]

Eliot omits any consideration of Poe's influence on Laforgue in "From Poe to Valéry," even though this connection is well known, and there is an obvious allusion to Poe's "Ulalume" and "Dream-Land" (poems singled out for comment by Eliot and Mallarmé) in Laforgue's "Complainte du roi de Thulé."[27] Laforgue may have been struck by Poe's accent at the end of "Thulé," which would suggest a Francophone locality, and was used only in one version of Poe's poem, published in Griswold's *Poets and Poetry of America* (1850). His use of the verb "ululer," meaning to ululate or groan, adds to the ever-expanding pool of possible etymologies for "Ulalume," and implicitly confirms Eliot's belief, shared by Poe and Laforgue, that diction is one of the richest sources of historical insight and self-understanding:

> Quand le Voile fut bien ourlé,
>   Loin de Thulé,
> Il rama fort sur les mers grises,
> Vers le soleil qui s'agonise,
>   Féerique Église!
>   Il ululait:
>
> "Soleil-crevant, encore un jour,
> Voux avez tendu votre phare
> Aux holocausts vivipares,
> Du culte qu'ils nomment l'Amour."[28]

[When the canvas was well stiched, / Far from Thule, / He rowed hard on the grey seas, / Towards the sun which was dying, / Fairy Shrine! / He groaned: // "Dying-Sun, still one more day, / You have shone your beacon / On viviparous holocausts / Of the cult they call Love."]

By calling attention to Laforgue, Eliot seems to distance himself from Whitman, a poet whose influence was constrained, he said, by the uniqueness and limited applicability of his idiom. But as critics such as Betsy Erkkila have observed, when the young Eliot turned abroad for influences he would have encountered Whitman's style indirectly, through Laforgue.[29]

Translations of Whitman's work were widely known in French intellectual circles by the early 1870s. In 1872, translated passages of such poems as "Starting from Paumanok" appeared in two articles on Whitman in *La Renaissance Artistique et Littéraire* and *Revue des Deux Mondes*.[30] Having first been introduced to Whitman by the American-born poet F. Vielé-Griffin,

Laforgue translated ten poems by Whitman in the summer of 1886, the first to receive wide circulation in France, all of which appeared in Gustave Kahn's *La Vogue*, a leading Symbolist review.[31] Laforgue collaborated with André Gide, Valéry Larbaud and others, translating poems for the 1918 volume *Œuvres choisies de Walt Whitman* published by the *Nouvelle Revue Française*, and this experience inspired his subsequent experimentation with free verse.[32] Evidently, Laforgue was so taken by Whitman he planned a complete translation of *Leaves of Grass*, and even went so far as to secure permission from Whitman to do it. "If Laforgue's premature death in 1887 had not prevented this project from being realized," writes Erkkila, "Jules Laforgue would have performed the same function for Whitman in France as Baudelaire had earlier performed for Edgar Allan Poe."[33]

Of course, there are essential differences between Whitman and Laforgue. Laforgue is more skeptically ironical than Whitman, even when we take into consideration Whitman's later, darker poems of doubt and mourning. Laforgue never wrote sexually explicit, passionate poems like those found in Whitman's *Calamus* section, nor does he in any way endorse Whitman's affirmative vision. Still, in poems composed after Laforgue made his translations, he emulates Whitman's lineation and habitual reliance on the incantatory, liturgical effect and closural force of anaphora.

One basis for affinity between Whitman and Laforgue is their shared awareness of the irreducible hybridity of New World cultures. In "Starting from Paumanok," the first poem by Whitman that was published in French translation and, possibly, read by Laforgue, Whitman is centrally concerned with the history of imperialism, migration and colonial settlement on the American prairies. Self-consciously intermixing French, Spanish and Amerindian diction with English, Whitman's poet–speaker emphatically celebrates his absorption of a diverse European cultural legacy in the Americas, as well as an Amerindian heritage of chanted place names. He gleefully describes this new, hybrid prairie idiom as a "melange mine own":

> Chants of the prairies,
> Chants of the long-running Mississippi, and down to the
>   Mexican sea,
> Chants of Ohio, Indiana, Illinois, Iowa, Wisconsin
>   and Minnesota
> . . .
>
> Melange mine own, the unseen and the seen,
> Mysterious ocean where the streams empty,
> Prophetic spirit of materials shifting and flickering around me

> Living beings, identities now doubtless near us in the air
>   that we know not of
> Contact daily and hourly that will not release me,
> These selecting, these in hints demanded of me.[34]

Elsewhere, in "Night on the Prairies," Whitman throws in a little French slang in his penultimate line:

> How plenteous! how spiritual! how resumé!
> The same old man and soul – the same old aspirations, and the
>   same content.[35]

Matthiessen, who hated Whitman's "Night on the Prairies," said it bordered on the "intense inane." This was, he argued, yet another unfortunate instance of Whitman's "odd habit of introducing random words from other languages"; Whitman's "resumé" was a French borrowing he had ignorantly "picked up" while traveling south.[36] But Whitman's French slang is more than just a confused effort to talk big. Helen Vendler once showed that, in Whitman's lexicon, "resumé," as distinguished from "history," is more "complete" because it involves only that which the poet writes for himself.[37] Slang, for Whitman, is not just an elemental source of poetic vitality, it also registers a regional history of colonial settlement that inexorably hybridized the language of the American frontier. In *Specimen Days*, Whitman noted that "The word Prairie is French, and means literally meadow."[38] The prairies – a vast grassy region spanning the Mississippi River and the Rocky Mountains, from Texas to Saskatchewan, and reaching eastward to northern Indiana – were part of the Louisiana Purchase of 1803, a Middle Western frontier that had been taken, settled and named by the French.

Unlike Whitman, Laforgue never explicitly mentions his New World origins in his poetry, and recalled very little about his youth in Montevideo – except his first recorded memory, a short visit with his grandmother.[39] But in "Albums," published in the posthumously titled volume *Derniers Vers*, Laforgue closely resembles Whitman in his fascination with the slang that germinates on the frontiers of New World cultures. Amalgamating English and Spanish with French in his opening lines, his speaker imagines a landscape based on hearsay ("On m'a dit"), as his stuttering reiteration ("là-bas, là-bas, je serai roi!") ambivalently commemorates the history of French imperial involvement in the region:

> On m'a dit la vie au Far-West et les Prairies,
> Et mon sang a gémi: "Que voilà ma patrie! . . ."
> Déclassé du vieux monde, être sans foi ni loi,

Desperado! là-bas, là-bas, je serai roi! . . .
Oh! là-bas, m'y scalper de mon cerveau d'Europe!
Piaffer, redevenir une vierge antilope,
Sans littérature, un gars de proie, citoyen
Du hasard et sifflant l'argot californien!
Un colon vague et pur, éleveur, architecte,
Chasseur, pêcheur, joueur, au-dessus des Pandectes![40]

[Someone told me about life in the Far-West and the Prairies, / And my blood
moaned: "There is my country! . . ." / Declassed from the Old World, to be
without faith or law, / A *Desperado*! Over there, over there, I'll be king! . . . /
Oh! Over there, to be scalped of my European brain! / To paw the ground, to
become a virgin antelope, / Without literature, a guy of prey, citizen / Of chance
and whistling California slang! / A settler distant and pure, a breeder, architect /
Hunter, fisher, player, above the Pandectes!]

Conjoining the "Far-West," the "Prairies" that comprise the Middle
Western frontier, and the Southwestern frontier (suggested by "*Desperado*"), Laforgue's ambiguous topography evokes his speaker's self-ironical,
imperialistic yearning to encompass this New World as a mythic totality.
"[A]u-dessus des Pandectes" sounds like a reference to an exotic mountain
range, but actually implies his desire to transcend the authority of Roman
civil law, laws of the Pandects, which emphatically affirmed the principle of
dividing property into equal parts. The presence of Spanish slang is fitting
when we recall that Uruguay was discovered in the early sixteenth century
by Spanish seamen searching for the strait linking the Atlantic and Pacific
oceans; that Spain eventually gained control of the region after vying for
it with Portugal; and that, by 1726, Montevideo had become the port and
station of the Spanish fleet in the South Atlantic. From 1860 to 1868, around
the time Laforgue would have been living in Montevideo, the European
immigrant population rose from 48 to 68 percent, and a great majority of
the immigrants were Basques of Spanish or French nationality.

Another, earlier lyric by Laforgue, "Cythère," from *Des Fleurs de bonne
volonté*, also elucidates his concern with hybridity and the American frontier. Like Baudelaire in "Un Voyage à Cythère," a work to which Laforgue
pays homage, Laforgue elliptically renders his New World landscape as "un
bois trop sacré," a too-sacred wood. Here, too, the lyric speaker knows
some Spanish slang ("ma sieste"), and the untold freedoms of this idealized
"hermétique Cythère" are depicted on tattoos, one depicting dances that
are completely unknown to the civilized world – dances that are, in a word,
"inédites":

Oui, fleurs de vie en confidences,
Mains oisives dans les toisons aux gros midis,
Tatouages des concettis;
L'un mimant d'inédites danses,
L'autre sur la piste d'essences . . .
– Eh quoi? Nouveau-venu, vos larmes recommencent![41]

[Yes, flowers of life in confidences, / Idle hands in hair at midday, / Tattoos of conceits / One depicting unheard of dances / The other following the trail of essences . . . / – And what? Newcomer, your tears began again!]

Laforgue indulges in telling self-reference here. The original, rhythmical "inédites danses" are also performed within the hermetic space of his own lyric, which would remain "inédit" insofar as *Des Fleurs* was never published during Laforgue's lifetime. It is likely, furthermore, that, taken together, "Cythère" and "Albums" illustrate the formative presence of Whitman in Laforgue's later work. We know, for example, that *Des Fleurs* represents an important turning point in Laforgue's stylistic development; that he stopped working on it in 1886, when he began translating Whitman; and that "Cythère" may well have inspired "Albums," because Laforgue often incorporated elements from *Des Fleurs* into the free-verse poems that would later be collected in *Derniers Vers*.[42] Both "Cythère" and "Albums" contain Spanish slang, both refer to an exotic frontier setting, and both include a bitterly ambivalent condemnation of "civilized" systems of moral and social classification.

To what extent is the history and hybrid legacy of the prairies present in Eliot's poetry? The difficulty of Eliot's multiple and contradictory regional affiliations, as well as his ambivalent feelings of kinship for Whitman and Laforgue as New World antecedents, are clearer when we situate his early poetry within this broader context. No stranger himself to the prairies, Eliot would have been well aware of the diverse, global influences on frontier cultures and the American language. In "Lune de miel" – an early French lyric that first appeared in the July 1917 issue of *Little Review*, and was subsequently published in *Poems* (1919), *Ara Vos Prec* (1920) and *Poems* (1920) – Eliot may even have drawn inspiration from Laforgue. As in "Albums," in Eliot's poem the ambiguous topography asks whether, and how, places, poems or people are ever "known" ("connue"): the suggestive density and reticence of the emblem sculpted on a public monument – the acanthus set on the column of a basilica known even to amateurs – is, like Eliot's own style, designed to resist the touristic gratification of swift, dismissive paraphrase. The commingled presences of Laforgue and Whitman are also indicated, albeit obliquely, by the fact that Eliot tries his hand at free alexandrines, a French equivalent to free verse in English:

> Ils ont vu les Pays-Bas, ils rentrent à Terre Haute;
> Mais une nuit d'été, les voici à Ravenne,
> . . .
> Moins d'une lieue d'ici est Saint Appollinaire
> En Classe, basilique connue des amateurs
> De chapitaux d'acanthe que tournoie le vent.[43]

[They have seen the Low Countries, they return to the High Land; / But one summer's night, there they are in Ravenna, / . . . Less than a mile away is Saint Apollinaire / In Classe, basilica known by amateurs / Whose capitals bear acanthus turned by the wind.]

The poem's place names appear, on first reading, to describe a typical American's honeymoon itinerary through Europe: they have seen the Low Countries, and now return to the "high land" of Italy. But the setting also works like a palimpsest, weirdly imposing European geography on American prairie landscapes. There were, and still are, two American prairies – one in the grassy highlands of the Western Great Plains, the other in the alluvial lowlands of the Mississippi River basin. If "Terre Haute" refers to the city in western Indiana, "Pays-Bas," on the alluvial lowlands near the Mississippi, could also be St. Louis, Eliot's hometown – a place whose limits, as Eliot recalled, were "on the verge of the Wild West," and whose name tacitly commemorates the lost French empire of "Albums."[44] Taken in this context, "Ravenne," the allegorical terrain of despair, also implies, by geographical juxtaposition, the cultural impoverishment of Eliot's Middle Western milieu. The name simultaneously refers to Ravenna, Italy (near the church of Saint Apollinaire), and Ravinia, Illinois, a tourist site on the outskirts of Chicago that was initially built in 1904 to encourage ridership on the Chicago and Milwaukee Electric Railroad, and which was, by 1917, known as America's summer opera capital.

Eliot's vigorous discernment of Francophone cultural influences in the region of his birth may have been further enhanced by the fact that his mother had, in an April 1910 letter, firmly opposed his trip to Paris, citing her lack of confidence in and admiration for the "French nation."[45] He was often humorously disparaging of the cultural hybridity recorded by place names associated with his native land and early life.[46] But the consequences of this hybridity were also painful. In a remarkable passage from a 1928 letter to Herbert Read, Eliot declared,

Some day I want to write an essay about the point of view of an American who wasn't an American, because he was born in the South and went to school in New England as a small boy with a nigger drawl, but who wasn't a southerner in the South because his people were northerners in a border state and looked down on all southerners and Virginians, and who so was never anything anywhere and who therefore felt himself to be more a Frenchman than an American and more an Englishman than a Frenchman and yet felt that the U.S.A. up to a hundred years ago was a family extension.[47]

Two other poems by Eliot, "Mélange adultère de tout" and "Ode," warrant consideration here. Both center on the theme of hybridity, and obliquely intertwine strains from Laforgue and Whitman, thus clarifying what Eliot found repellent, but so uncannily familiar, about Whitman's frontier poetic. Together with "Lune de miel" they form a cluster of early, relatively neglected lyrics, all written during the same period, collected in *Ara Vos Prec*, and showing the formal consequences of hybridity, of "never [being] anything anywhere."

In "The Music of Poetry," Eliot emphasized poetry's "immediacy" to the vernacular. Poetry, he said, remains

one person talking to another . . . Every revolution in poetry is apt to be, and sometimes to announce itself to be a return to common speech . . . No poetry, of course, is ever exactly the same speech that the poet talks and hears: but it has to be in such a relation to the speech of his time that the listener or reader can say "that is how I should talk if I could talk poetry."[48]

Eliot's racially stigmatized regional drawl, in other words, may have been forsaken, but his poetry could never afford to lose its contact with the ordinary language we use and hear. This insistence that poetry not stray too far from the language of everyday conversation explains why, in "Mélange adultère de tout," the disruptive consequences of transnational migration are depicted in such bitter terms. Eliot contends that the music of poetry should be latent in the common speech of its time: "And that means also that it must be latent in the common speech of the poet's *place*."[49] In "Mélange adultère de tout," displacement, which now threatens to destroy the music of poetry, presents an insoluble problem that must be accepted, not overcome.

The poem's syntax initially falls into a neat quatrain, highlighting the speaker's drastic self-division – ambivalences towards place and nationality that are intimately bound up with his search for a profession and poetic form:

En Amérique, professeur;
En Angleterre, journaliste;
C'est à grands pas et en sueur
Que vous suivrez à peine ma piste.[50]

[In America, a professor / In England, a journalist, / Only by leaping and sweating / Will you just barely follow my track.]

The pattern immediately disintegrates, however, as the poem wanders. The phrase "J'erre toujours" is richly connotative, suggesting, among other things, restless migration; dilettantism; error; Arthurian romance; and adulterous errancy resulting in hybridity. Like the speaker's bewildering catalogue of professions, shifting locations and genealogy, the poem's formal errancies and idiosyncratic associative leaps are difficult to track.

J'erre toujours de-ci de-là
A divers coups de tra là là
De Damas jusqu'à Omaha.
Je célébrai mon jour de fête
Dans une oasis d'Afrique
Vêtu d'une peau de giraffe.[51]

[I roam constantly here and there / With various steps of tra la la / From Damas to Omaha / I'll celebrate my Saint's day / In an African oasis / Wearing the skin of a giraffe.]

It is true, as Michael North says, that Eliot's poem is about fear of deracination.[52] His speaker's act of racial cross-dressing implies that traveling has exacerbated his condition of being an adulterate mixture. But Eliot's speaker is not only imagining a far-off African adventure after Rimbaud, as North and Grover Smith attest.[53] The striking presence of an Amerindian place name – Omaha, on the west bank of the Missouri River, one of only two Amerindian names in Eliot's entire oeuvre – establishes that the poem does not enforce a complete and total break from the symbolically resonant landscapes of Eliot's youth. The result is a palimpsest setting that illustrates historical continuities between Africa as a frontier of European empire-building and the American Middle Western frontier of Eliot's childhood on the verge of the Wild West.

Eliot's inclusion of "Omaha" in the composite setting of "Mélange" foregrounds another source of cultural hybridity, and shaping influence, in addition to English, French and Spanish settler cultures, on Eliot's hybrid frontier poetic. The inscription of dead Amerindian languages, not just in Eliot's Middle Western frontier landscape but throughout the United

States, recollects the violent history of imperial conquest, migration and the vanishing of native cultures. The presence of an Amerindian place name in Eliot's poem, his use of anaphora, cataloguing and the word "mélange" in his title, all bring to mind Whitman's "Starting from Paumanok," perhaps implicitly commemorating the passage of Whitman's hybrid prairie idiom into French Symbolist circles. Such an allusion would be apt insofar as Whitman was the first poet from the United States to declare openly his hybridity and introduce Amerindian names to Symbolists such as Laforgue.

Critics have long observed that Amerindian names are central to Whitman's poetics.[54] Like Longfellow, who once remarked in his diary that "the parallelism, or repetition, is . . . the characteristic of Indian . . . song," Whitman liked to insist that his chanted geographical catalogues authentically embodied an Amerindian cultural style.[55] In "Pioneers! O Pioneers!," for example, Whitman's resounding, falling rhythm, and mention of "primeval forests," bring to mind two of Longfellow's bestsellers, *Evangeline: A Tale of Acadie* and *The Song of Hiawatha*.[56] This formal resemblance, moreover, may not have been entirely coincidental. In many of Longfellow's unrhymed trochaic poems, we find parallelism that is similar to the syntactical technique Whitman developed in the 1855 edition of *Leaves of Grass*, just around the time Longfellow was composing *Hiawatha*.[57] And Tennyson presents a far more plausible, shared source for this use of reiterative devices than any Amerindian influence, since Tennyson was well known, during this period, for employing initial, terminal and internal patterns of repetition to regulate the architectural symmetries of his poetry.[58] Another common source for these cadences is, of course, the Bible, and both Longfellow and Whitman may well have ascribed to the popular belief that the Old Testament bore a direct developmental relation to Amerindian chants.[59]

This typical nineteenth-century view of the historical links between the incantatory styles of Amerindian chants and the Old Testament provides an illuminating background for the other reference to an Amerindian place name in Eliot's poetry. "Chicago Semite Viennese," in "Burbank with a Baedeker: Bleistein with a Cigar," also from *Poems* (1920), is a line that unleashes its hateful animosity, not only against Jews but also, more generally, against a fated diasporic condition of hybridity evinced by the commingling of cultures on the American frontier.[60] Eliot's awareness, moreover, of Whitman's conflation of Old Testament and Amerindian sources is evident in his allusion to Whitman's *Out of the Cradle Endlessly Rocking* in the ninth chorus from *The Rock*.[61] Conjoining echoes of Whitman and Ezekiel 2:1, Eliot's poem reveals that the incantatory style of the Old Testament is a far closer, more demonstrable source for Whitman's cadences than Amerindian chants:

> Son of Man, behold with thine eyes, and hear with thine ears
> And set thine heart upon all that I show thee.
> . . .
> The soul of Man must quicken to creation.
> Out of the formless stone, when the artist united himself with
> stone,
> Spring always new forms of life, from the soul of man that is
> joined to the soul of stone;
> Out of the meaningless practical shapes of all that is living or
> lifeless
> Joined with the artist's eye, new life, new form, new colour.
> Out of the sea of sound the life of music,
> Out of the slimy mud of words, out of the sleet and hail of verbal
> imprecisions,
> Approximate thoughts and feelings, words that have taken the
> place of thoughts and feelings,
> There spring the perfect order of speech, and the beauty of
> incantation.[62]

Here, as in "Mélange," Eliot acknowledges Whitman's poems as antecedents to his own and, in doing so, expresses the strongest possible difference between himself and Whitman concerning matters of tradition. In "Pioneers! O Pioneers!" Whitman credits the civilizational achievement of "elder races" only to dismiss the past altogether; Eliot, by contrast, labors to perceive the past's enduring presence. The seriousness of Eliot's concern with Amerindian cultural influences in the Americas is suggested by his active studies in academic anthropology and ethnography, including Lucien Levy-Bruhl's *Les Functions mentales dans les sociétés inférieures*, which Eliot read in French shortly after it appeared in 1910.[63] His effort to avoid "sentimentalizing the life of the savage" is evident in his contention that Amerindian cultures are as different, and as difficult to learn about, as the ritual practices of Christianity practiced in a bygone era. By recognizing our differences from these "others," Eliot argues, we will be better able to perceive the limitations of our own worldview:

And without sentimentalizing the life of the savage, we might practice the humility to observe, in some of the societies upon which we look down as primitive or backward, the operation of a social-religious-artistic complex which we should emulate upon a higher plane . . . The struggle to recover the sense of relation to nature and to God, the recognition that even the most primitive feelings should be part of our heritage, seems to me to be the explanation and justification of D. H.

Lawrence, and the excuse for his aberrations. But we need not only to learn how to look at the world through the eyes of a Mexican Indian – and I hardly think that Lawrence succeeded – and we certainly cannot afford to stop there. We need to know how to see the world as the Christian Fathers saw it; and the purpose of reascending to origins is that we should be able to return, with greater spiritual knowledge, to our own situation.[64]

Though we may quarrel with many aspects of Eliot's thinking here, it is a far cry from the stance towards Amerindian cultures taken by Whitman and many of his contemporaries. In "Starting from Paumanok," Whitman dramatizes a joyful absorption of Amerindian chants into his poetic "melange." In "Mélange," by contrast, Eliot's speaker projects a relation to Omaha, as both a name and a place, that is distanced and tenuous. Whereas Whitman emphatically celebrates his hybrid American heritage, Eliot equivocates between humorous self-ironical acceptance and disgust, rhyming "Omaha" with "de-ci de-là," a phrase that records the fact, but significantly evades the historical particularities and consequences, of New World migration.

We have seen that Eliot's style and diction in "Mélange" – his use of anaphora, the "mélange" in his title, the rare reference to an Amerindian place name and so on – bring to mind Whitman's "Starting from Paumanok," and may implicitly commemorate the passage of Whitman's hybrid prairie idiom into Laforgue's poetry as well as Laforgue's Symbolist milieu. Like Eliot, Whitman and Laforgue were centrally concerned with the diverse cultural influences on American diction. As in Eliot's "Mélange," in Whitman's poems and in Laforgue's "Cythère" and "Albums," cultural memories of European conquest of the New World are deeply etched in the prairie landscape.

There is, however, another clearer instance of Eliot's effort to cross the influences of Laforgue and Whitman: "Ode on Independence Day, July 4th, 1918."

> Tired.
>
> Subterrene laughter synchronous
> With silence from the sacred wood
> And bubbling of the uninspired
> Mephitic river.
>   Misunderstood
> The accents of the now retired
> Profession of the Calamus.
>
> Tortured.
>
> When the bridegroom smoothed his hair
> There was blood upon the bed.

Morning was already late.
Children singing in the orchard
(Io Hymen, Hymenæe)
Succuba eviscerate.

Tortuous.

By arrangement with Perseus
The fooled resentment of the dragon
Sailing before the wind at dawn.
Golden apocalypse. Indignant
At the cheap extinction of his taking-off.
Now lies he there
Tip to tip washed beneath Charles' Wagon.[65]

Suppressed, perplexing in its obscurity, the poem bears a significant relation to Laforgue, including the "bois trop sacré" from "Cythère," and draws on two characteristically Whitmanian symbols, the Calamus and the Hymen.[66] Critics such as Harold Bloom have interpreted "Ode" as a marriage poem that significantly revises Whitman's psychosexual symbolism and highlights Eliot's agonistic ambivalence towards Whitman.[67] Sexuality and marriage are central, but we should also consider the richly intimate geographical implications of Eliot's allusions to Whitman, implications that are brought to the fore when we examine the poem's evocation of landscape. "Ode" portends the procedures Eliot would employ in later works such as "Landscapes" and "The Dry Salvages," even though the lyric's regional references to America are much more obscure than in poems published during the 1930s. For example, the Laforguean symbolic setting of a "sacred wood," recalling medieval romance and pilgrimage, is not given a historical correlative (in Southeast Wales) until "Usk."[68] The unspecified orchard (a word whose place is designated only in its rhyming with "tortured") does not find an explicit regional correlative until "New Hampshire," and the seacoast, barely insinuated here, is not rendered with particular concreteness as a New England setting until "Cape Ann" and "Marina."

Reading "Ode," our immediate sense is that landscape functions as a symbolic embodiment of the speaker's inner life, not as precisely concrete representation. The progression from "Tired" to "Tortured" to "Tortuous" dramatizes how shifting regional externalities correspond to changes in emotional point of view. Topography, sensibility and style are presented without any logic of cause and effect: a tortuously oblique style is inextricably correlated to being tired and tortured; the desire to be torturous finds sanctioned expression in a tortuous form that slowly winds its way around meanings like a mephitic river.

Only when we consider Eliot's juxtaposition of two images, the mephitic river and the Calamus, do we begin to arrive at a realistically rendered, regional orientation within this chaotic composite setting. By itself, the slow, foul-smelling (and presumably muddy) river could be anywhere – the Thames or the Ganges (as in *The Waste Land*); the Rivanna River at Charlottesville described in "Virginia"; the Charles River in Cambridge, Massachusetts (as suggested by the reference to "Charles"); the River Cam in Cambridge, England (as suggested by "Charles' Wagon," a British name for the constellation "the Big Dipper"); or the Mississippi as depicted in "The Dry Salvages."

Placed, however, near the Whitmanian Calamus, the river begins to bear regional connotations that are specifically American. Much has already been written about Whitman's sexual politics in the *Calamus* poems, and his emphasis on love between men, or "adhesiveness," as a means of ministering to the national crisis in the years before and during the Civil War.[69] Less well known are the implied regional significances of the Calamus plant itself. In addition to being a by now notoriously explicit phallic symbol, the Calamus is also a botanical metonymy – a species of grass, often called Sweet Flag, that grew in both the Northern and the Middle States. "Calamus," Whitman writes:

is the very large and aromatic grass, or rush, growing about water ponds in the valleys – spears about three feet high; often called Sweet Flag; grows all over the Northern and Middle States, the recherché or ethereal sense of the term, as used in my book, arises probably from the actual Calamus presenting the biggest and hardiest kind of spears of grass, and their fresh, aquatic, pungent bouquet.[70]

In Eliot's "Ode," the Whitmanian Calamus retains this botanical significance, confirming hidden continuities with Whitman, and figuratively conjoining the alluvial lowland prairie of Eliot's childhood with a tract of land following the northeast corridor from New York to Massachusetts that Eliot shared with Whitman.

In addition to the Calamus, there is an allusion in "Ode" to Whitman's "O Hymen! O Hymenee" where Eliot corrects Whitman's orthography, recovering a Latin syllable, "æ," which Whitman drops so that "hymenee" rhymes ominously with "kill me."

> O HYMEN! O hymenee! why do you tantalize me thus?
> O why sting me for a swift moment only?
> Why can you not continue? O why do you now cease?
> Is it because if you continued beyond the swift moment you
>   would soon certainly kill me?[71]

Orthographic details, Eliot noted, are essential to preserving a word's history: "I am averse," he said, "to simplified spelling which destroys all traces of a word's origin and history."[72] In Eliot, the strangely parenthesized wedding song sung by children in the orchard, "Io Hymen, Hymenæe," accurately records, with devastating irony, Whitman's lost allusion to Spenser's *Epithalamion*, a poem that in turn alludes to the wedding song's source, the first of Catullus's two *epithalamia, Carmina LXI*. The restorative work of Eliot's poem implies that Whitman's stylistic revolution was, as Eliot once put it, "unwholesome."[73] But it also indicates Eliot's principled acknowledgment of continuity with Whitman, particularly with regard to their shared interest in American landscape. "Hymenæe" not only corrects a false etymology in Whitman, it also emphasizes hidden, precise geographical connotations of Whitman's symbolism. Whitman's spelling, "Hymenee," suggests that the word derives from Greek, and is related to "Hymen" which, in turn, is variously defined as the god of marriage in ancient mythology, a marriage, a wedding song or poem, a pellicle enclosing the flower of a bud, or the membrane which represents physical proof of virginity – a quintessential frontier trope. But as Eliot's orthography makes clear, Whitman's symbol also harbors meanings that are concretely regional. "Hymenæa," which derives not from Greek but from the Latin word for marriage ("hymenæus"), is a genus of tropical timber tree found in Southern states as well as the Caribbean. Like Whitman's Calamus – a symbol that connoted, among other things, Whitman's dream of unifying the Northern and Middle states – Eliot's Hymenæa also works symbolically to enact a hemispheric unification, evoking continuities (historical, floral, geographical, cultural and so on) between regions in the American South and the Caribbean.

It would be easy to assume that in "Ode" Eliot unequivocally condemns Whitman's break with tradition, a break that resulted, in part, from his misunderstanding of the languages in which earlier poems by Spenser, Catullus and others were written. But the poem actually hints that "The accents of the now retired / Profession of the Calamus," Whitman's apparent mishandling of Latin accents, would be "misunderstood." As Eliot remarks, such eventful misunderstandings as Whitman's must be accepted as part of the history of literature, insofar as he hybridized and enriched the American idiom, thereby forming an inescapable foundation for the subsequent emergence of poetry, including Eliot's own:

In the history of versification, the question of whether poets have misunderstood the rhythms of the language in imitating foreign models does not arise: we must accept the practices of great poets of the past, because they are practices upon which our ear has been trained or must be trained. I believe that a number of foreign influences have gone to enrich the range and variety of English verse.[74]

American poetry, like English poetry, has always represented a hybridized "amalgam" of cultures:

What I think we have, in English poetry, is a kind of amalgam of systems of divers sources (though I do not like to use the word "system" for it has a suggestion of conscious invention rather than growth): an amalgam like the amalgam of races, and indeed partly due to racial origins . . . As with human beings in a composite race, different strains may be dominant in different individuals, even in members of the same family, so one or another element in the poetic compound may be more congenial to one or another poet or to one or another period.[75]

Though we may balk at Eliot's insistence on race as a guiding metaphor, his concern with amalgamation anticipates, and illuminates, the hybridization of English-language poetry in the Caribbean and elsewhere.

ELIOT, ST.-JOHN PERSE AND THE WHITMANIAN POETICS OF THE *FRONTIÈRE*

In *T. S. Eliot and American Poetry*, Lee Oser shrewdly perceives the importance of Whitman's frontier for Eliot's poetic development. "Vis-à-vis Whitman," he writes, "Eliot cultivates a mode of spiritual self-inquiry in which the frontier has been internalized."[76] As we have seen, the lurking presence of Whitman, as well as Eliot's Middle Western frontier, figure significantly in a cluster of poems from *Ara Vos Prec*, even though Eliot's references are often obscure. By 1930, the same year his translation of St.-John Perse's *Anabase* first appeared, Eliot had become more sharply and publicly aware of the frontier as a poetic resource. In a letter to the *St. Louis Post-Dispatch*, he said: "I have spent many years out of America altogether; but Missouri and the Mississippi have made a deeper impression on me than any other part of the world."[77]

Given the relevance of these remembered prairie settings, it is notable that the actual word "frontier" does not appear in any of Eliot's poems until 1930, in his translation of "frontière" in Perse's *Anabase*. Published eight years after the opening Song of *Anabase* first appeared in an April 1922 issue of the *Nouvelle Revue Française*, Eliot's translation was painstakingly revised in subsequent editions. A year after the unbound copies of the 1930 edition were reissued in England in 1937, Eliot made changes for an American printing, and further changes for the second edition in 1949. Regarding the final, 1959 edition, Eliot informs us, all revisions were done at the request of Perse himself, tending "to make the translation more literal than in previous editions."[78] Eliot's frontier initially surfaces, then, in a translation where Perse was so closely involved that Eliot identified him as a "half-translator," and the time and effort involved in the collaboration indicate his strong admiration for Perse's poem.[79] In 1927, he wrote a letter in French to Perse saying "The poem is one of the greatest and most original in modern times, and if I can render a translation worthy of such a masterpiece, I shall be completely satisfied." Three years later, weighing the importance of *Anabase* in his 1930 Preface, Eliot raised a telling comparison with Joyce's *Finnegans Wake*.[80]

In an interview with the journalist Pierre Mazars, Perse once said that he wanted his work to evoke "la ressource humaine," the reservoir of human potentialities. To do this, he would have to focus on solitude in action ("la solitude dans l'action"), not only action taken in society ("parmi les hommes"), but also action of the spirit towards itself ("de l'esprit envers soi-même").[81] In *Anabase*'s eighth canto, the word "frontier" occurs as part of a metaphor, but the situation is that of a real anabasis, a military expedition up and into the continental interior. This literal migration to the Western frontier is, in Perse's poem, also a figurative journey to "les frontières de l'esprit," an image that evokes the speaker's striving to realize the fullest limit of his potential, for comprehension as well as action.

Non que l'étape fût stérile: au pas des bêtes sans alliances
(nos chevaux purs aux yeux d'aînés), beaucoup de choses
entreprises sur les ténèbres de l'esprit – beaucoup de choses à
loisir sur les frontières de l'esprit – grandes histoires sé-
leucides au sifflement des fronds et la terre livrée aux expli-
cations . . .
Autre chose: ces ombres – les prévarications du ciel contre
la terre . . .
Cavaliers au travers de telles familles humaines, où les
haines parfois chantaient comme des mésanges, lèverons-nous
le fouet sur les mots hongres du bonheur? – Homme, pèse
ton poids calculé en froment. Un pays-ci n'est point le mien.
Que m'a donné le monde que ce mouvement d'herbes? . . .

*   *   *

Jusqu'au lieu dit de l'Arbre Sec:
et l'éclair famélique m'assigne ces provinces en Ouest.
Mais au delà sont les plus grands loisirs, et dans un grand
pays d'herbages sans mémoire, l'année sans liens et sans

anniversaires, assaisonnée d'aurores et de feux. (Sacrifice
au matin d'un cœur de mouton noir.)

* * *

Chemins du monde, l'un vous suit. Autorité sur tous les
signes de la terre.
  Ô Voyageur dans le vent jaune, goût de l'âme! . . . et la
graine, dis-tu, du cocculus indien possède, qu'on la broie!
des vertus enivrantes.

* * *

Un grand principe de violence commandait à nos mœurs.[82]

In 1930, 1937, 1938 and 1949, Eliot rendered Perse's "frontière de l'esprit" as "marches of the spirit," even though Perse's frontier image resonates with Eliot's much earlier use of the metaphor in 1919, when "frontier of metaphysics" appeared in "Tradition and the Individual Talent."[83] By 1959, however, Eliot's translation of the passage – a translation whose sole purpose, he says, is to "assist" the English-speaking reader "who wishes to approach the French text," and not to interpose Eliot's own idiom between Perse's text and the reader – would read as follows:

Not that this stage was in vain: to the pace of the beasts
akin to none (our pure bred horses with eyes of elders) many
things undertaken on the darkness of the spirit – infinity of
things at leisure on the frontiers of the spirit – great selucid
histories to the whistling of slings and the earth given over to
explanations . . .

And again: these shadows – the prevarications of the sky
against the earth . . .
Cavaliers, across such human families, in whom hatreds
sang now and then like crested tits, shall we raise our whip
over the gelded words of happiness? – Man, weigh your
weight measured in wheat. A country here, not mine. What
has the world given me but this swaying of grass? . . .

* * *

To the place called the Place of the Dry Tree:
and the starved lightning allots me these provinces in the
West.

But beyond are the greater leisures, and in a great
land of grass without memory, the year without ties or
anniversaries, seasoned with dawns and heavenly fires. (Sacri-
ficed, in the morning, the heart of a black sheep.)

* * *

Roads of the world, we follow you. Authority over all the signs of the earth.

O Traveller in the yellow wind, lust of the soul! . . . and the seed (so you say) of the Indian cocculus possesses (if you mash it!) intoxicating properties.

*   *   *

A great principle of violence dictated our fashions.[84]

Perse's metaphor was, evidently, on Eliot's mind when he employed "frontiers of the spirit" a year after the American printing of *Anabase*, in an April 1939 prose commentary written for the *New English Weekly*, the same journal that would publish "The Dry Salvages" two years later. Here, as in Perse, the frontier trope depicts the poet's effort to draw on a reservoir of human potentialities, regaining "under very different conditions, what was known to men writing at remote times and in alien languages."[85]

The winter following the publication of Eliot's piece in the *New English Weekly*, a French translation by Georges Linbour of "Difficulties of a Statesman," the second part of the *Coriolan* sequence, appeared *en regard* with the original in *Commerce* – a periodical, as I mentioned in the previous chapter, for which Perse served as an anonymous but active member of the editorial staff. The lyric would be Eliot's final contribution to *Commerce*, and was published in the last issue of the review, although Eliot had begun planning the *Coriolan* sequence (which he never completed) almost a decade earlier.

Musgrove pointed out long ago that there is an allusion to Whitman's "Pioneers! O Pioneers!" in "Difficulties," but the significance of the echo is much clearer when we consider that Eliot may also have been recalling Perse's adaptation of the Whitmanian frontier setting in *Anabase*:[86]

> Cry what shall I cry?
> All flesh is grass: comprehending
> The Companions of the Bath, the Knights of the British Empire,
> 　　the Cavaliers,
> O Cavaliers! of the Legion of Honour,
> The Order of the Black Eagle (1st and 2nd class),
> And the Order of the Rising sun.
> Cry cry what shall I cry?[87]

Eliot replaces Whitman's "Pioneers" with the more obviously militaristic "Cavaliers" employed by Perse, whose frontier setting in Canto 8 circumscribes a dense constellation of Whitmanian symbols. The newly discovered prairie landscape in Canto 8 is full of swaying grass; there is a westward migration to the frontier; and, juxtaposed to the image of a prairie landscape we find an open road, Whitman's cherished symbol of democracy and progress.

Elsewhere in "Difficulties," Eliot deliberately reworks the stunningly encyclopedic, Whitmanian catalogue of vocations and pastimes from Perse's tenth canto.[88] In Eliot the homologous series incorporates a smith – his translation of Perse's "le forgeron" – as well as "fletchers" that call up Perse's image of a man dragging a dead eagle whose plumage is given, not sold, for fletching ("est donnée, non vendue, pour l'empennage des flèches").[89] The borrowing is highlighted not only insofar as Eliot's rendering of Perse produced two characteristically English names that are, as Christopher Ricks observes, jarringly anachronistic in the context of his own poem;[90] but also because the Romans, who were modernizing their weaponry and giving up the spear in favor of the sword during the period of conflict with the Volscians, never would have resorted to arrows ("des flèches"):

A commission is appointed
For Public Works, chiefly the question of rebuilding the fortifications.
A commission is appointed
To confer with a Volscian commission
About perpetual peace: the fletchers and javelin-makers and smiths
Have appointed a joint committee to protest against the reduction of orders.[91]

One reason Eliot may have been especially drawn to Perse's frontier setting in *Anabase* is that it lays bare Perse's ambivalent affinity with Whitman and, in so doing, brings Eliot one step closer to a *rapprochement* with a poet who represented all that Eliot had tried hardest to avoid in his American past. Perse was a close friend of Valery Larbaud, a poet–critic whose *Poèmes par un riche amateur* had been extensively influenced by Whitman, and who (at the suggestion of André Gide) wrote the first article on Perse's poetry for *La Phalange* in December 1911, where he actually compared Perse's style to Whitman's.[92] Perse owned and annotated Léon Bazalgette's two-volume translation of Whitman, which first appeared in 1909, as well as a 1919 English edition of *Leaves of Grass and Democratic Vistas*, but he would also have been familiar with André Gide's edition of selected poems by Whitman, with translations by Laforgue, Larbaud and Gide himself.

In "The Muse of History," Walcott mentions the influence of Whitman on Perse's style. "The sources of [Perse's] diction are both ancient and contemporary," he argues, "the bible and the tribal ode as well as French surrealist poetry, the proletarian hymns of Whitman, and the oral or written legends of other civilizations."[93] Like Whitman, Perse was vitally interested in the vocabulary of trades and vocations. Both poets attempted to reconcile the presence of concrete realistic details with a mythologizing stance and an incantatory style; both were concerned to write poems commemorating conquest, and the end of a war; both make frequent use, as Erkkila notes, of "exclamation, parentheses, dashes, present participles, conjunctions, prepositions, [and] initial repetitions."[94] And though Perse will, on occasion, avoid Whitman's end-stopped lines, his verse abounds with expansive catalogues, a "trademark" of his technique that is strikingly reminiscent of Whitman's.[95] In Perse, as in Whitman, the practice of accumulative amplification is a formal means of expressing an endlessly excited desire for territorial expansion. Glissant also comments on this Whitmanian procedure in Perse's poetry: "The techniques of listing used in Saint John Perse's poetics and that I use a lot in my work, those interminable lists that attempt to exhaust reality not in a formulaic way but by accumulation, accumulation used precisely like a rhetorical device."[96]

Perse was always careful to note his differences from Whitman. In a 1955 letter to Katherine Biddle, he thanked her for distinguishing his "rigorous," "exacting" and "precise" internal metrics from Whitman's free verse.[97] But, eight years later, in a public eulogy for President Kennedy, Perse alluded to the apostrophic second section of *When Lilacs Last by the Dooryard Bloom'd* ("O shades of night! – O moody, tearful night! / O great star disappear'd – O black murk that hides the star"), implicitly comparing his own task as a poet to that of Whitman, who had written such a beautiful elegy on the death of Lincoln.[98] During his years of exile in New York and Washington, Perse clipped and saved many articles about Whitman from American newspapers and magazines, and he consciously regarded Whitman's New World epic as a precursor to his own encyclopedic, enumerative, American epic *Vents*, published in 1945.[99]

Despite Perse's differences from Whitman, echoes of Isaiah, chapter 40, in Eliot's "Difficulties" ("The voice said, Cry. And he said, What shall I cry? All flesh is grass, / and all its beauty is like the flower of the field") disclose a biblical antecedent for prairie-grass imagery that Eliot shared with both Whitman and Perse, a reminder that, violent history notwithstanding, American frontier landscapes also summon up nostalgic associations with peace, solitude and perfect communion with divine nature.

> "Rising and falling, crowned with dust," the small creatures,
> The small creatures chirp thinly through the dust, through the night.
> O mother
> What shall I cry?
> We demand a committee, a representative committee, a committee of
>   investigation
>   RESIGN RESIGN RESIGN[100]

Eliot himself observed echoes of *Anabase* in "Journey of the Magi," and critics have observed that "Triumphal March" alludes to Perse's Leader.[101] But "Difficulties" is also indebted to *Anabase* insofar as it centers on the meditations of a leader at a moment when he reluctantly turns once again to burdensome affairs of state. Read in this light, Eliot's echoes of Isaiah show the necessity of Perse's language of incantation, for the making of poetry, and the survival of individuals and entire cultures in dark times. But whereas in *Anabase* Perse's Leader turns resolutely away from the seductive satisfactions of dreaming and introspective withdrawal, affirming the priority of political action, the primary "difficulty" confronted by the statesman and lyric speaker in Eliot's poem is his effort to salvage an adequately ritualized language of self-purification, meditation and renewal amidst the nightmarish, impossibly faction-ridden rhetorical rubble of contemporary politics. The small creatures that chirp thinly in Eliot's closing lines, recalling Isaiah's grasshoppers as well as the voice among the bones in *Ash-Wednesday*, evoke the trial of statesman and poet alike striving for speech that will meet a spiritual need.

As in *Ash-Wednesday*, in "Difficulties" Eliot portrays his speaker's yearning for a still moment symbolically evoked by the presence of a feminine, saving dove, but the formal resemblance also poignantly highlights what Eliot did not know about the political future of Europe at the time when he wrote the earlier poem. And, unlike Eliot's highly stylized, allegorical description (rendered in dimeter) of the Rose Garden in *Ash-Wednesday* (ii), in "Difficulties" we are presented with long lines and an accumulation of concrete imagery in homologous series that are reminiscent of both Perse and Whitman:

> O hidden under the . . . Hidden under the . . .
> >   Where the dove's foot rested and locked for a moment,
> A still moment, repose of noon, set under the upper branches of
> >   noon's widest tree
> Under the breast feather stirred by the small wind after noon
> There the cyclamen spreads its wings, there the clematis droops over
> >   the lintel.[102]

Richard Abel, who noted that Eliot's images in this passage bear the mark of Perse's influence, does not go on to show how they promise concreteness while at the same time putting this solidity into question through symbolic resonance and ambiguity, creating an ambience that is highly characteristic of Perse.[103] Although "cyclamen" is the scientific botanical name for a genus of plants, the figurative context in which the word occurs ("spreads its wings") could lead an unknowing reader to the assumption that Eliot literally refers to a kind of bird. Even when we realize that the cyclamen is a tuberous plant, and the phrase "spreads its wings" is a figurative description of blooming (an image that recalls the dried tubers in April of *The Waste Land*'s opening lines, as well as "(Why should the aged eagle stretch its wings?)" in *Ash-Wednesday*), ambiguities still proliferate.[104] Because the genus *Cyclamen* is notable for the fact that it includes species that flower every month of the year, we cannot be sure of the passage's seasonality; and although the plant has strong national associations with English gardens, in the wild they are also found in other parts of Europe, as well as western Asia and North Africa, so the geographical setting is also unclear.

Unlike Eliot's cyclamen, the clematis in "Difficulties" acquires a more literal and precise topographical referent when we remember Eliot's visit, with Emily Hale, to the garden of *Burnt Norton* in September 1935: "Will the sunflower turn to us, will the clematis / Stray down, bend to us; tendril and spray / Clutch and cling?"[105] In "Difficulties," however, the clematis is drooping and past its peak, figuratively evoking spiritual exhaustion and despair, or perhaps a seasonal setting some time in late summer or late fall, depending on the species. Still, the plant's appearance remains altogether ambiguous, insofar as the genus *Clematis* comprises over 200 species, all bafflingly diverse with regard to form, color, bloom season and height, not to mention the vast number of existing garden hybrids.[106]

Remarking that Eliot had offered both "Triumphal March" and "Difficulties of a Statesman" for publication in *Commerce*, Sophie Levie explains that Marguerite Caetani and the editorial staff would probably have found the former too militaristic, and too political, for Europe in the 1930s.[107] It is true that there are fewer obvious political references in "Difficulties" than there are in "Triumphal March," but when we look closely at the poem's correlations with Perse's political career and struggles against fascism during the late 1930s, some unexpectedly powerful political meanings are brought to light.

By the time Perse published *Anabase* in 1924, he had already spent a decade immersed in public affairs, having entered the French diplomatic service in 1914, where he was known by his given name, Marie-René-August Aléxis Saint-Léger. Serving first in China, and later as Cabinet Chief for the statesman Aristide Briand, Perse's own difficulties as a statesman began in 1933, when he became Secretary General of Foreign Affairs, the highest position in the French Foreign Office, three years after the Nazi party had begun its rise to power. From 1933 to 1940, he served under a succession of Foreign Ministers who were, in his view, unable to follow "the

great rules of French diplomacy" and who did not share his commit-
ment to forming international alliances and adamant opposition to the
policy of "appeasement."[108] Engaged, reluctantly, in negotiations first with
Mussolini, and later with Stalin and Hitler (who tried to insult Perse by
calling him a black man or *martiniquais*), and vocal in his resistance to
Nazism, Perse was dismissed from his post shortly after the Second World
War broke out in 1939, only a few weeks before the defeat of France by
Nazi Germany.[109] The Vichy government passed against him a sentence
of "national indignity" and, as a result, he lost his citizenship and all his
property in France. The Gestapos ransacked his apartment, destroying
all his precious, unpublished manuscripts and, by June 1940, stripped of
his job, his property, his life's work as a poet, as well as his French citizenship, he prepared to leave French soil. During his wartime exile in
the United States, he worked as a consultant on French literature in the
Library of Congress, and turned to the poetic vocation he would never again
relinquish.[110]

Eliot's "We demand a committee . . . of investigation," and especially
the ambiguous concluding statement "RESIGN RESIGN RESIGN" fit well with
what we know to be Perse's experience during this period, with regard both
to his career and to his spiritual and political exile. The report issued by
a postwar investigation commission blamed Perse and his colleagues for
France's disastrously inadequate foreign policy during the war years, charging him with "intellectual acrobatics" and "rigid adherence to a system
rather than political views grounded on realities."[111] Elizabeth Cameron
observes that neither Perse's intellectual clarity nor his liberal political philosophy would spare him "the execution of policy decisions which he dis-
approved." She continues:

Léger was no willing accomplice of the champions of appeasement . . . Yet hating
both the tawdry politics and unforeseen damages of surrender to Nazi demands, he
nevertheless followed a line which hewed closely to that of the appeasers on the need
for concessions to Germany in Czechoslovakia. At the time he was convinced that
even a French government dedicated to resistance would have had no alternative
to diplomacy by conference . . . It can be argued that Léger, at odds with the
trimming policies of successive Foreign Ministers, should have resigned his post,
before Rome in 1935, before London in 1936, or before Munich in 1938 . . . Yet
it can also be argued, and perhaps with a greater cogency, that by remaining he
could still hope to exercise a restraining influence, a small but valid function of
prevention even on the road to surrender.[112]

Perse scrupulously separated his activities as a statesman from his
acclaimed work as a poet. Still, it is illuminating to consider Perse's

opposition to Hitler's militant racial nationalism, and his ardent condemnation of the "mentality of prewar imperialist Germany," given *Anabase*'s emphasis on the violence of imperialism and the resulting hybridity of frontier cultures.[113] Perse, like Eliot, was well aware of the inescapable cultural hybridity of his childhood in Guadeloupe. His friend Valery Larbaud, in the same article comparing Perse to Whitman, emphasized the mixing of European national cultures in Perse's Antillean milieu.[114] Although Columbus had given the island a Spanish name after a monastery in Guadeloupe, Extremadura, the French claimed possession after 1635, vying intermittently with Britain for control until the Treaty of Vienna in 1815. Guadeloupe, like many Caribbean locales, was originally inhabited by Amerindians, first Arawaks and then Caribs, until the French came and wiped most of them out. African slaves were used to cultivate sugar cane, and Indians and Chinese were brought in as indentured laborers in the post-emancipation period, so Guadeloupean culture was a complex blend of European, African, Asian and Amerindian elements.

The commingling of bloods and cultures on the frontier is vividly and intimately described in Canto 6 in *Anabase*: the same canto that significantly influenced Eliot's imagery in "Journey of the Magi"; the first place where "frontière" appears in Perse's poem; and the only instance where the word is employed literally. Here, the Leader tells a messenger to recruit the cavaliers – people sitting idly amidst the crops on the slopes, dismounted from their horses ("démontés") – and invites them to practice their "habitudes de violence" on the weaker, economically vulnerable western provinces of the frontier ("Aux pays épuisés"). In contrast to Canto 8, where the actualities of conquest are hidden behind a veil of Whitmanian symbols and figures, in this passage the Leader expresses great joy in realizing the limit of his power – power, that is, to hybridize, perpetuating new families and lines of descent; to invent an entirely new culture by suppressing and unifying diverse peoples (whom he compares to caged birds, "comme des encagées d'oiseaux siffleurs") through the violent imposition of an imperial order.

Whereas, in all the printings of the first edition, Eliot translated Perse's metaphorical "frontière de l'esprit" in Canto 8 as "marches of the spirit," in Canto 6 "frontière" was rendered as "frontier."

. . . Pour nous qui étions là, nous pro-
duisîmes aux frontières des accidents extraordinaires, et
nous portant dans nos actions à la limite de nos forces, notre
joie parmi vous fut une très grande joie:
"Je connais cette race établie sur les pentes: cavaliers

démontés dans les cultures vivrières. Allez et dites à ceux-là:
un immense péril à courir avec nous! des actions sans nombre
et sans mesure, des volontés puissantes et dissipatrices et le
pouvoir de l'homme consommé comme la grappe dans la
vigne . . . Allez et dites bien: nos habitudes de violence, nos
chevaux sobres et rapides sur les semences de révolte et nos
casques flairés par la fureur du jour . . . Aux pays épuisés
où les coutumes sont à reprendre, tant de familles à com-
poser comme des encagées d'oiseaux siffleurs, vous nous
verrez, dans nos façons d'agir, assembleurs de nations sous
de vastes hangars, lecteurs de bulles à voix haute, et vingt
peuples sous nos lois parlant toutes les langues . . .[115]

In the 1938 American printing of the first edition, Eliot's translation reads as follows:

> . . . For us who were there, we caused at the frontiers ex-
> ceptional accidents, and pushing ourselves in our actions to
> the end of our strength, our joy amongst you was a very
> great joy:
> "I know this folk squatting on the slopes, horsemen dis-
> mounted among the food crops. Go say to them: a great risk
> to run with us! deeds innumerable unmeasured, puissant
> and destructive wills, and the power of man brought to
> fruition like the grape in the vine . . . Go and say truly:
> our habits of violence, our horses staid and swift upon the
> seeds of sedition and our helmets sniffed by the fury of the
> day . . . In the faint lands where the ways of life are to be
> remade, so many families to be composed like cages of whis-
> tling birds, you shall see us, the way we do, gatherers of na-
> tions under vast shelters, readers aloud of decrees, and
> twenty peoples under our law speaking all tongues . . ."[116]

In all three editions, Eliot loosely translates Perse's "établir" (a verb that means to settle or to establish) with the same American frontierism, "squatting," he used in "Gerontion." Perse's frontier setting in this canto may also have been of particular interest to Eliot insofar as *frontière* accurately registers the etymological derivation of "frontier" from Old French ("faire frontière"), thereby preserving the word's explicit connotations of military attack, resistance and territorial conquest. This is in keeping with their shared commitment to realism, historical sense and stylistic acknowledgment of tradition. Although, like Whitman, Perse creates a mythically transcendent world, in this passage he is more frankly specific about the frontier's violent actualities than Whitman in these lines from "Starting from Paumanok":

Omnes! omnes! Let others ignore what they may,
I make the poem of evil also, I commemorate that part also,
I am myself just as much evil as good, and my nation is –
    and I say there is in fact no evil,
(or if there is I say it is just as important to you, to the land
    or to me, as any thing else.)[117]

In a preface by Hugo von Hofmannsthal that was appended to the 1949 edition of Eliot's translation, Perse's *Anabase* is described, somewhat misleadingly, as having been "created . . . in the spirit of our day, that alert and heroic spirit of contemporary France which is . . . founding a new colonial empire before its southern gates."[118] It would be more accurate to add that Perse's mythopoesis also accommodates a domain of historical fact; and that Richard Slotkin's conclusion that "the first colonists saw in America an opportunity to regenerate their fortunes, . . . but the means to that regeneration ultimately became the means of violence," is entirely apposite to the frontier landscape of *Anabase*.[119] In Perse, "a great principle of violence" not only dictates the "moeurs" (that is, the morals, manners or, as Eliot puts it, "fashions" of the conquerors), and the suggestively revealed inner landscape of Perse's poetry; it also highlights the violence that took place on the frontiers of empire, transcultural contact zones of the Americas.

Valery Larbaud, describing the effects of Guadeloupe's hybrid culture on Perse's formation as a poet, refers to the "old blood of the New World," a primitivist acknowledgment of the island's Amerindian past.[120] According to Rigolot, many of Whitman's poems in Perse's Bazalgette edition, but especially "Starting from Paumanok," are heavily annotated in Perse's hand.[121] Evidently, Perse was drawn to the poem – the first by Whitman, as we have seen, to be published in French translation and possibly read by Laforgue, a work Eliot may have recalled when he confronted the inescapable fact of a New World cultural *mélange*. Comparing Amerindian names to "calls as of birds . . . in the woods," Whitman may even have helped to elicit Perse's striking simile, "tant de familles à composer comme des encagées d'oiseaux siffleurs":

The red aborigines,
Leaving natural breaths, sounds of rain and winds, calls as of
    birds and animals in the woods, syllabled to us for
    names,
Okonee, Koosa, Ottawa, Monongahela, Sauk, Natchez,
    Chattahoochee, Kaqueta, Oronoco,
Wabash, Miami, Saginaw, Chippewa, Oshkosh, Walla-Walla,
Leaving such to the States they melt, they depart, charging
    the water and the land with names.[122]

In *Vents* – an epic poem that is, like *Anabase*, about the history and figurative possibilities of the frontier – Perse expresses, in Whitmanian fashion, the desire to forget and disperse all history. Speaking of *Vents*, Perse once said the poem expresses "a general impatience towards all accomplishments, all the ashes and acquisitions of the human environment."[123] Despite this impatience and his poem's compulsive forward momentum, in *Vents* (IV) Perse's speaker labors to commemorate the Amerindian presence, while the winds of destruction momentarily subside. Though the frontier and the reference to an Amerindian in his canoe are metaphorical, figures that evoke a desire to forget and take refuge in the pleasures of the flesh, still we are left with traces that suggest the literal actualities of frontier history:

> . . . *C'était hier. Les vents se turent. – N'est-il rien*
> *que d'humain?*
> *"À moins qu'il ne sa hâte, en perdra trace ton*
> *poème . . ." Ô frontière, ô mutisme! Aversion du dieu!*
> *Et les capsules encore du néant dans notre bouche de*
> *vivants.*
> . . .
>
> *Et certains disent qu'il faut rire – allez-vous donc les*
> *révoquer en doute? Ou qu'il faut feindre – les confondre?*
> *Et d'autres s'inscrivent en faux dans la chair de la*
> *femme, comme étroitement l'Indien, dans sa pirogue*
> *d'écorce, pour remonter le fleuve vagissant jusqu'en ses*
> *bras de fille, vers l'enfance.*[124]

[It was yesterday. The winds silenced themselves. – Is there nothing but a human thing? "Unless you hurry, your poem will lose track of it . . ." Oh frontier, oh muteness! Aversion of god! And still capsules of nothingness in our mouth of the living . . . And certain people say that we have to laugh – are you therefore going to doubtfully dismiss them? Or that we must dissemble – are you going to confound them? And others, denying this, take refuge in the flesh of a woman, like an Indian in his bark canoe, in order to go upriver wailing until they are in the woman's arms, towards infancy.]

Like *Vents*, *Anabase* calls attention to the inescapability of the past: in Canto 8, Perse hints at the Amerindian legacy when his speaker describes the act of mashing an "Indian cocculus" (or seed-containing berry), combined with the image of a "yellow wind" used as an evocation of soulful lust, to intimate conquest on the frontier, and the resulting hybridity that culminates in Perse's own poem and idiom. Because *Anabase's* topography is so ambiguous, however, we cannot be sure whether Perse refers to Indians from India or to indigenous peoples in the New World. The inhabitants of Perse's frontier lack modern technology and appear, on first reading, to live in a remote, pre-industrial epoch. Perse omits the recent mechanized phases of history, Knodel says, in order to "place man against the background of the more elemental forces that are always present but that mechanization tends to obscure."[125] But the assumption that the poem's action takes place in a pre-industrial era is overturned by the presence of one vivid and concrete reference in Canto 5 to the Bielids, a meteor-shower occurring in late November whose name is derived from that of Wilhelm von Biela (1782–1856), a German astronomer – a foray into fact which suggests that the poem's era may be closer to our own.[126]

Many readers, including Eliot, have speculated that *Anabase* is set somewhere on the Asiatic continent. "The poem," he said in 1930, "is a series of images of migration, of conquest of vast spaces in Asiatic wastes, of destruction and foundation of cities and civilizations of any races or epochs of the ancient East."[127] Some details of the poem (the journey on horseback, caravan routes, desert-wastes) recall Perse's experiences as a diplomat in China from 1916 to 1921, the early years of the Chinese Revolution. We know that he composed the poem in China after seeing the Gobi desert. There are also recollections of Xenophon's *Anabase*, which chronicles the battle of Cunaxa and the retreat of the Persian Army of Ten Thousand, after the death of Cyrus the Younger in 401 BC, along the plains between the Tigris and the Euphrates rivers in Upper Asia. Perse himself claimed that his poem had nothing to do with Xenophon, but Rigolot contends that "the 'family of Cyrus' preoccupied Perse from very early . . . In *Anabase*, under a title reminiscent of Xenophon and the Persians, Saint-John Perse founds his own poetic Persepolis."[128]

The topographical ambiguity of *Anabase* suggests that Poe was another New World antecedent Perse shared with Eliot, exerting as strong an influence on this poem as on Perse's *Images à Crusoé, Pour fêter une enfance* and *Éloges.* Like Poe's *Al Aaraaf,* which obliquely refers to Persepolis, the capital of ancient Persia that was burned to the ground by Alexander the Great in 330 BC, Perse's poem evokes an Asiatic setting. In Canto 5 of *Anabase,* the Leader mentions the "Mers Mortes" over the course of his nocturne and, similarly, Poe's "The City in the Sea" recalls the ruins of the Cities of the Plain that sank in the Dead Sea. Like Poe, Perse creates the effect of concreteness that is curiously lacking in specificity.[129] In Canto 4 of *Anabase,* for example, Perse describes the building of a city, dedicated "sous les labiales d'un nom pur," but, though we are given this precise detail about the city's name, the name itself is never mentioned.

Despite strong indications of an Asiatic setting, the dry plains that are so memorably rendered in *Anabase* also bring to mind Whitman's Edenic New World frontier.[130] We know that Perse visited the United States in 1921, and was deeply affected by the vast frontier spaces and natural phenomena he encountered during the trip.[131] His opening canto in *Anabase* shows the founding of a new social order in a coastal region, and the nomad Leader describes a seedless or virgin soil ("la terre sans amandes") that delivers an incorruptible sky ("ce ciel incorruptible") to the conquerors, who build a city there.

Anabase's mythic evocation of the frontier is, moreover, strikingly concretized in Canto 10 when, during the course of a long Whitmanian catalogue of vocations and pastimes, Perse's speaker suddenly mentions a man who is eating beetle-larvae from the cabbage-palm, a Guadeloupean delicacy ("celui qui mange . . . des vers de palmes"). As Perse himself wrote to André Gide in a 1911 letter:

And have the Botanists further told you that it is this tall palmtree, the handsomest of its race, that is doomed to death by having its heart cut out, that is, the leaves, still white and tender, that are curled at the centre of the crown, which are eaten, chopped up in an extraordinarily good salad? And then, two months later, one has a fine harvest of "cabbage-palm worms," fat larvae of a beetle (calandra palmarum) that lays its eggs in the tree-pith. You eat them alive or slightly roasted, always in a salad, with lemon-juice, pepper, and salt.[132]

Another sudden, strikingly precise reference to New World fauna occurs in Canto 8, where Perse describes a species of bird, "les mésanges" (the black-capped chickadee, *Poecile atricapilla*), found only in Canada and the upper two-thirds of the United States. The geographical distribution of the chickadee has historical resonance insofar as it covers a region spanning contested frontier colonial territories repeatedly fought over by Britain and France (for example, during the French and Indian Wars, 1689–1763), and, in 1812, by the USA as well. Equally striking is Eliot's mistranslation of Perse's "les mésanges": in the first and second editions he rendered the word as "tomtits," a widely distributed European titmouse; and in the third edition – a revision, presumably, made at the request of Perse – as "crested tits." *Baeolophus bicolor*, the tufted titmouse, also goes by such names as crested titmouse, crested tomtit, tufted chickadee and tufted tit, and it is common east of the Great Plains, in the woodlands of the southeastern United States, the Midwest and southern Ontario. But although, like the common chickadee, this is a New World species, its geographical range is far broader and more ambiguous than the chickadee's, since it is also endemic to Greenland, the Canadian Arctic islands, and all of the North American continent as far south as the highlands of central Mexico.[133] "In his translation of *Anabase*," writes Bush, "Eliot is concerned to heighten the opacity of the verse and emphasize the exoticism of Perse's central images."[134] We see here that Eliot's emphasis on exoticism may also have led him to obscure Perse's precise description of a well-known North American bird.

Although the concluding cantos of *Anabase* portray a joyous, passionate reception of the conquerors by women of the new country, the poem as a whole expresses deep ambivalence towards the hybrid fruits of such cross-cultural encounters, and especially the resulting proliferation of undocumented lines of descent in frontier societies. "O généalogiste sur la place!" Perse writes in Canto 10, "Combien d'histoires de familles et de filiations?" According to Albert Henry, this question is parenthetically elaborated in the manuscript of *Anabase*, illustrating that Perse's fascination with lineage is far greater than we can see in the final version of the poem.[135] *Anabase* is, as Rigolot has argued, "threaded with allusions to lineage . . . A preoccupation with ancestry weaves itself through the poem from beginning to end, as the poet-narrator grapples with questions of chronology and with his relation to an inherited culture."[136]

Earlier in this chapter, I observed that Eliot's "Mélange" intimates a theme of promiscuous adultery and undocumented hybrid lineages, not only because of the lyric speaker's deracination and absorption of diverse cultures, but because the poem's formal errancies and idiosyncratic range of allusion make it very difficult to follow. In Perse's *Anabase*, as in Eliot, hybridity entails the destruction of genealogies; as such, it marks a tragic loss of a pure, known racial identity, something Perse himself valued, as he characteristically praised a work of art saying it was "très racé, très français" ("très racé, très français"), a "work of race and lineage" ("une oeuvre de race et de lignée").[137] At the same time, however, hybridity is associated with positive, equally prized qualities, especially Perse's singularity. Regarded in this light, it involves much-yearned-for transgressions that would enact a liberating break from conformity to tradition.

Noting how influential negative connotations of "hybridity" have been in imperial and colonial discourse, Homi Bhabha has reinterpreted the term so that it calls into question any claims to cultural purity and authority.[138] Perse, too, is aware of the tenuousness of such claims to purity, given the historical consequences of transculturation on the frontier. This inescapable fact of hybridity also helps to explain Perse's constant return to the theme of transgression, including sexual transgression, in *Anabase*. The Leader in the poem habitually expresses a contradictory desire to affirm his own individuality through acts of transgression and to offer ritual commemorations of the Dead: in Canto 2, at high noon, he and his party step over the drying linen of the Queen and her daughter, dramatizing forbidden passion for a wife as well as her daughter. In Canto 3, we are told that women in the community have begun to exhibit a sexual preference for animals; in Canto 4, there is a subtle reference to prostitution where a child solicits for his older sister; and in Canto 9, we witness a startling scene where young women stand on the frontier and urinate.[139] The very resolve to migrate, conquer and transgressively hybridize is evoked in response to the achievement, as Knodel puts it, of "a ripeness verging on over-ripeness," decadence and contentment verging on boredom.[140]

Eliot's abiding memory of Perse's Whitmanian frontier landscape in *Anabase*, like his earlier, formative efforts to cross the influences of Whitman and Laforgue, calls attention to his engagement with a more accurate, global conception of the frontier. In this and many other respects, as I have tried to show, *Anabase* directly addresses the concern of much recent Americanist criticism to reconceive the Whitmanian frontier by placing it within the international, comparative framework of European empire-building in the Americas. The very obliquity, furthermore, of Eliot's reference to Whitman's frontier in his early poems raises a suggestive, revealing comparison with what Glissant describes as Perse's "dilemma of the White Creole."[141] Like Perse, Eliot is caught between, on the one hand, "a metropolitan history that often does not 'include' him (and that he, in reaction, claims meticulously and energetically as his legitimate ancestry)," and, on the other, a Whitmanian, New World frontier heritage that "engenders new points of growth" but towards which he feels tortuously ambivalent.[142]

Taken together, Perse's *Anabase* and Eliot's translation work to illuminate Whitman's presence in the Francophone Caribbean, a much-neglected subject given the ample body of scholarship that is devoted to Whitman's influence on Pablo Neruda, José Martí and other Spanish American writers.[143] Still, we are left with questions regarding the effect on Eliot of his encounter with Perse. Did Eliot's translation prompt a new line of poetic exploration in his later poetry? More specifically: did Perse's poetry help Eliot to clarify his own relation, not just to Missouri, the Mississippi and other landscapes of the American frontier, but to his unlikeable, unavoidable "relative," Whitman?

NEW WORLD QUARTET: HISTORY AND THE MUSIC OF PLACE IN
"THE DRY SALVAGES"

On June 20, 1930, shortly after he put finishing touches to his portrayal of the granite shore and sails flying seaward at the end of *Ash-Wednesday*, Eliot identified Massachusetts as his ancestral home. Two years later, he paid his first visit to America since 1915, having taken up the Charles Eliot Norton professorship at Harvard for the academic year.[144] It therefore makes sense that the poems written during the 1930s are replete with returning images of the New England shorescape. In the opening lines of "Marina," composed the same year as *Ash-Wednesday*, Eliot's imagery is clear but ambiguous; though the landscape is reminiscent of the Massachusetts coast, the "marina" of the title could just as well be elsewhere. In his original draft, Eliot mentioned that the specific place he had in mind was Rogue Island at the mouth of the New Meadows River in Casco Bay, Maine, a favorite destination of sailing ventures during his childhood.[145] "Marina" is a poem of restored vision and arrival, even though we cannot say exactly in "what" small harbor the miracle, a miracle of "grace dissolved in place," happened:

> What seas what shores what grey rocks and what islands
> What water lapping the bow
> And scent of pine and the woodthrush singing through the fog
> What images return
> O my daughter.[146]

"Cape Ann," by contrast, is a poem whose title immediately informs us that its setting is off the Massachusetts coast. Whereas "Marina" is about the rejuvenation of sight, "Cape Ann" calls our attention, not to a particular view of the land but to a variety of bird dances and music of commingled birdsong that summon up remembrances of Eliot's New England childhood.

> O quick quick quick, quick hear the song-sparrow,
> Swamp-sparrow, fox-sparrow, vesper-sparrow
> At dawn and dusk. Follow the dance
> Of the goldfinch at noon. Leave to chance
> The Blackburnian warbler, the shy one. Hail
> With shrill whistle the note of the quail, the bob-white
> Dodging by bay-bush. Follow the feet
> Of the walker, the water-thrush. Follow the flight
> Of the dancing arrow, the purple martin. Greet
> In silence the bullbat. All are delectable. Sweet sweet sweet

> But resign this land at the end, resign it
> To its true owner, the tough one, the sea-gull.
> The palaver is finished.[147]

Part of the *Landscapes* sequence, written in December 1935 during Eliot's stay in America, this is a lyric where, in contrast to the woodthrush of "Marina" – a focus for quickened emotion – the beautifully expansive, geographically accurate, chanted catalogue of sparrows (all members of the family *Emberizidae*, New World sparrows found in the region of Cape Ann) confirms abundant nature as a source for Eliot's poetry while at the same time establishing his expertise and devotion to birdwatching, something he had often done as a youth.[148] As a child in Missouri, Eliot recalled, he habitually "missed the song sparrows, the red granite and the blue sea of Massachusetts."[149] Most of the birds mentioned in this poem – "goldfinch," "purple martin" and "bob-white" (which in this context modifies "quail," since the poem refers to the Northern Bobwhite, a member of the New World Quail family) – are common in New England.[150] But this precise bird imagery cohabits in the poem with "palaver" – idle nonsense words such as "bay-bush" and "bullbat," where melody matters more than sense, and the juxtaposition of scientific precision and sonorous incantation is reminiscent of Perse.

Earlier on, we saw that Eliot echoes Whitman's *Out of the Cradle Endlessly Rocking* in the ninth chorus from *The Rock*, completed roughly a year before "Cape Ann" was written, and his allusion suggests that the Old Testament is a far more plausible source for Whitman's cadences than Amerindian chants. Here, too, the musical, nonsense aspects of Eliot's poem contain hidden references to the history of transculturation in the Americas. Consider, for instance, the word "palaver," which passed into colloquial usage from nautical slang picked up by English sailors some time in the early 1770s. It is related to the word "Palavra" used by Portuguese traders on the coast of Africa, and the first definition listed in *The Oxford English Dictionary* is not "idle talk," but "A talk, parley, conference; chiefly applied to conferences between uncivilized natives."[151] "Dancing arrow," furthermore, is not a local name for the purple martin, and the formulaic quality of the metaphor recalls Longfellow's incantatory poetics and questionable translation of Ojibwa chants in *The Song of Hiawatha*.

Eliot once observed that nonsense elicits a pleasurable "feeling of irresponsibility towards the sense," but, insofar as the theoretical goal of *la poésie pure* is "one that can never be reached," subject matter will always retain its value, and the poet should aspire to a comprehensible order of commonplace speech, in addition to a beautifully new, incantatory form.[152] In "Cape Ann" he layers, in musical unison, regionally precise description; beautiful nonsense; impersonal exhortation; self-distancing irony (as in "the palaver is finished"); as well as the acutely personal but universal symbolism, present in "Gerontion" and *Ash-Wednesday*, of the triumphant and free gull – all implicit reminders that the poem's layering of names emerged from a history of regenerative frontier violence. Particular settings objectify personal emotion in Eliot's *Landscapes*, and "Cape Ann" is "pure" insofar as we never intuit a unifying personal or dramatic presence in the poem as we read.[153] What is more, the lyric fulfills this indispensable condition of impersonality while at the same time prompting us to contemplate the desolate truths of frontier history, the bittersweet realization that even the most fondly remembered Eden of childhood, personal or national, had already been violated by experience. The concluding, cryptic exhortation to "resign this land at the end, resign it / To its true owner" recalls not only the speaker's self-admonishment in "Marina" to "Resign my life for this life"; but also, in "Difficulties of a Statesman," the ambiguous cry "RESIGN RESIGN RESIGN," which intimates, among other things, a surrender of will in the face of the uncontrollable, tragic unfolding of political events. The question of ownership also calls up the sustained conflict, and cross-cultural exchanges, that took place between British settlers and the Agawam Indian nation in the New World during the seventeenth century, as well as the naming of Cape Ann after Ann of Denmark.[154]

"The Dry Salvages" – the only other poem by Eliot, besides his translation of Perse, where the frontier is explicitly mentioned – resembles "Cape Ann" insofar as it opens with a memorable, precise rendering of landscape. A little over four miles offshore from Rockport, this group of three rocks was the last landmark Eliot would see when he used to sail from Cape Ann to Maine.

(The Dry Salvages – presumably *les trois sauvages* – is a small group of rocks, with a beacon, off the N.E. coast of Cape Ann, Massachusetts. *Salvages* is pronounced to rhyme with *assuages*. *Groaner*: a whistling buoy.)

I

I do not know much about gods; but I think that the river
Is a strong brown god – sullen, untamed and intractable,
Patient to some degree, at first recognized as a frontier;
Useful, untrustworthy, as a conveyor of commerce;
Then only a problem confronting the builder of bridges.
The problem once solved, the brown god is almost forgotten

By the dwellers in cities – ever, however, implacable,
Keeping his seasons and rages, destroyer, reminder
Of what men choose to forget. Unhonoured, unpropitiated
By worshippers of the machine, but waiting, watching and waiting.
His rhythm was present in the nursery bedroom,
In the rank ailanthus of the April dooryard,
In the smell of grapes on the autumn table,
And the evening circle in the winter gaslight.

The river is within us, the sea is all about us;
The sea is the land's edge also, the granite
Into which it reaches, the beaches where it tosses
Its hints of earlier and other creation:
The starfish, the hermit crab, the whale's backbone;
The pools where it offers to our curiosity
The more delicate algae and the sea anemone.
It tosses up our losses, the torn seine,
The shattered lobsterpot, the broken oar
And the gear of foreign dead men. The sea has many voices,
Many gods and many voices.[155]

Like "Cape Ann," and the sea itself, the poem sounds, in unison, many different voices – different ways of speaking and writing, each of which implies a distinct worldview – creating a music that comes very close at times to nonsense. The first movement, for example, counterpoints a conversational, explanatory headnote; regionally particular, historically suggestive imagery (the river, the April dooryard, the ailanthus); a colloquial, at times journalistic and clichéd idiom ("worshippers of the machine"); orderly generalization and social commentary; fleeting reminiscences of childhood; and words overheard as a solitary speaker gravely reasons with himself about "our losses."

In contrast to "Cape Ann," however, here Eliot evokes not just the seaboard but a picture of the Atlantic itself, and his poem's landscape is a composite, conjoining two frontiers – the Mississippi River in St. Louis and the land's edge off the New England coast – unifying places and cultural perspectives that in Eliot's earlier writings were portrayed as separate and irreconcilable. In a 1960 lecture given at the American Academy of Arts and Sciences, Eliot discussed the influence of this composite, personal landscape, a landscape bearing traces of every environment in which he had lived, on his development as a poet. His interest in such landscapes, he said, may shed light on works such as "The Dry Salvages":

I came East . . . , at the age of seventeen, to a school not remote from Brookline; and as far back as I can remember and before, my family had spent every summer on the New England coast. So my personal landscape is a composite . . . My urban imagery was that of St. Louis, upon which that of Paris and London have been superimposed . . . My country landscape, on the other hand, is that of New England, of coastal New England, and New England from June to October. In St. Louis I never tasted an oyster or a lobster – we were too far from the sea. In Massachusetts, the small boy who was a devoted bird watcher never saw his birds of the season when they were making their nests . . .

What I have been saying was, in its first intention, merely an elaboration of the simple "Thank you." But I hope that my words will shed some light upon the poem I am about to read; and also substantiate, to some degree, my claim to being, among other things, a New England poet. You will notice, however, that this poem begins where I began, with the Mississippi; and that it ends, where I and my wife expect to end, at the parish church of a tiny village in Somerset.[156]

Eliot understood that the very sound of his title's name, like all place names, bore particular historical associations, and he expressed concern that "The Dry Salvages" should be recognized as an actual locale. In response to John Heyward's query he wrote:

"The Dry Salvages" is a place name (rhymes with "rampages"). It is ("Les trois sauvages") the name of a group of three rocks off the eastern corner of Cape Ann, Massachusetts, with a beacon: convenient for laying a course to the eastward, Maine or Nova Scotia. It happens to have just the right denotation and association for my purpose; and therefore I am the more disturbed by your comment. It doesn't matter that it should be obscure, but if it is going to lead people quite on the wrong track, then something must be done.[157]

The Dry Salvages have just the right denotation and association for Eliot's poem, not only because, as a geological formation, they represent both a unity and a composite assembly. Also they are submerged and hidden at high tide, unlike the Big Salvage (the other ledge of the reef) which is always out of the water – and, according to local legend, the danger they posed reminded settlers of Amerindian "savages." Eliot denied any authenticity for his presumed derivation of "salvages," and recalled that it was simply the pronunciation he had learned from his brother. But, according to Admiral Morison, the name:

may possibly be owing to Champlain who, in his account of his exploration of 1605, describes Cape Ann (which he called *Cap au Isles*) with its islands and reefs, and tells how near it he caught sight of a canoe in which "were five or six Indians (*sauuages*)" who came towards his pinnace, but then "went back to dance on the beach."[158]

Eliot's substitution of one rhyme word for another ("assuages," instead of "rampages") insinuates a great deal about the inextricable relation between frontier violence and cultural exchange, both in his headnote and in "The Dry Salvages" as a whole.[159] Facing the Atlantic, reaching out to nations beyond the sea, as a frontier of empires the three rocks bear powerful associations that are transnational and comparative. Like the poem itself, they remind us that frontier violence is historically related, and similar, to violence wrought by ethnic nationalist conflict and World War. Both result in "waste" and leave an enduring mark, not just on the landscape, but on the consciousness and culture of succeeding generations. In this respect, Eliot's evocation of the frontier may have owed something to James Fenimore Cooper. In 1953, Eliot remarked: "Cooper has suffered, like Walter Scott, from being read in early youth, and by many people never again."[160] D. H. Lawrence, in what Eliot described as "probably the most brilliant of critical essays on [Cooper]," describes this legacy of frontier violence:

A curious thing about the Spirit of Place is the fact that no place exerts its full influence upon a newcomer until the old inhabitant is dead or absorbed. So America. While the Red Indian existed in fairly large numbers the new colonials were in a great measure immune from the daimon, or demon of America. The moment the last nuclei of Red life break up in America, then the white men will have to reckon with the full force of the demon of the continent. At present the demon of the place and the unappeased ghosts of dead Indians act within the unconscious or under-conscious of the white American, causing the great American grouch, the Orestes-like frenzy of restlessness in the Yankee soul, the inner malaise which amounts almost to madness.[161]

In his portrayal of the Mississippi, as in his portrayal of the Dry Salvages, Eliot relates his acute personal reminiscence of loss to communal losses and collective acts of violence, not just in the United States, or in Europe, but on national frontiers throughout the world. In addition to this stern admonishment, however, the form of Eliot's opening lines in "The Dry Salvages" also attests to his participation in an American literary tradition idealizing the frontier as a mythic place of intercultural exchange. Though Eliot refrains from using the actual Amerindian name, Mississippi, within the text of his poem, his participial endings and hexameters recall the infamously inauthentic but nonetheless alluring "chants" of his American predecessor, Longfellow. Whereas the "dancing arrow" of "Cape Ann" echoed Longfellow's adaptation of Amerindian epic formulae, "The Dry Salvages" recalls Longfellow's *Evangeline*, a poem that also opens with a memorable evocation of the turbulent Mississippi. The allusion suggests that frontier history, the New World's hybrid cultural legacy, like the experience of war, are an inescapable part of Eliot's past. "One imagines that this rhythm," Gardner comments, "the rhythm of *Evangeline*, came almost unconsciously here among memories of early childhood."[162]

Whereas the banks of the Mississippi are barely hinted at by the "Pays-Bas" of "Lune de miel," or the slow-moving rivers of Eliot's other early works, "The Dry Salvages" begins, in Eliot's phrase, "where I began," and every figurative aspect of the poem's lowland prairie setting bears the full weight of the past.[163] The poem is centrally about the shaping effect of history on poetic form, and the poet's imperfect effort to arrange, reflect on and thereby experience a life that would otherwise be hastily lived, and wasted, amidst a meaningless welter of details. The audible echo of these forms (sonnet, sestina, catalogue, rhyme), like the "ghost of some simple metre" lurking behind Eliot's free verse, represents a creative, volitional choice to confer meaning on a small handful of remembered images encountered over the course of a lifetime of peregrination.[164] Regarded in the light of history, even the most minute of stylistic decisions may come to represent the independence of the pioneer, on what Eliot called, echoing Perse in 1939, the "frontiers of the spirit" or, three years later, the "frontiers of consciousness beyond which words fail, though meanings still exist."[165] Insofar as these decisions show a desire for meaning, and enhance our experience of orderly beginnings and endings, they offer an illuminating contrast to the powerfully dictatorial natural force Eliot once attributed to the Mississippi River as the setting appears in Twain's *The Adventures of Huckleberry Finn*:

A river, a very big and powerful river, is the only natural force that can wholly determine the course of human peregrination. At sea, the wanderer may sail or be carried by winds and currents in one direction or another; a change of wind or tide may determine fortune. In the prairie, the direction of movement is more or less at the choice of the caravan . . . But the river with its strong, swift current is the dictator to the raft or to the steamboat . . . Huck Finn must come from nowhere and be bound for nowhere. His is not the independence of the typical or symbolic American Pioneer, but the independence of the vagabond. His existence questions the values of America as much as the values of Europe; he is as much an affront to the "pioneer spirit" as he is to "business enterprise" . . . He has no beginning and no end . . . Like Huckleberry Finn, the River itself has no beginning or end. In its beginning, it is not yet the River; in its end, it is no longer the River . . . At what point in its course does the Mississippi become what the Mississippi means?[166]

There is a consensus among critics that Eliot's style in "The Dry Salvages" suggests a concern with the frontier between poetry and prose – a concern that was most explicitly addressed in Eliot's 1930 preface to *Anabase*, but which was raised two years earlier (significantly, in connection with Whitman's style) in the introduction to Pound's *Selected Poems*, and hinted at over two decades earlier in "Ode," where Eliot's compressed style, economy of phrase, and reference to a "sacred wood" within the poem's composite landscape all implicitly commemorate the concentrated critical prose of *The Sacred Wood*, written during the same period.[167] Kenner, for example, observes that:

There is nothing in the last three-quarters of "The Dry Salvages," not the materials handled, the mode of ideation, nor the process by which instance yields formulation, that is beyond the scope of a sensitive prose essayist . . . The poem leads us out of "poetry" – the river and the sea – down into small dry air in which to consider in an orderly fashion what "most of us" are capable of.[168]

Christopher Ricks comments on a related point, the importance of rhyme as a means of creating, and dramatizing, an "elemental continuity" between the first, tidepool-like couplet of "The Dry Salvage" and the ambience of the passage where it occurs.[169] Insofar as the couplet offers us momentary relief from the feeling of fated necessity evoked by the strong flow of narrated consciousness in "The Dry Salvages," rhyme proves essential to the poet's design, marking a frontier between poetry and prose. The significant work performed by rhyme is also revealed by the headnote, where rhyme actively preserves the traditional pronunciation of an obscure place name. Unlike Whitman's simplified spelling "Hymenee," which destroys traces of the word's history, here Eliot's enforcement, through rhyme, of the French pronunciation of "Salvages" admonishes us to remember, in Gardner's phrase, the "permanence of past agonies" inscribed on the symbolically conjoined frontiers of Eliot's childhood.[170]

Although the river is highlighted as a frontier setting in "The Dry Salvages," Eliot's evocation of the sea's voices heard from the land's edge off Cape Ann inspires far more beautiful, memorable poetry. The delicate intermingling of seascape and landscape – the salt on the briar rose, the fog in the fir trees – creates natural forms as strangely new as Eliot's own intermingling of poetry and prose.

> . . . The sea has many voices,
> Many gods and many voices.
> The salt is on the briar rose,
> The fog is in the fir trees.
> The sea howl
> And the sea yelp, are different voices

Often together heard; the whine in the rigging,
The menace and caress of wave that breaks on water,
The distant rote in the granite teeth,
And the wailing warning from the approaching headland
Are all sea voices, and the heaving groaner
Rounded homewards, and the seagull:
And under the oppression of the silent fog
The tolling bell
Measures time not our time, rung by the unhurried
Ground swell, a time
Older than the time of chronometers, older
Than time counted by anxious worried women
Lying awake, calculating the future,
Trying to unweave, unwind, unravel
And piece together the past and the future,
Between midnight and dawn, when the past is all deception,
The future futureless, before the morning watch
When time stops and time is never ending;
And the ground swell, that is and was from the beginning,
Clangs
The bell.[171]

The permeability of the frontier between poetry and prose in "The Dry Salvages" immeasurably broadens possibilities for reminiscence. Like a Gloucester fisherman's seine, or the Mississippi River, the poem gathers a richly diverse choir of voices comprising the American cultural landscape, accommodating rhythms and images that disclose Eliot's very beginnings as a poet. We know, for example, that Eliot's earliest rendering of the heroic sea voyage to the Grand Banks by Gloucester fishermen in "The Dry Salvages" had been cut by Pound (who called it "bad") from the "Death by Water" section of the *Waste Land* manuscript:

> We beat around the cape and laid our course
> From the Dry Salvages to the eastern banks.
> . . .
> Said one of influence amongst the rest,
> "I'll see a dead man in an iron coffin,
> "With a crowbar row from here to Hell, before
> "This vessel sail to windward".
> So the crew moaned; the sea with many voices
> Moaned all about us, under a rainy moon,
> While the suspended winter heaved and tugged,
> Stirring foul weather under the Hyades.

Eliot's sea, moaning with many voices, his reference to the Hyades (a cluster of stars named after the sisters or daughters of Hyas who died mourning his death), and the rhythms of the passage call up the heroic sea voyage in search of a Newer World from Tennyson's *Ulysses*.[172]

There are also memories of Whitman's *Sea Drift* lyrics, with their reminiscences of "briers" on the seashore, the sea's dirge composed of "voices of men and women wreck'd," the "loud admonition" of a "warning bell" ringing by the sea reefs, as well as the birth of poetic sensibility on Paumanok's shores.[173] Like Eliot, Whitman is centrally concerned in these poems with the frontier between poetry and prose, form and formlessness – the seashore evoking a "dividing line, contact, junction, the solid marrying the liquid – that curious, lurking something . . . which means far more than its mere first sight."[174] Equally significant is Whitman's antiphonal design, especially in *Out of the Cradle Endlessly Rocking* where, as Kerry Larsen has shown, the deliberate interweaving of echoes "softens any sense of agonistic encounter among its personae: by establishing a serial, complementary interdependence among its voices the poem skillfully evades the competition for power or influence such as might transpire between an 'I' and a 'you,' between the singer and his speech, or between a 'me' and 'the real Me.'" Although Eliot, unlike Whitman, dispenses with personae in *Four Quartets*, the music of "The Dry Salvages" results, as in Whitman's best work, from the intimate harmonious orchestration of voices – not from the dominance of any personal voice, or in the beauty or particularity of what is said. "It is string music," Kenner reminds us, "more closely analogous to the human voice than any other instrumentation, but still not to be confused with either quotidian discourse or with a particular person speaking."[175]

Published in 1941, two years after the declaration of yet another World War and a year after the Blitz, "The Dry Salvages" also recalls Whitman's wartime elegy, *When Lilacs Last by the Dooryard Bloom'd*. Like Whitman's poem, which was written to console and unify a grieving, broken nation in the aftermath of Civil War, Eliot's "The Dry Salvages" was written in response to war's destruction of hope in a collective cultural life. Critics such as Charles Feidelson, David Moody and Harold Bloom have identified Whitman as the source of Eliot's frontierism, his "dooryard"; Moody finds echoes of Whitman's "With the tolling tolling bells' perpetual clang"; and close readers have been struck, more generally, by the Whitmanian tone of the poem's memorable exhortation, "fare forward."[176] The seasonality of Eliot's dooryard setting may remember as well a more hidden and ambivalent tribute to the power of Whitman's lilac symbolism in *The Waste Land*:

"Beneath all the declamations," Eliot wrote in 1926, "there is another tone, and behind all the illusions there is another vision. When Whitman speaks of lilacs or of the mocking-bird, his theories and beliefs drop away like a needless pretext."[177]

By the time Eliot was writing "The Dry Salvages," he had given himself over to a careful study of Whitman, and found something of tremendous value, more important even than perfect craft. Speaking at the Churchill Club in 1944, he offered this telling contrast between Whitman and Tennyson, praising Whitman for his endless effort to realize, and communicate, his intuitive perception of communal responsibility, and "a relationship between individuals by which he wanted society to be governed":

He is a greater poet than Tennyson: Tennyson is a great craftsman, but there is something more in Whitman's account of John Paul Jones's seafight in *Song of Myself* – a greater depth and universality – than in Tennyson's "Revenge," or any other of his military and patriotic poems. Whitman is more like Wordsworth, a poet of a particular intuition which took possession of him. In Whitman, this goes much deeper than mere social or political views. It is a perception, of strange intensity, of a relationship between individuals by which he wanted society to be governed and which he spent his life communicating to others . . . I shan't attempt to explain this – any more than Wordsworth's feeling – but it is essential to grasp this to understand the poet.[178]

Whitman's delineation of the "old-time sea fight," the 1779 Revolutionary War battle between John Paul Jones's *BonHomme Richard* and a British vessel, the HMS *Serapis*, was drawn from "the yarn" he heard, not from his "grandmother's father," as his poem relates, but from his mother's mother, whose father had served under Jones, and from the narrative of Jones himself in a report to Benjamin Franklin and the Continental Congress that had been printed in *Old South Leaflets*.

> Would you hear of an old-time sea-fight?
> Would you learn who won by the light of the moon and stars?
> List to the yarn, as my grandmother's father the sailor told it to me.[179]

The vivid dramatic monologue of section 35, which conveys details of the seafight, is notable in and of itself, but even more unforgettable is Whitman's rendering of Jones's mode of conquest. At the end of section 35 we hear that the British surrendered; section 36 opens with a remarkable portrait of the victors the moment before Jones and his men board the captured ship, a passage that reveals how impossible it is ever to "win" a war of independence that was also, in effect, a Civil War:

Toward twelve there in the beams of the moon they
    surrender to us.
. . .
Stretch'd and still lies the midnight,
Two great hulls motionless on the breast of the darkness,
Our vessel riddled and slowly sinking, preparations to pass
    to the one we have conquer'd,
The captain on the quarter-deck coldly giving his orders
    through a countenance white as a sheet,
Near by the corpse of the child that serv'd in the cabin,
The dead face of an old salt with long white hair and
    carefully curl'd whiskers,
The flames spite of all that can be done flickering aloft and
    below,
. . .
A few large stars overhead, silent and mournful shining,
Delicate sniffs of sea-breeze, smells of sedgy grass and fields
    by the shore, death-messages giving in charge to survivors . . .
. . .
These so, these irretrievable.[180]

Whitman's account of the seafight may well have been on Eliot's mind when he was writing "The Dry Salvages," where Eliot not only refers topically to Navy experiences, but also draws images from his own political journalism.[181] In 1937, writing about the Spanish Civil War, Eliot had associated the figure of Arjuna with the "balance of mind" of extraordinary, informed individuals whose partisanship, even in combat, would be held with "reservations, humility and misgiving":

Now an ideally unprejudiced person, with an intimate knowledge of Spain, its history, its racial characteristics, and its contemporary personalities, might be in a position to come to the conclusion that he should, in the longest view that could be seen, support one side rather than the other . . . and even any eventual partisanship should be held with reservations, humility and misgiving. That balance of mind which a few highly-civilized individuals, such as Arjuna, the hero of the Bhagavad Gita, can maintain in action, is difficult for most of us even as observers, and, as I say, is not encouraged by the greater part of the Press.[182]

The ideal of such balance, as well as the ideal of reconciliation iconically embodied in the Dry Salvages, and formally dramatized by Eliot's composite landscape technique and musical orchestration of voices, are further confirmed by Eliot's allusive practice in the poem. For Eliot of the *Four Quartets*, writes Ricks, "an essential quest becomes where and how to discover an animation, in the very words, which would not have its deepest source in animosity," and this new, reconciliatory practice is at one with Eliot's changed method of allusion to poets such as Tennyson. As when discussing Tennyson (whom he first compared to Whitman in a 1926 essay and again in a talk almost two decades later), in selecting for remembrance Whitman's greatest poetry, Eliot alludes without anger or disfigurement.[183]

Insofar as "The Dry Salvages" marks a new, reconciliatory phase in Eliot's relations with Whitman, this may well have been helped by his involved collaboration with Perse. Richard Abel has observed that, after the translation of *Anabase*, Eliot tends more often to employ precise plant, animal and topographical imagery drawn from his childhood experiences in New England and St. Louis. Abel argues that – although this change in style can be explained, in part, by Eliot's return to the United States in the early 1930s, and by Eliot's growing acceptance, after his conversion, of a natural, embodied world he had previously treated with pained ambivalence – still "the diverse and startling imagery of *Anabase* . . . probably also helped in its immediacy and concreteness to stimulate the recovery of that youthful world."[184] The regional topography and natural imagery of "The Dry Salvages" are far more vivid than in earlier poems such as "Lune de miel" or "Ode." In "Lune de miel," for example, Eliot eruditely mentions the Acanthus, a genus of flowering plant found throughout the Mediterranean region that was also a conventional symbol in classical Greek architecture, and in medieval and Renaissance sculpture – a plant which, in the Victorian language of flowers, symbolized art. In "Ode," the American regional connotations of Eliot's floral diction (*Calamus* and *Hymenaea*) would have been unfamiliar to most readers. In "The Dry Salvages," by contrast, Eliot's "rank ailanthus," otherwise known as *Ailanthus altissima*, Tree-of-Heaven or Chinese sumac, directly recalls a tree that stood very near the house where Eliot played as a young boy.[185]

Here, as in his allusions to Whitman and Tennyson, Eliot recalls the name of this tree without animosity or disfigurement. Commenting on the fact that in the earliest manuscript Eliot had put "efflorescence" before eventually changing it to "rank ailanthus," Ricks proposes that:

part of Eliot's enterprise . . . is the redeeming of his prejudicial predation in "Whispers of Immorality" . . . "Effluence," "rank," "smell," and "drawing-room" have come (via "efflorescence") to be recollected, in tranquillity this time, as "the rank ailanthus," "the smell of grapes" and "the nursery bedroom." The vulgarized foreign ("Grishkin has a maisonnette") had been, as it always will be, a focus for prejudice . . . But in *Four Quartets* there are only three occurrences of a foreign language and none of them is an irruption.[186]

Eliot very likely would have known that "ailanthus" is a Latinized version of a much more exotic word: *aylanto*, or *ailanto*, meaning "tree-of-heaven," in a language spoken on the island of Ambon, in eastern Indonesia, in the Moluccas near Ceram. Historically, the tree illustrates the intricate, world-wide system of commerce, cultural exchange and migration that formed part of the legacy of imperialism. First introduced into England from China in the mid eighteenth century as an ornamental plant, Tree-of-Heaven was not only imported to the United States, in 1784, by a gardener in Philadelphia; it was also brought into California by Chinese immigrants during the goldrush in the mid-1800s. Set in this rich context, the precision and suggestiveness of the image illustrate a point Moody once raised – that Eliot's range of American material was vital but drastically limited, thus it is all the more evident that Eliot enhances the connotative power of each image each time he puts it to fresh use: "'The Dry Salvages' might be called Eliot's *New World Quartet*, not only because it returns to his American sources, but because it discovers a new meaning in them."[187]

CONCLUSION

Tapping into the American wellsprings of his poetry, Eliot shows that he is, above all, "a poet of places."[188] In Eliot, as in Whitman and Laforgue, the frontier landscape figuratively embodies not only states of mind, but also the hidden, regional history of colonial settlement and the hybrid cultural legacy recorded by names of places in the New World. Whitman is a crucial American antecedent to Eliot's renderings of the frontier, because he emphasized the essential hybridity of New World cultures, and the eventful contact and commingling of national cultures encrypted in the very cadences of American place names. In his earlier engagements with Whitman, Eliot seeks, through allusion, to restore historical and literary contexts of Whitman's verse, contexts from which Whitman, in an "unwholesome" revolution against tradition, had adamantly declared his independence. But "The Dry Salvages" represents an important departure in Eliot's relations with Whitman, as well as other American sources that mark his very beginnings as a poet, and it is likely that this *rapprochement* was inspired, in part, by his experience of translating Perse's *Anabase*.

CHAPTER 3

From Harlem to Haiti: Langston Hughes, Jacques Roumain and the avant-gardes

INTRODUCTION

In an essay published six years before his death, Langston Hughes described his formative first encounter with modern American poetry at Central High School in Cleveland. "We read Sandburg, Millay, Masters, and other American poets who wrote of the things we knew about," Hughes said,

we could identify their poetry with our lives . . . The aim of the teacher must be to stimulate the individual to create freely and individually – regardless of the great models of the past or present. Actually, the younger the student, the easier it is for him to express himself . . . If children wait to start writing in high school they're apt to be too inhibited to write freely . . . If they don't start writing until college, they'll try to be young T. S. Eliots.[1]

It is well known that Hughes's poetics follows a line of development in twentieth-century American poetry that Pound denounced for its "general floppiness" – a line that extends from Whitman to Sandburg, Edgar Lee Masters, E. A. Robinson, Edna St. Vincent Millay and Amy Lowell.[2] Whitman would always be, for Hughes, "the greatest of American poets"; and, as early as 1927, he explicitly distanced himself, and all the other writers in Alain Locke's *New Negro* anthology, from Poe as the forerunner of Eliot's modernist craft.[3]

Apart from this sole caveat about Eliot's inhibiting effect on college-age writers, Hughes assiduously avoided any public mention of Eliot, and certainly never claimed him as an influence. Thus it is understandable that scholars such as George Hutchinson, Craig Werner and Arnold Rampersad have depicted Hughes as part of a literary camp that starkly opposed and rivaled Eliot's modernism.[4] Critics have dwelt at length on Hughes's importance to the aesthetic philosophy of the Harlem Renaissance, as well as on the cultural distinctiveness of his sources and idiom. Steven Tracy and James Emanuel, for instance, have studied the centrality of the blues to Hughes's lyric practice, and Richard Barksdale, R. Baxter Miller and

Onwuchekwa Jemie have shown how Hughes adapted vernacular forms at a time when folk literature and song were unjustly derided and neglected by a black literary establishment bent on assimilation with the mainstream.[5] At first glance, then, Hughes's poetics fits well with what recent commentators on modernism, such as T. J. Clark, Wanda Corn and Walter Benn Michaels, have, with misleading generalization, described as the purism and cultural nationalism of the modernist movement.[6]

But in emphasizing Hughes's blackness, or the teleological, nativist dimensions of modernism, we lose sight of how Hughes's work, like that of Eliot and other modernists, expresses a sustained, generative ambivalence towards the expressive constraints of cultural nationalism. Studies by Rampersad, Faith Berry and Edward J. Mullen indicate that Hughes not only read Conrad, Joyce, D. H. Lawrence and other important modernist writers of his day, he was also involved in an extensive transnational literary network including Carsen McCullers, Marianne Moore, W. H. Auden, André Malraux, Louis Aragon, Bertholt Brecht, Ernest Hemingway, Diego Rivera, Nicolás Guillén, Alejo Carpentier, Jacques Roumain, Pablo Neruda, Jorge Borges, Leopold Sedar Senghor and Aimé Césaire.[7] Hughes even maintained a correspondence with Pound over the course of many years, and in 1932 wrote a letter to Pound saying "I have known your work for more than ten years and many of your poems insist on remaining in my head."[8]

Hughes's adaptation of folk sources laid a foundation for the flourishing of twentieth-century African-American literature, and even the briefest poems in his poetic oeuvre engage sociohistorical contexts such as slavery, Reconstruction, the Great Migration and the pernicious threat of racial violence against African-Americans. While maintaining a clear sense of Hughes's cultural distinctiveness, however, in this chapter I will also examine Hughes's close affinities with Eliot's transnational modernism, affinities that help explain Hughes's contribution to the rise of black internationalism and the hybridity of the Harlem Renaissance, as well as the volatile interplay of influences between the Renaissance and other avant-garde movements in the USA, Europe and the Caribbean.

The fact that Hughes never directly acknowledged Eliot's influence does not mean that he was entirely unaffected by modernist formal practices and principles. As we shall see, the deceptive simplicity of Hughes's early lyrics obscures a concern with craft and stylistic innovation he shared with his modernist contemporaries, and his engagement with the European avant-gardes, and poets such as Laforgue and especially Baudelaire, was deeper and more extensive than has previously been shown. Like Eliot, Hughes was born in Missouri and led the life of an expatriate in Paris at a critical moment in his coming of age as a poet. Like Eliot, whose attraction to vaudeville and jazz is now becoming better understood, Hughes was vitally concerned with the relations between poetry and music, and he described his modern poetics as "Jazz . . . putting itself into words."⁹ Like Eliot's poetry, Hughes's work crosses, and to some degree obviates, the divide between "high" and "low" culture.

Finally, and most important for the larger argument of this book, Hughes's influence, like Eliot's, extends to the Caribbean – not just in the work of the Martinican poet Aimé Césaire but also in the earlier work of the Haitian poet and novelist Jacques Roumain. As we shall see, Hughes's relations with Roumain established a cross-current of New World influences that, like Eliot's relations with Perse, would foster the cultivation of modernism and *Négritude* in the Francophone Caribbean. In the previous chapters I remarked how Eliot's influence on Perse was aided by their earlier encounters with French modernism. Here, too, the rapport between Hughes and Roumain was nurtured, in part, through their shared affinity with Baudelaire and Laforgue, as well as Louis Aragon, who had previously been influenced by Perse. Studying this dense, surprising matrix of transatlantic and hemispheric convergences will enhance our understanding of Hughes's associations with avant-gardists of the 1920s, as well as his contribution to the subsequent growth of Caribbean modernisms.

BLACK PIERROT: HUGHES, LAFORGUE AND THE AVANT-GARDES

During the 1920s, and throughout the interwar period, American writers and intellectuals flocked to the Left Bank, searching for artistic community as well as the freedom embodied by the myth of Paris, a city once described by Henry James as "the most brilliant . . . in the world."¹⁰ Arriving at the Gare Saint-Lazare in February 1924, Hughes traced a transatlantic path well worn by his American antecedents and contemporaries. "I began to say to myself I guess dreams do come true and life sometimes makes its own books," he reminisced in *The Big Sea*, "Because here I am, living in a Paris garret, writing poems."¹¹

Unlike Eliot, Perse and many others, Hughes would never frequent Sylvia Beach's Shakespeare and Company. Although he admired the *Little Review*, he never went to the bookstore to meet the editors because, as he confided to Alain Locke in 1923, he thought his own poetry was not "eccentric enough" to be appreciated there.[12] Still, for Hughes, as for Frederick Douglass, James Weldon Johnson, Locke and generations of African-Americans, the ideal of freedom evoked by Paris meant as much as, if not more than, it did to Euro-American expatriates. Ever since Douglass recounted his meeting, in Paris, with the "venerable and philosophic" French senator who had been directly involved in the emancipation of slaves in the French colonies, the myth of Paris as a non-racist city remained an ineluctable source of its attraction for African-American writers.[13] "From the day I set foot in France," Johnson remarked of his trip there in 1905, "I became aware of the working of a miracle within me . . . I was suddenly free; . . . free to be merely a man."[14] Locke, too, regarded the city as free but in a different way, as a haven for sensuous enjoyment far from the constraints of American homophobia, and other deep-seated, cultural taboos.[15] Even Hughes's father, hearing that Alexandre Dumas was a black man who had made his living as a writer, had been taken by the myth: "Yes," he said, "but he was in Paris, where they don't care about color."[16]

If Paris symbolized freedom, the realization of such freedom was intimately associated in Hughes's mind with the act of learning to read French. "I found that my high school French didn't work very well, and that I understood nothing anyone said to me," he remembers, "They talked too fast. But I could read French." It is likely Hughes understates his proficiency, since by this time he had studied French for two and a half years at Columbia and Lincoln University, in addition to two years in high school. Hughes's French would have improved, moreover, as a result of his trip to Senegal in 1921.[17] Elsewhere in *The Big Sea*, Hughes describes himself chatting comfortably in French with a dock watchman from Rotterdam, during his second transatlantic voyage to Holland in 1923.[18] By Hughes's own account, the mysterious, transnational experience of reading Guy de Maupassant in French first inspired him to become a writer: "I will never forget the thrill of first understanding the French of de Maupassant . . . I think it was de Maupassant who made me really want to be a writer and write stories about Negroes, so true that people in far-away lands would read them – even after I was dead."[19]

Comparing the jazz poems Hughes composed before and after his first visit to France, we see that his lyric practice was unquestionably affected by his time spent in Parisian nightclubs. "Jazzonia," published in *Crisis* six months before his trip, exhibits a style that highlights its own status as "literature." Hughes alludes to Cleopatra and Eve, and employs compounded figures of speech in a way that even Pound, discussing the virtues of craft in his early essays, would have approved of:

Oh, silver tree!
Oh, shining rivers of the soul!

In a Harlem cabaret
Six long-headed jazzers play.
A dancing girl whose eyes are bold
Lifts high a dress of silken gold.

Oh, singing tree!
Oh, shining rivers of the soul!

Were Eve's eyes
In the first garden
Just a bit too bold?
Was Cleopatra gorgeous
In a gown of gold?

Oh, shining tree!
Oh, silver rivers of the soul!

In a whirling cabaret
Six long-headed jazzers play.[20]

Hughes's refrain, "Oh, silver tree! / Oh, shining rivers of the soul!" is a compound trope, metaphor embedded in apostrophe, that seeks to construe musical meanings in broader, more widely accessible terms. Like jazz, Hughes's idiom crosses cultural and social boundaries, a transgression that is implicitly observed by the bold dancer's action of lifting her dress. At the same time, however, the cryptic rhetorical questions and reticent density of Hughes's imagery suggest his aversion to explicit, public revelation in poetry.

In poems such as "Negro Dancers," inspired by the Paris nightclub scene, Hughes's "Brown-skin steppers" recall the "long-headed jazzers," the dancing girl and the Harlem cabaret in "Jazzonia." But where "Jazzonia" emphasizes how language may breach frontiers of culture and works stylistically to clarify the meanings of jazz, "Negro Dancers" is polyvocal, fragmented and oblique, evading ready comprehension by a wide, culturally diverse readership:

"Me an' ma baby's
Got two mo' ways,
Two mo' ways to do de buck!
Da, da,
Da, da, da!
Two mo' ways to do de buck!"

Soft light on the tables,

Music gay,
Brown-skin steppers
In a cabaret.

White folks, laugh!
White folks, pray!

"Me an' ma baby's
Got two mo' ways,
Two mo' ways to do de buck!"[21]

"Jazzonia" confirms, above all, the freedoms of poetry; "Negro Dancers," by contrast, stresses a tension between the desire to speak freely across frontiers of culture, and the constraints imposed by social conditions and the inherent limitations of language as an expressive medium. And though Hughes avoids the figurative complication of "Jazzonia," "Negro Dancers" offers other dizzying forms of ambiguity. We are not given the cabaret's locale, for example, and the identities of the poem's various speakers are shifting and ambiguous. Unlike "Jazzonia," which self-reflexively illustrates the poet–speaker's effort to communicate the meanings of jazz to a diverse readership, "Negro Dancers" dramatizes an apparent failure to communicate across racial and cultural lines. The dancer's interpretation of the music is lost on "white folks," and the speaker's exhortation to laugh and pray communicates anger and a threat of violence against them.

In "Negro Dancers," Hughes relies on nonsensical, rhythmic sounds ("Da da, / Da, da, da!") that call attention to the poem's embattled effort to become a medium as "pure" as music. In at least one version of the poem, published as "Charleston" in *Vanity Fair*, this phrase appears in italics, emphasizing a sustained tension between voice and the mechanics of print.[22] Was Hughes aware of *la poésie pure* as a central concern in French modernism? His poem's formal audacities, montage aesthetic and implied ambivalence towards a popular audience offer a startling parallel with other jazz-influenced works of avant-garde literature and art during the 1920s.

We know that when Hughes returned to Paris for the International Writers' Congress in the summer of 1937, he met the Romanian artist, Tristan Tzara, founder of the transnational Dadaist movement, who was largely responsible for bringing Dadaism from Zurich to Paris in collaboration with poets such as Guillaume Apollinaire, André Breton and Louis Aragon; Aragon, in turn, would in the 1930s become a friend of Hughes and an active promoter of his work.[23] Though Tzara's name is never mentioned in *I Wonder as I Wander*, Hughes vividly recalls how the Writers' Congress strengthened his ties to other writers from abroad.[24] Would Hughes have known about the Dadaist movement, whose influence extended into poetry, the visual arts and music, and which had reached its height in Paris during the 1920s when many of its main practitioners converged there? With its complex obliquities, "Negro Dancers" does convey the aversion to mass audiences prescribed by Tzara; like a Dadaist painting, it poses a threat of violence, evades all efforts at meaningful explanation and, in doing so, affirms the poet's freedom.[25]

Douglas Clayton has shown that Decadent aspects of turn-of-the-century European culture were manifested in the 1920s cult of primitivism, jazz and ragtime. In poems such as "Negro Dancers" Hughes raises an analogous, suggestive continuity between the advent of Dadaism and the European attraction to jazz.[26] It is difficult, reading the poem all by itself, to relate Hughes's work to developments among the avant-gardes in Paris during the 1920s. Still, when we closely examine Hughes's involvement with modernism in France, some surprising parallels with Eliot and Pound come to light.

Both Eliot and Pound, for example, admired the craftsmanship, and especially the quatrains, wrought by the French poet, novelist, dramatist, journalist and literary critic, Théophile Gautier. Eliot was drawn to Gautier in part because the syntactic diversity of his quatrains illustrates the "volatility" of technique, which involves much more than following rules.[27] Like Eliot, who tried to perfect his quatrains in "Whispers of Immortality" and six other poems published in the 1920 collection *Ara Vos Prec*, Hughes worked to refine techniques associated with this stanzaic form. Not all of Hughes's quatrains are adapted from blues stanzas. Is it possible he was aware of Gautier? When we realize that Hughes actually mentions Gautier in, of all unlikely places, a 1966 essay on "The Negro and American Entertainment," the connection seems far more plausible.[28]

Though little has been said about Hughes's links to French Surrealism, we know that his poems appeared regularly in French avant-garde periodicals during the 1930s and, as mentioned earlier, he had a close, sustained friendship with Aragon, one of the founding members of the Surrealist group and a leading practitioner of Dadaism in the early 1920s. In 1933, Hughes first met Aragon and his wife in Moscow and, hearing Aragon recite his revolutionary poem "Magnitogorsk," Hughes was inspired to translate it. *Littérature internationale* published the translation, Hughes's first from French, later that year.[29] In the summer of 1937, Hughes traveled to Europe once again – this time as a foreign correspondent for the *Baltimore Afro-American*, the *Cleveland Call and Post* and the *Globe*, under assignment to cover the Spanish Civil War – and met Aragon in Paris at the Second International Writers' Congress. The US State Department had denied Hughes permission to travel to Spain for the assignment, and it was Aragon who helped him acquire the necessary papers from the French *préfecture de police* for entry there.[30] Aragon introduced Hughes to George Adam, who had translated Hughes's short stories into French, and to Nancy Cunard, with whom Hughes had previously corresponded about his inclusion in her *Negro* anthology, and who subsequently became an influential supporter of Hughes's work.[31] In a 1937 radio speech broadcast from Madrid, Hughes praised Aragon and other members of Alianza, the Alliance of Antifascist Intellectuals, for doing work that is "useful, entertaining, and beautiful in a living, vital way."[32]

There is another, far better-known source of French modernist influence which Hughes shares with Eliot: the poetics of Jules Laforgue. "By the age of 23," writes Rampersad:

[Hughes] could speak both French and Spanish. In 1923 he was writing poems about Pierrot (a *black* Pierrot, to be sure), after Jules Laforgue, like Edna St. Vincent Millay in Aria da Capo, and another young man who would soon concede that he was a poet manqué and turn to fiction to confront the gap between lowly provincialism and modernism – William Faulkner.[33]

What Rampersad does not mention is that, in choosing to write after Laforgue, both Millay and Faulkner were following the example set by Eliot and Pound.[34]

Hughes's Pierrot poems are collected in a section of the volume *The Weary Blues* entitled "The Black Pierrot," and Laforgue's example would have attracted him for many reasons. Part of Pierrot's appeal, for Laforgue as well as Hughes, is that he usually appears as a slave or a servant, and played an important role in the emergence of popular, lowbrow cultural forms in nineteenth-century Paris, including the circus, street performance and music-hall comedy. A famous French acrobat pantomime, Jean-Gaspard Deburau, first popularized the image of Pierrot as the moonstruck, tragic clown, and Deburau's performances in the Théâtre des Funambules on the Boulevard du Temple may well have reminded Hughes of the Parisian nightclub scene, insofar as they were regarded as being for the common people, subverting the "official" theatre of the Comédie-Française.[35]

Furthermore, the Pierrot figure was closely connected with a cherished vernacular tradition of song and legend. Laforgue's "Complainte de cette bonne lune" opens with an imitation of "Sur le pont d'Avignon," and in "Complainte de Lord Pierrot" Laforgue adapted a burlesque form of the *complainte* that was both spoken and sung in the sixteenth century, as well as a popular contemporary folk song, "Au clair de la lune."[36] The rhythms of popular song aided Laforgue's effort to disengage from the Alexandrine and other formal elements of traditional prosody.[37]

In both Laforgue and Hughes, the Pierrot persona is closely linked to Decadence and religious skepticism. Like Laforgue, whose adaptation of the Pierrot in *L'Imitation de Notre-Dame la lune* contains elements of religious parody in its portrayal of a cult of moon-worship, poems such as "March Moon" in Hughes's *The Weary Blues* humorously undermine the conventional, divine, feminine connotations of moon imagery.[38] Similarly, in "Pierrot," which concludes the "Black Pierrot" sequence, Hughes explores the liberating Decadence of a Pierrot "steeped in sin": the poem reads like a folk ballad, but expresses the religious skepticism and sexual freedom of Paris during the 1920s.[39]

Madhuri Deshmukh contends that Hughes's transatlantic encounter with Laforgue's Pierrot allows him to "recreate the aesthetic space that minstrelsy in the U.S. had stolen from black creativity."[40] Laforgue's involvement with Decadence, vernacular tradition, burlesque forms of the *complainte*, comedy and music-hall performance was no doubt a source of his attraction for Hughes. Equally important, however, is the fact that Laforgue's Pierrot poetics marks a significant turning point in the emergence of realism in modern French poetry. Anne Holmes has shown how Laforgue deftly reconciles technique with the contingencies of contemporary history: his poems would have provided an invaluable model for Hughes, first and foremost because his Pierrots affirm modernist principles of lyric artifice and impersonality while at the same time never losing their grip on reality.[41] Like Laforgue's poems, Hughes's raise questions about stultifying critical binarisms that for years have pitted modern realism against modernist anti-realism, tradition against the avant-garde, political content against artistic form.[42]

In "A Black Pierrot," the first poem in the "Pierrot" sequence, Hughes tacitly honors Laforgue's achievement as a lyric realist. A milestone in the formation of Hughes's transnational poetics, the poem was, along with "Negro," Hughes's first international publication, appearing in the July 1924 issue of René Maran's *Les Continents*. Like many of Laforgue's Pierrots, Hughes's Black Pierrot is a frustrated lover, and his effort to reject the real world is formally expressed as an avant-garde flight from verisimilitude. Notably, however, Hughes dramatizes that the Black Pierrot's escapist striving for figurative transcendence is destined to fail. In doing so, he intimates time-bound social realities that are his poem's main subject:

> I am a black Pierrot:
>   She did not love me,
>   So I crept away into the night
>   And the night was black, too.
>
> I am a black Pierrot:
>   She did not love me,
>   So I wept until the dawn
>   Dripped blood over the eastern hills
>   And my heart was bleeding, too.
>
> I am a black Pierrot:
>   She did not love me,
>   So with my once gay-colored soul
>   Shrunken like a balloon without air,
>   I went forth in the morning
>   To seek a new brown love.[43]

We never experience a full-fledged metaphor, or the illusory identification with nature such a metaphor would imply. The poem progresses from an explicit comparison between the blackness of the Pierrot and the blackness of night, to the bloody metaphor of dawn that is explicitly compared to the Pierrot's heart, to the shrunken balloon simile that is, again, explicitly compared to the Pierrot's soul. The implied narrative structure of the lyric exhibits a disquieting openness to the realities of racism and inequality. The bloodiness of the eastern hills not only hints at the sorrow and suffering of slaves, it also anticipates, obliquely, the violence of the lynch mob Hughes would depict in later realist works.

Though Hughes's simile of a deflated balloon illustrates his Pierrot's failure to trope, and highlights the limitations imposed on the poet by a social context that must always be accounted for, the very presence of this figure, like the poem as a whole, affirms a victory of style. The "blackness" of the Pierrot is a mask, like the poet's, that simultaneously conveys the speaker's individual identity as an African-American, while also transcending such particularities by evoking his melancholy mood. What is more, a fruitful ambiguity in Hughes's closing line delineates the complex social dynamics of color consciousness and sexuality but also leaves open the more hopeful possibility of self-transformation and transcendence. If the Pierrot ventures forth in the morning to find a *new* brown love, this implies that the woman who rejected him was also brown and, capitulating to the racist norms of her day, preferred a white man, or a lighter-skinned brown man, over the Black Pierrot. If, on the other hand, he searches for a new *brown* love, this means he has left the psychological legacy of slavery behind him, and stopped yearning for white women who do not love his blackness. The juxtaposition of "Black" with this more literal brownness in the closing line – in combination with the fact that the gender of the new love is never grammatically specified – heightens the richly ambiguous, transgressive social significance of Hughes's Pierrot.

HUGHES AND BAUDELAIRE: FIGURES IN BLACK

Hughes's attraction to Laforgue's realism illustrates how the internationalism implied by his practices as a lyricist lead to some provocative, surprising transatlantic comparisons. As with Laforgue, the social fragmentation evoked by Hughes's realism is ordered within the constraints of significant form, and this suggests that even the most chaotic aspects of contemporary life may prove socially viable and morally redeemable. Insofar as both poets write lyrics that figuratively transcend frontiers of consciousness and culture, they fulfill a cherished criterion of modernism; and this modernism, in turn, serves the moral ends of realism by allowing them to encompass, order and preserve history. Stylistically, however, Hughes's poems are very different from Laforgue's. Laforgue does not adhere closely to the forms of vernacular song the way Hughes does. Contrasting with Laforgue's jarring rhythms, dense concentration of exclamation points, complex structures of rhyme, wrought syntax and exotic diction, poems like Hughes's "Pierrot" are formally simple, almost balladic, and relatively easy to read.

Perhaps most important of all, the use of blackness as a metaphor – an innovation that is central to the entire enterprise of Hughes's "The Black Pierrot" – never appears in Laforgue. The metaphor does, however, occur in Baudelaire, a poet who wrote numerous poems about interracial love and dusk, or "les ténèbres," as a trope that suggests the erotic beauty of blackness, no doubt partly inspired by his lifelong love affair with an Afro-French *comédienne*, Jeanne Duval. Baudelaire was also influenced by Deburau's performances as Pierrot, though this is less known of his work than it is of Laforgue's.[44]

Hughes himself remarked in a January 1926 essay published in *Crisis* that the fascination of dusk purpling to night outside his windows in Montmartre inevitably summoned up Decadent associations, not with Laforgue but with Baudelaire:

Springtime – Paris – Dusk, opalescent, pale, purpling to night – Montmartre. The double windows of my high little attic room open to the evening charm of the city . . . And we search for the things we know and watch the lights come out beneath us and the stars above . . . And I think of the many illustrious ones who, through the centuries, have been her lovers, – the strange satanic Baudelaire; Wilde, and the gorgeous Bernhardt.[45]

The importance of Baudelaire's dusky imagery for Hughes's coming of age as a poet also helps to account for the way Hughes translates parts III and IV of Aragon's "Magnitogorsk." There are many reasons why, in addition to the relative simplicity of Aragon's style, Hughes would have been drawn to this poem. The substitution of human for divine agency in the story of creation, Aragon's reference to the conquest of masters, his ardent celebration of people who till the earth, and the blurring of distinctions between blacks and whites are all in close keeping with Hughes's worldview. And given Hughes's own affinities with Baudelaire, it is telling and apt that Hughes, by selecting this particular excerpt for translation, indirectly calls attention to Aragon's own use of the dusk as a quintessentially Baudelairean trope. In Aragon the two parts are entitled, respectively, "Hymne" and "1930," but in Hughes's version the two parts are untitled and conjoined. Part III, "Hymne," is rendered as follows:

> . . . il s'agit maintenant de la transformer [it's now a matter of change]
> Karl Marx
> They have given man back to the earth
> They have said You shall devour all
> and you shall devour all
>
> They have thrown sky to earth
> They have said The gods shall die
> and the gods shall die
>
> They have put in ferment the earth
> They have said Times shall be good
> and times shall be good
>
> They have dug a hole in the earth
> They have said Fire shall burst forth
> and fire shall burst forth
>
> Addressing the masters of the earth
> They have said You shall be conquered
> and you shall be conquered
>
> They have taken in their hands the earth
> They have said Black shall be white
> and black shall be white
>
> Glory to the land and the earth
> in the sun of bolshevik days
> and glory to the bolsheviks[46]

Hughes's version, like the original, is syntactically straightforward, with simple diction, and only two metaphors. The first occurs when Aragon compares the earth to a worker, writing "Ils ont mis en chantier la terre," "They have put the earth to work." Hughes translates this with another metaphor of his own choosing, comparing the earth to fermenting grapes: "they have put in ferment the earth." Hughes's merging of "Hymne" and "1930," moreover, draws attention to Aragon's second, more hidden metaphor, his use of blackness, the color of dusk in the village, as an image that evokes the hope, ability to survive and latent power of downtrodden workers of the earth:

> In the little houses of black earth lived
> the human mole
> In the little houses of black earth laughed
> the child with the slanting eyes
>
> In the little houses of black earth sleeps
> the woman on the smoky hearth
> In the little houses of black earth one day more
> is dead
>
> One day more in the little houses of black earth
> One day more in the shadow of the church or the mosque
> One day more to sew on the dead days like coins
> on the breasts of the women here
> . . .
>
> The agitator comrade from the Komsomols
> in the dusk of the village
> re-tells in one breath the modern legend
> Marx, October and Lenin
> . . .
>
> he explains the world
> he explains what will be
> Magnitogorsk, Magnitogorsk
> Do you hear Magnitogorsk
>
> At his feet little naked children crawl in the black earth
> One day more in the little houses of black earth
> one day more.[47]

The idealization of blackness and the tropics that recurs throughout Baudelaire's poetry helps to explain why his work figures so prominently in the tradition of literary primitivism that flourished in Europe, and derives from the earliest cross-cultural encounters between Europeans and natives in the New World, Asia and Africa. Recounting the emergence of primitivism in French literature during the late eighteenth and early nineteenth centuries, Michael Dash claims that Baudelaire's poetry represents a prime example that was vital to the formation of European modernisms.[48] Whereas, in its earlier forms, the discourse of primitivism was used to mask the exploitative, violent realities of contact on the frontiers of empire, some modernists tended to employ tropes of the primitive in a fundamentally different way. The "primitive" began increasingly to be associated not with the tropics but with the European city; "savagery" was used to describe the urban phenomenon of the crowd. Modernist primitivism, in short, entailed a diverse range of ideological stances: despite the realities of racism in Europe and the violence of colonialism, some representations of the primitive during the 1920s expressed a salutary critique of staid convention.[49]

Reminiscing about Baudelaire's Paris at dusk, Hughes may have been thinking of Baudelaire's portrayal of dusk's black shadows as a desirable, voluptuous woman in "Les Ténèbres" (the lyric that opens the sequence "Un Fantôme"), or this apostrophe to the twilight in "Le Crépuscule du soir":

> Ô soir, aimable soir, désiré par celui
> Dont le bras, sans mentir, peuvent dire: Aujourd'hui
> Nous avons travaillé![50]

[Oh night, lovely night, so desired by one / Whose arms, without falsehood, can say: Today / We have labored!]

But when we recall Hughes's "Dream Variations," it is clear the most memorable and important poem of all would have been Baudelaire's "La Fin de la journée," with its mysterious dance, symbolic confrontation of light and darkness, and rest amidst the cool, refreshing shadows ("rafraîchissantes ténèbres") as voluptuous night comes on:

> Sous une lumière blafarde
> Court, danse et se tord sans raison
> La Vie, impudente et criarde.
> Aussi, sitôt qu'à l'horizon
>
> La nuit voluptueuse monte,
> Apaisant tout, même la faim,
> Effaçant tout, même la honte,
> Le Poïete se dit: "Enfin!
>
> Mon esprit, comme mes vertèbres,
> Invoque ardemment le repos;
> Le coeur plein de songes funèbres,

Je vais me coucher sur le dos
Et me rouler dans vos rideaux,
Ô rafraîchissantes ténèbres!"[51]

[Under a leaden sun / She runs, dances and twists without reason / Life, impudent and gaudy. / But as soon as, at the horizon, // Voluptuous night arises, / Appeasing all, even hunger / Effacing all, even shame, / The Poet tells himself: "At last! // My spirit, like my backbone / Ardently calls for repose; / My heart full of mournful dreams, / I will lie on my back / And roll myself in your curtains, / Oh refreshing shadows!"]

In "Dream Variations," selected by Alain Locke (along with "Youth" and "Our Land") for inclusion in the special March 1925 issue of *Survey Graphic* that would become the *New Negro Anthology*, Hughes brilliantly adapts Baudelaire's primitivist longing and imagery for his own special purpose, a celebration of blackness. Though the poem is set in an idealized, geographically unspecified tropical setting – "some place of the sun" – the poet–speaker closely identifies with the dancer, who is never perniciously objectified, as dancers are in "Jazzonia" and "Negro Dancers," by a racist gaze. Both the dance and the poem illustrate how Baudelaire's poetics offered Hughes new-found expressive freedom. Here, as in Baudelaire and "The Black Pierrot," blackness is a figure evoking the promise of paradisal peace, rest at the coming of night, and a longing for gentle death:

> To fling my arms wide
> In some place of the sun,
> To whirl and to dance
> Till the white day is done.
> Then rest at cool evening
> Beneath a tall tree
> While night comes on gently,
>   Dark like me –
> That is my dream!
>
> To fling my arms wide
> In the face of the sun,
> Dance! Whirl! Whirl!
> Till the quick day is done.
> Rest at pale evening . . .
> A tall, slim tree . . .
> Night coming tenderly
>   Black like me.[52]

It is possible, furthermore, that Hughes also recalls Laforgue in this poem. Though the imagery of "Dream Variations" is reminiscent of Baudelaire, the syntactical parallelism, Hughes's repetition of verbs in the infinitive, bears a striking, close resemblance to the syntax of Laforgue's unapologetically primitivist "Complainte des nostalgies préhistoriques." In both poems, the series of infinitives sustains a tension between physical stasis and yearning for free, self-expressive action. But, whereas in Hughes's lyric the dance is an impassioned, erotic declamation of self-love, in Laforgue the speaker nostalgically dreams of liberated, dance-like sex at nightfall with a childlike primitive:

> Heurter . . .
> Une enfant bestiale et brûlée
> . . .
>
> Livrer aux langueurs des soirées
> Sa toison . . .
> . . .
>
> Un moment, béer, sans rien dire,
> . . .
>
> Puis, . . .
> Nous prendre . . .
> . . .
>
> Et, nous délèvrant de l'extase,
> . . .
>
> Fous, nous renverser sur les reins,
> Riant, battant des mains![53]

[To collide . . . with a native, bestial and burning . . . To let down her hair in the languor of evening . . . To gaze for a moment, without saying a thing . . . Then . . . To embrace . . . And, delivering ourselves from ecstasy, . . . To turn over on our backs, crazy, laughing, clapping our hands!]

It is tempting to read Hughes's poem solely as an affirmation of racial and cultural difference, but the symbolic confrontation and commingling of day and dusk in "Dream Variations" – like Hughes's fertile, transatlantic crossing of influences with French poets such as Gautier, Laforgue, Baudelaire and Aragon – belies such oversimplification. Certainly, Hughes's work is grounded in the distinctive idiom of African-American vernacular culture, but it would be a terrible mistake to overlook the presence of these other, equally vital influences. As Hughes himself once said:

I do not believe there were ever any beautiful "hate" poems. I think the dreams in my poems are basically everybody's dreams. But sometimes, on the surface, their complexion is colored by the shadows and the darkness of the race to which I belong. The darkness has its beauty, and the shadows have their troubles – but shadows disappear in the sun of understanding.[54]

HUGHES, ELIOT AND THE RISE OF JAZZ MODERNISM

A great deal has already been said about the "modernity" of African-American music and, in particular, about the centrality of jazz to Hughes's lyric practice. Walter Farrell and Patricia Johnson have argued that be-bop offered Hughes a way of building a long poem out of many shorter poems. Tracy raises a similar claim, but goes on to argue, like Robert O'Brien Hokanson, that Hughes's method was adapted from modernists such as Eliot.[55] More recently, David Chinitz has contended that Eliot anticipates the musical techniques that would be exploited by Hughes.[56] There is, however, much to be learned about how Hughes's jazz poetics fits in the larger development of the modernist lyric, both in the USA and in Europe; and, conversely, how Hughes's engagement with various forms of modernism contributed to the development of his technique.

Jazz appealed to Hughes, as it did to Eliot and other avant-gardists during the 1920s, in part because the music affirmed their cosmopolitan outlook, enabled their struggle against conformity with tradition, and aided their engagement with vernacular resources.[57] "Jazz Band in a Parisian Cabaret," first published in *Crisis* in December of 1925, and the only jazz poem collected in *Fine Clothes to the Jew*, opens with a Whitmanian catalogue of audience members that dramatizes how shared love for the music breaches national boundaries and dismantles hierarchies of class and color. Unlike the blues poems collected in the same volume, which probe the meanings of migration, the folk idiom and the legacy of slavery in a national context, "Jazz Band in a Parisian Cabaret" resituates the problem of black mobility along a transnational axis.[58]

> Play that thing,
> Jazz band!
> Play it for the lords and ladies,
> For the dukes and counts,
> For the whores and gigolos,
> For the American millionaires,
> And the school teachers
> Out for a spree.
> Play it,
> Jazz band!
> You know that tune

> That laughs and cries at the
> same time.
> You know it.[59]

Hughes was drawn to jazz's universal appeal, but his poem also implies, emphatically, that this music, like Hughes's own idiom, will not be apprehended by everyone who hears it.[60] As with Eliot and many other avant-gardists, Hughes's open-mindedness towards popular culture was qualified by a contradictory aversion to mass forms of entertainment where the mind was "lulled," in Eliot's phrase, "by continuous senseless music and continuous action too rapid for the brain to act upon."[61] Like Eliot's *The Waste Land,* and works associated with Dadaism, Surrealism and many other avant-garde movements of the 1920s, Hughes's multilingualism in "Jazz Band in a Parisian Cabaret" not only affirms the possibility of transnationalism. It also imposes a barrier to easy comprehension, and deepens the cultural divide between an elite who knows "it" and the majority of readers who, like many people who may enjoy jazz without grasping its meanings, do not. In this crucial sense, Hughes's poetics is a modernist poetics par excellence:

> May I?
> Mais oui.
> Mein Gott!
> Parece una rumba.
> Play it, jazz band!
> You've got seven languages to speak in
> And then some,
> Even if you do come from Georgia.
> Can I go home wid yuh, sweetie?
> Sure.[62]

Hughes's modernist affinities with Eliot are even clearer when we recall that, for both poets, Laforgue's involvement with vernacular musical traditions and songs from the French music hall provided a model for incorporating popular music into poetry. The close kinship between Laforgue's Pierrot and the persona who would eventually become Eliot's Prufrock is evident, for example, in "Suite Clownesque," a 1910 poem from the early notebook published in 1996 as *Inventions of the March Hare*. Like Laforgue, whose lyrics quote popular songs such as "Au clair de la lune" and "Sur le pont d'Avignon," Eliot's "Suite Clownesque" (iii) alludes to "By the Light of the Silvery Moon" and reveals the influence of jazz-inflected popular song on the formation of his style, accurately capturing cadences from Tin Pan Alley.[63]

If you're walking down the avenue,
Five o'clock in the afternoon,
I may meet you
Very likely greet you
Show you that I know you.[64]

The following year, Eliot would compose an untitled poem, also written after Laforgue, that is, like Hughes's "Jazz Band," set in a Parisian cabaret:

The smoke that gathers blue and sinks
The torpid smoke of rich cigars
The torpid after-dinner drinks
The overpowering immense
After dinner insolence
Of matter "going by itself"
Existence just about to die
Stifled with glutinous liqueurs
Till hardly a sensation stirs
The overoiled machinery . . .

What, you want action?
Some attraction?
Now begins
The piano and the flute and two violins
Someone sings
A lady of almost any age
But chiefly breast and rings
"Throw your arms around me – Aint you glad you found me"
Still that's hardly strong enough –
Here's a negro (teeth and smile)
Has a dance that's quite worth while
That's the stuff!
(Here's your gin
Now begin!)[65]

Like Hughes, Eliot is here concerned with the confluence of disparate worldviews in poetry and in musical performance. Both poets raise questions about the possibility of comprehensible cultural translation in popular forms of music; and both register vexed discontent with the relations between poetry and song, highlighting how layers of biased interpretation affect the audience's reception of musical performance. Beyond this, however, there are key differences. In Eliot, the fascinated condescension and urban sophistication of avant-garde audience members starkly contrasts with the naïve, shallow, primitive worldview these same audience members perceive in the musical allusion. Eliot's avant-garde audience questions whether African-American performers mean anything at all; Hughes's poem asks, conversely, whether and under what conditions an African-American's performance would be comprehensible to a white, multinational audience.

There are also important stylistic differences. Hughes's "Jazz Band" is formally suffused by the rhythms of jazz, with only a brief, oblique indication of a writerly frame. In "The smoke that gathers blue and sinks," by contrast, Eliot frames the performed fragment of song – a line, notably, from "Cubanola Glide," Harry von Tilzer's rewriting of African-American vernacular song for a minstrel show – with obtrusive punctuation such as italics, quotation marks and parentheses.

Both poets employ metonymy as a mainstay of their realist poetics, but to very different effect. Eliot's metonymies show how difficult it is to see and hear clearly enough to comprehend fully the significance of jazz; his poem's swift proliferation of fragments obscures the agency and personhood of the performers. Piano, flute, violins, breast, rings and fragment of song are jumbled up with an African-American dancer who has been stylistically cordoned off and reduced to a mere "(teeth and smile)."

By contrast, in jazz poems such as Hughes's "Trumpet Player," originally entitled "Trumpet Player: 52nd Street" when it was first published in 1947, realist metonymy emphasizes the African-American performer's personhood, history and expressive freedom. Even when the lyric speaker refers to the uses of metaphor in describing the "old desire" expressed in the trumpet's rhythm, he does so to highlight the far more meaningful surfaces of the trumpet player's face and body. As an expression of weariness, traces of a personal and collective history of oppression have been artfully, and figuratively, inscribed on the trumpet player's body as "dark moons of weariness" beneath his eyes. What metaphors we do find undergo a series of metamorphoses that only serve to highlight their catachretic, dissonant complexity. Music, for example, is initially a metonymy situated near the trumpet at the player's lips, but swiftly modulates to honey mixed with fire, another metaphor for alcohol:

> The Negro
> With the trumpet at his lips
> Has dark moons of weariness
> Beneath his eyes
> Where the smoldering memory
> Of slave ships
> Blazed to the crack of whips
> About his thighs.

. . .

The music
From the trumpet at his lips
Is honey
Mixed with liquid fire.
The rhythm
From the trumpet at his lips
Is ecstasy
Distilled from old desire –.[66]

Like a held chord, Laforgue's Pierrotic "longing for the moon" is sustained and, at the same time, transmuted into a "spotlight / In his eyes." As an evocation of Whitmanian, infinitely expansive desire for transcendence and death, the metaphorical sea has been reduced, and literally condensed, into a metonymic bar-glass, sucker size:

Desire
That is longing for the moon
Where the moonlight's but a spotlight
In his eyes,
Desire
That is longing for the sea
Where the sea's a bar-glass
Sucker size.[67]

The implications of Hughes's jazz modernism are clearest in late works such as "Dream Boogie," part of the book-length sequence *Montage of a Dream Deferred*, published in 1951. It is likely that Hughes was acutely aware of Eliot at this time, since his own reputation was being eclipsed by Melvin Tolson, who was fast becoming known as a rising star, the first African-American to adapt the techniques of Eliot's modernism. A year before Hughes's *Montage* appeared, Allen Tate had published a Preface to Tolson's *Libretto for the Republic of Liberia*, where he praised Tolson, saying that his poem marked "the first time, it seems to me, a Negro poet has assimilated completely the full poetic language of his time, and, by implication, the language of the Anglo-American tradition."[68]

Like *The Waste Land*, Hughes's "Dream Boogie" is not designed to meet our interpretative expectations; it contains no meaning that, as Eliot says, would readily satisfy a "habit" of the reader:

Good morning, daddy!
Ain't you heard

The boogie-woogie rumble
Of a dream deferred?

Listen closely:
You'll hear their feet
Beating out and beating out a—

You think
It's a happy beat?

Listen to it closely:
Ain't you heard
something underneath
like a—

What did I say?

Sure,
I'm happy!
Take it away!

Hey, pop!
Re-bop!
Mop!
Y-e-a-h![69]

Blues, ragtime, syncopated vaudeville music, minstrel songs, "symphonic jazz," as well as the "hot" New Orleans style now identified as jazz would all have been regarded, in broad generic terms, as "jazz" in Britain, France and America during the 1920s.[70] Michael North and David Chinitz have persuasively documented the fact that Eliot was familiar with jazz in these various manifestations, in part through his patronage of music halls and dance halls in Britain during the 1910s and 1920s.[71] The musical allusions cut from the final version of *The Waste Land* are of particular interest, since many of them cryptically encode the composite regional landscapes and irreducibly hybrid cultures evoked by American popular music.

Eliot's fascination with jazz in the broadest sense is best understood in light of his effort to grasp the idea of "purity" in poetry – that is, the peculiar effect of works that direct the reader's attention primarily to style, and virtually exclude consideration of their subject matter.[72] According to Eliot, the music of modern poetry should intensify our emotional response to poems verging on the frontier of consciousness, arriving at meanings that have not yet been put into words.[73] In "Dream Boogie," Hughes's jazz idiom achieves "purity," in the sense adduced by both Eliot and Valéry, because the lyric pushes towards this frontier. But although "Dream Boogie" self-reflexively dramatizes its own embattled effort to become pure as music, escaping history and verisimilitude, and although Hughes refuses to state clearly and explicitly the meanings encoded in jazz, it nonetheless remains, like Eliot's *The Waste Land*, anchored in realist historical particularities. Hughes once remarked that the rhythms of jazz, an art form that "for all its gaiety, remembered Africa, the Middle Passage, whips, chains, the slave market, the lifetimes of work," were anything but happy.[74] The italicized question in Hughes's poem marks a crucial confrontation with these meanings of jazz – meanings, so to speak, on the frontier of America's social consciousness.

The horrors of lynching, racial segregation, disenfranchisement and migration spurred hybrid formal innovation in works by Hughes and other African-Americans in a way parallel to, if distinctly different from the Great War for Eliot and other transatlantic modernists.[75] Both Hughes and Eliot seek, above all, to protect the historical implications of poetic forms, and both are concerned about the danger posed to humanity when readers, shackled by habit, fail to perceive social truth in the realm of art.

HUGHES, JACQUES ROUMAIN AND THE EMERGENCE OF CARIBBEAN MODERNISMS

The parallels between Eliot and Hughes are suggestive. Both poets are centrally concerned with craft; both were profoundly moved by their experiences in Paris; both were influenced, early on, by Baudelaire, Gautier and Laforgue; both were involved with French avant-gardists during the 1920s and 1930s; and, despite their shared distrust of mass reproduction, both were receptive to the fullest possible range of cultural forms, popular or embedded in revered tradition. Both, in short, were more culturally flexible than critics have previously surmised. Eliot's engagement with jazz and other vernacular musics questions critical preconceptions of his elitist, "high" modernism in much the same way that Hughes's involvement with French avant-gardes prompts us to redefine his reputation as the voice of cultural nationalism. But there is another similarity we have yet to explore: that Hughes, like Eliot, contributed to the emergence of Caribbean modernisms.

Hughes traveled extensively in the Caribbean, and his awareness of poet-critics such as A. J. Seymour in Guyana, "one of the most exciting of the many interesting poets of Negro blood now writing in the Caribbean area," shows that, although he was primarily involved with Cuba, Mexico, Martinique and Haiti, by the late 1940s he was also closely watching developments in Anglophone regions.[76] In 1947, Hughes traveled to Jamaica, meeting writers such as Roger Mais and Vic Reid, and his long essay on Jamaica expresses his attraction to the island's "English-African charm" – not just its people, music, beaches and easy way of life but also the local creole. "The peasants speak an intriguing kind of Afro-Creole-Cockney with little musical lilts to each word," Hughes writes; "It's hard to completely understand the average person at first, but gradually the language grows on you. For instance, folks say things like 'Him thump him down,' instead of 'He knocked him down.' And . . . 'Goodnight' does not necessarily mean that you have gone. It may mean that you have just arrived – a kind of 'Howdy-do.'"[77] In the late 1950s, Hughes lectured in Trinidad, where he met Eric Williams, C. L. R. James and Derek Walcott, and his lifelong effort to popularize Caribbean writing culminated in anthologies such as *The First Book of the West Indies*, published in 1956.

Hughes does not mention, as he does in reference to contemporary Africa, the influence of modernism on emerging poetry in the Caribbean, and he never discusses the influence of Caribbean poetry on his own work.[78] But Léopold Sédar Senghor, one of the principal theorists of *Négritude*, remarked that Hughes's poetry shared rhythmic similarities not just with modern French poetry, but with the work of Perse, the Guadeloupean poet whose significance for the rise of Caribbean modernisms was examined in previous chapters of this book. "You will find [Hughes's] rhythm in French poetry," Senghor said, "you will find it in Péguy, you will find it in Claudel, you will find this rhythm in St. John Perse . . . And it is this that Langston Hughes has left us with, this model of the perfect work of art."[79]

The transmission of Perse's modernism to Hughes could have come indirectly, through Eliot and Pound. But, as we have seen, Hughes was also directly involved with avant-garde contemporaries such as Aragon. If, as the sustained relations between Aragon and Hughes suggest, Hughes was influenced by Aragon, he would also have absorbed the influence of Perse: like other Surrealists, Aragon's poetics derived, in part, from his reading of Perse's *Éloges*.[80]

Hughes was also extensively involved with the *Négritude* movement, and Perse's substantial, if comparatively neglected, role in the emergence of *Négritude* poetry is well worth considering in light of the way his influence on Senghor, Léon Damas and Aimé Césaire commingles, surprisingly, with Hughes's.[81] Senghor commented extensively on both Hughes and Perse, and Michel Fabre and others have documented Hughes's influence on Césaire.[82] Césaire's conceptualization of *Négritude*, as well as his *Cahier d'un retour au pays natal*, were, as he openly acknowledged, indebted to Hughes.[83] Late in his life, Hughes himself contemplated the extent of this influence, praising the transnational scope of Césaire's idiom: "Césaire's 'Cahier' takes all that we have, Senghor, Guillén and Hughes, and flings it at the moon, to make of it a space-ship of the dreams of all the dreamers in the world."[84]

In addition to absorbing Hughes's influence, Césaire would have come to know Perse's poetry, not just through Senghor, but as a result of Perse's influence on Surrealism.[85] James Arnold has shown how, early on, Césaire placed himself alongside André Breton as the heir to Rimbaud, revealing close relations to Surrealism.[86] And Walcott, in turn, has described how, despite or because of their vast differences from one another, Perse and Césaire are conjoined by a shared New World sensibility:

Now here are . . . two poets whose formative perceptions, whose apprehension of the visible worlds of their very different childhoods, were made numinous by their elation in the metropolitan language, and whose very different visions created indisputable masterpieces . . . without doing violence to the language itself, in fact perpetuating its grandeur through opposite beliefs . . . Perse and Césaire, men of diametrically challenging backgrounds, racial opposites, to use the language of politics, one patrician and conservative, the other proletarian and revolutionary, classic and romantic, Prospero and Caliban, all such opposites balance easily, but they balance on the axis of a shared sensibility, and this sensibility, with or deprived of the presence of a visible tradition, is the sensibility of walking to a New World.[87]

In "Cérémonie vaudou pour Saint John Perse . . . ," for example, Césaire affirms his animosity as well as his indebtedness to Perse. Playing with the scientifically accurate botanical terminology Perse loved ("Curaçao asclepias," "asphodel," "Haemanthus" and so on), Césaire adapts Perse's infernal frontier setting ("des prairies infernales") and psalm-like, incantatory style, offering ambivalent words of praise for his fellow Antillean and exile, as one who searched for long-vanished cultural origins ("le chercheur de sources perdues").[88] In the poem's elated, visionary and obscure closing lines, Césaire's imagery of natural cataclysms and conquest evokes the speaker's ambivalent desire to honor the past and, as Walcott puts it, perpetuate the grandeur of an imperial, metropolitan tradition, the "ultimate Conquistador." To do so, the poem implies, there must be a fertile crossing of oceans, races, classes and national cultures, as each poet works to acknowledge and answer the other:

> et que l'arc s'embrase
> et que de l'un à l'autre océan
> les magmas fastueux en volcans se répondent pour
> de toutes gueules de tous fumants sabords honorer
> en route pour le grand large
> l'ultime Conquistador en son dernier voyage.[89]

[and may the arch be set ablaze / and from one ocean to another / may the sumptuous volcanic magmas respond to each other in order / to honor, with all gules and all portholes smoking / sailing for the high seas / the ultimate Conquistador on his final voyage.]

There is yet another plausible conduit by which Perse, and French modernism more generally, could have reached Hughes: Jacques Roumain, a Haitian poet and novelist whom Hughes first met briefly in 1931, on the day of his departure from Haiti back to the United States after spending the summer there. Their meeting sparked a friendship that would last a lifetime. Eight years after his encounter with Hughes, Roumain would reject the modernist ideal of *la poésie pure*, calling it an escapist "fanaticism for pure sound" that effectively isolates the poet from the people.[90] But despite, or even in light of, Roumain's explicit rejection of Mallarmé's poetics, there is overwhelming evidence of modernist influence in Roumain's writings early on in his career.

Critics such as Maurice Laraque, D'Henock Trouillot, Roger Dorsinville and Carolyn Fowler have all detected traces of modernism in Roumain's early poetry.[91] Dorsinville has shown that "Les Indigenistes," a movement in Haitian poetry co-founded by Roumain, adapted lyric practices established by their modernist contemporaries in France, including Aragon, Tzara, André Breton and Apollinaire. Paradoxically, these Caribbean innovators, in their effort to resist conformity with tradition, ended up imitating their modernist antecedents.[92] Rather than being centrally preoccupied with Africanity, Dorsinville explains, the group sought to demystify, and clarify, their region's cultural association with metropolitan France, and to develop a conception of "Antillanité" that would highlight distinctive qualities of Caribbean poetics.[93] *La Revue indigène*, the journal most closely associated with the movement, which ran for six issues from July 1927 through February 1928, regularly published works by Valéry and other avant-gardists, as well as a poem by Roumain himself that carried an epigraph from Apollinaire.[94] In a 1943 interview with René Depestre, Roumain identified a number of modernist influences, ranging from Faulkner and Joyce to Kafka, Hemingway and Lorca.[95]

The scope of Roumain's transnational modernism extends not just to Rimbaud and Surrealism but, significantly, to Perse, a Caribbean heir to modernism in both France and the United States. The points of intersection among Roumain, the Surrealist group, and Perse and his circle are too numerous to describe in detail. We know, for example, that the October 1927 issue of *La Nouvelle Revue française* noted the first publication of *La Revue indigène*, and that Roumain was influenced by Arthur Rimbaud, who had previously been influenced by Perse.[96] Roumain was also associated with another revue, *Commune*, which ran briefly from July 1933 through August 1939 and whose personnel included Surrealists such as André Gide, and Roumain's friend, Louis Aragon, who was instrumental in the publication of Roumain's *Gouverneurs de la rosée*. In 1925 Philippe Thoby-Marcelin, a poet and close colleague at *La Revue indigène*, initiated a long correspondence with Valery Larbaud, the poet-critic who was one of the first and strongest promoters of Perse's work, and Larbaud helped Thoby-Marcelin publish poems in the December 1928 issue of *La Revue européenne*.

Roumain's self-consciousness as a New World poet makes him an important figure not just for the narrative of Hughes's involvement with modernism, but also for studying the hemispheric cross-currents of modernist influence documented in this book as a whole. Like Perse and Eliot, in his early poems "Le Buvard: orage" and "À jouer aux billes" Roumain draws on frontier imagery, amalgamating topographically ambiguous landscapes that bear simultaneous reference to the Caribbean and the United States.[97] Like Perse, his verses are at times long and Whitmanian; like Perse, following Poe, Roumain avoided the use of creole dialect in his early poetry; like Perse, Roumain was simultaneously committed to complex stylization and to scientific observation; like Perse, Roumain belonged to an elite social class, worked for a time as a statesman, and was eventually driven into exile. "Créole," a poem Roumain published in *Haiti-Journal* in July 1931, evokes the standpoint of a white "Creole" reminiscent of Perse's speakers in *Pour fêter une enfance* and *Éloges*.[98] In 1939, at the same banquet-reception where he would meet Hughes for the last time before his own death, Roumain expressed his commitment to internationalism, political action and art in terms that could well have been employed by either Perse or Hughes. "At this very moment," he said:

the entire world, because of the war, is facing problems which affect our fate in a most fundamental manner: Politically the facts cannot remain localized and isolated any longer in time and space. They are immediately internationalized by the very substance of a war for a new redivision of the world. They have made as one the destiny of all mankind, no matter to what country or race they may belong . . . We writers, who like to believe ourselves to be reflecting the consciousness of the universe, have once and for all lost the right – if ever it was ours – to the artifice of solitude and to the mysticism of introspection. This more or less subtle phraseology is but a screen of smoke, hiding, imperfectly a panic to desert. It is a renunciation of the primordial mission of a man of thought: *to be a man of action*.[99]

In contrast with the relatively straightforward narrative concerning Hughes's influence on Césaire, the murkier and more complex story of Hughes's relations with Roumain, which began almost a decade earlier, has yet to be fully understood. Hughes had relatively little contact with Césaire, and even refused a request from Alioune Diop asking him to translate Césaire's *Cahier* into English.[100] By contrast, he was persistently involved in all aspects of Roumain's life and work, translating two of Roumain's best-known poems, "When the Tom-Tom Beats" and "Guinea," as well as his posthumously published novel, *Gouverneurs de la rosée*.[101] In 1934 and 1935, Hughes published appeals for Roumain's release in the *New Republic* and *New Masses*, after a Haitian tribunal sentenced Roumain to three years in prison for his activities as a member of the Communist Party. Celebrating Roumain as "the finest living Haitian writer," Hughes called upon "all writers and artists of whatever race who believe in the freedom of words and of the human spirit, to protest immediately . . . the uncalled for and unmerited sentence to prison of . . . one of the few, and by far the most talented of the literary men of Haiti."[102] In his speech at the final session of the Second International Writers' Congress delivered on July 17, Hughes paid a warm tribute to Roumain, saying that his work represents "the great longing that is in the hearts of the darker peoples of the world to reach out their hands in friendship and brotherhood to all the white races of the earth."[103]

Critics such as Naomi Garrett, Martha Cobb and Carolyn Fowler have noticed uncanny similarities between Hughes and Roumain but, as Trouillot observes, scholars have not ascertained the extent of Hughes's influence in any detail.[104] After the American occupation of Haiti ended in 1934, a "Langstonienne" zeal spread to many poets on the island.[105] In a 1929 issue of *La Revue de Paris*, Franck Schoell published an article on the Harlem Renaissance, as well as French translations of Hughes's "Our Land" and "I, Too" that were widely read by Haitian poets. And two years later, the Haitian anthropologist and man of letters Jean Price-Mars published an influential series of articles on the Harlem Renaissance, one of which included Schoell's Baudelairean rendering of Hughes's "Our Land."[106]

It is possible Roumain also played a vital role in raising awareness of Hughes's work in the region. The two poets corresponded and saw each other twice after their first meeting in Port-au-Prince: in Paris at the Second International Writers' Congress in 1937, during a time when Roumain was studying at the Institut de Paléonthologie Humaine and the Musée de l'Homme, and in 1939, five years before Roumain's death when he was living in exile in New York City.[107]

Hughes said he visited Haiti to "get away from my troubles," but he was even more troubled and shocked by the poverty he found there.[108] Deploring the misery of "va-nu-pieds," poor people without shoes, he immediately dashed off a letter to the editor of *New Masses*, castigating Haiti's elite for not meeting their people's most basic needs. This point was elaborated in a longer *New Masses* piece published three months later, which was translated into French for the local Port-au-Prince newspaper *Haiti-Journal*.[109] Hughes also wrote about Haiti for the *Crisis* and the *New Republic* and even composed (with Arna Bontemps) a children's story about Haiti, *Popo and Fifina: Children of Haiti*, a year after his first visit.[110] In 1935, *Drums of Haiti* appeared, a work that was retitled *Emperor of Haiti* in 1938 and would form the basis for Hughes's three-act opera, *Troubled Island*, first staged in Cleveland in 1936, and published in 1949.

Fowler reports that Hughes and Roumain were already familiar with each other's work when they met in 1931.[111] Though Hughes was something of a recluse in Haiti, he did pay a visit to Roumain on the last day of his trip. Roumain was very disturbed to hear that Hughes had been in the area for the entire summer, and quickly organized a delegation, who surprised and embarrassed Hughes, who was eating lunch, coatless and shirtless, on the deck when the assembly of dignitaries arrived. "I was caught greasy-handed, half-naked – and soxless – by an official delegation of leading Haitians," Hughes writes; "I arose from my table on the cargo hatch, wiped my hands on my trousers, and was introduced by Roumain as 'the greatest Negro poet who had ever come to honor Haitian soil.' Each man bowed gravely. I bowed, too."[112]

Immediately after Hughes's departure from the island, Roumain wrote a tribute to Hughes for *Haiti-Journal*. The piece, which appeared in early August and was written without much time for research, demonstrates Roumain's detailed knowledge of Hughes's influences and life's work, including the fact that Knopf had published Hughes's first two volumes of poetry, and even the specific journals where his poems first appeared. "Langston Hughes is the greatest black poet in America," Roumain wrote:

And there is no other writer of his race, in my view, who rivals him as a novelist . . . He was discovered in Harlem by the excellent black writer Walter White who introduced him to Carl Van Vechten. The Negro periodicals *Opportunity* and *Crisis*, the great white revues *Survey Graphic*, *Vanity Fair*, and the *World Tomorrow* published his poems.

Alfred Knopf, the great editor in New York, published his volumes of poetry: The Weary Blues, Fine Clothes to the Jew, his novel Not Without Laughter, assuring him of the success he deserved. Langston had opened vast new horizons to his poetic experience:

J'ai connu des rivières aussi vieilles que le monde et plus vieilles que le flot du sang humain dans les veines de l'homme.
Mon âme est devenue profonde comme les rivières.

[I've known rivers ancient as the world and older than the flow of human blood in human veins. / My soul has grown deep like the rivers.]

A beautiful, great Whitmanian movement runs through these lines.[113]

Studying in Switzerland and Spain in the 1920s, Roumain would doubtless have been aware of contemporary avant-garde activities in Paris during this period.[114] He may have heard from friends such as Thoby-Marcelin, who was in Paris at the time, that Hughes's "Negro" and "A Black Pierrot" appeared in a July 1924 issue of a Paris-based periodical, *Les Continents*. Or he may have learned about Hughes two months later, when Hughes was mentioned by Alain Locke in an essay, also published in *Les Continents*, on recent trends in African-American poetry. In any event, by 1927, upon his return to Haiti, in an interview with Antonio Vieux that was published in the September 1927 issue of *La Revue indigène*, Roumain had evidently done considerable research on African-American literature. He was, as Garrett notes, the first of the "Indigenistes" to intuit and explain the full significance of the Harlem Renaissance for the subsequent Renaissance of poetry in Haiti.[115] In 1928, the same year Jean Price-Mars published *Ainsi parla l'oncle*, an anthropological analysis of African-American culture that would profoundly influence Haitian literature, Roumain wrote an essay called "Comment on traite les nègres aux États-Unis" that appeared in *Le Petit Impartial*.[116] And in January 1933, Roumain mentioned in a letter to Tristan Rémy, subsequently published in *Haiti-Journal*, that he was preparing a translation of poems by African-Americans such as Hughes.[117]

For readers already familiar with Hughes, encountering Roumain's poetry for the first time may bring on an eerie feeling of *déjà vu*. But sometimes, as in Roumain's "Le Buvard: insomnie," it is difficult to make a watertight case for Hughes's direct influence:

> Clarté indécise.
> La nuit
> entre dans la chambre, sombre voile
> brodé d'étoiles.
> La lune est un gros fruit
> se balançant à mon insomnie.
> Les rossignols de Hafiz
> sont morts. Silence bleuâtre.

Nuit interminable . . .

. . .

Je tends les mains
vers toi et j'étreins
le ciel
— et le vide.[118]

[Indistinct clarity. / Night / enters the bedroom, a dark veil / embroidered with stars. / The moon is a large fruit / balancing on my insomnia. / Hafiz's nightingales / are dead. Blueish silence. / Interminable night . . . / . . . / I reach with my hands / for you and embrace / the sky / — and nothingness.]

The cadences and line breaks in Roumain's poem, his speaker's isolation and angst-ridden insomnia, and the reference to a blue mood ("Silence bleuâtre") — a mood, notably, that comes on when Hafiz's nightingales, poems that were put to music, fall into deathly silence — all bring to mind the opening stanza of Hughes's "Summer Night." In Hughes, as in Roumain, the lyric speaker restlessly perceives an existential void when the music stops, and night seems endless:

> The sounds
> Of the Harlem night
> Drop one by one into stillness.
> The last player-piano is closed.
> The last victrola ceases with the
> "Jazz Boy Blues."
> The last crying baby sleeps
> And the night becomes
> Still as a whispering heartbeat.
> I toss
> Without rest in the darkness,
> Weary as the tired night,
> My soul
> Empty as the silence,
> Empty with a vague,
> Aching emptiness,
> Desiring,
> Needing someone,
> Something.[119]

It is possible Roumain read "Summer Night" before composing his poem, which was published in *La Revue indigène* in September 1927, almost two years after Hughes's poem first appeared in the December 1925 issue of *Crisis*, and a year after it was collected in *The Weary Blues*. All by itself, the chronology of publication may not be convincing. But when we consider, in addition to the internal evidence, that "Summer Night" proved to be one of Hughes's best- and earliest-known poems in Haiti, singled out as the very first (along with "Negro") to be translated into French by René Piquion and published as "Nuit d'été" in the June 1, 1933, issue of *La Relève*, the resemblances seem more than accidental.

The question of influence is further complicated by Roumain's and Hughes's shared affinities, not just with mutual friends and politically engaged writers like Aragon (to whom Roumain refers in the 1939 speech at the Harlem banquet where Roumain and Hughes had their final face-to-face encounter), but with Baudelaire and Laforgue. Mercer Cook and Fowler have noted Roumain's debt to turn-of-the-century French Decadents in his fiction, but the influence of Baudelaire's "Correspondances" pervades Roumain's early poems, especially in "Le Buvard: calme" and "Midi," where his speaker describes "Des fleurs irréelles" [unreal flowers], and a rhythm of silence "embalmed" by incense.[120] In 1929, Roumain praised Baudelaire's "Femmes damnées," observing that Baudelaire's sensuality is rendered in his verse with astonishing, almost onomatopoeic, exactitude.[121] Like Hughes – who three years earlier had paid tribute to Baudelaire's suggestive renderings of pale dusk purpling to night in his piece written for *Crisis* – Roumain, in poems such as "Noir," published in the August 1927 issue of *La Revue indigène*, was, judging from the text, drawn to Baudelaire's figurations of blackness.[122]

Another poem, "Créole," published in late July, about three weeks after Roumain had met Hughes, not only contains one of the very few creole expressions ("A vot' sèvice, moussié") in Roumain's poetic oeuvre, but also shows Roumain adapting, perhaps even in conscious emulation of Hughes, the Baudelairean image of shadow or shade, to portray the blackness of a woman, "fraîche et nue comme l'ombre" [fresh and naked as the shade], whom the white Creole speaker endlessly desires.[123]

If the Baudelairean antecedents lead to some startling family resemblances between Hughes and Roumain, their combined admiration for Laforgue makes for even more startling similarities. Like Hughes, in "La Danse du poète-clown" Roumain adapts Laforgue's pierrotic poetics to his own ends.[124] And in "S'échapper," a version of which was published as "Échapper" in March 1928, not only does Roumain draw elements from Laforgue's "Complainte des nostalgies préhistoriques," but also the poem bears an uncanny resemblance to Hughes's "Dream Variations" which was, as we have seen, also influenced by Laforgue's poem. In Roumain, as in Laforgue and Hughes, the central grammatical structure is a series of infinitives; all three poems express a nostalgic yearning for the freedom to dance ecstatically in an exotic, tropical realm; all three hint at the possibility of restful escape through death. But Hughes and Roumain also evoke memories of hard labor under the sun (for example "les mains qui saignent / d'avoir halé" [hands that bleed from having hauled]); and Roumain's poem is unique in its explicit reference to an American frontier setting:

> Se croire solitaire et joyeux
> dans la savane et
> cow-boy
> lancer son lasso aux chimères
> sans voir
> les mains qui saignent
> d'avoir halé jusqu'au coeur
> le Vide amer.
> Courir dans les champs de cannes
> parmi
> le hérissement des sabres d'argent
> au soleil,
> se croire plante
> devenir plante
> sentir la caresse des bras multipliés
> Y mêler ses bras multipliés
> écouter naître en soi une musique
> qui ayant couru
> d'horizon à horizon
> reviendra mourir en soi.[125]

[To believe oneself to be alone and joyful / in the savannah and / a cow-boy / thrusting his lasso at chimeras / without seeing / his hands which bleed / having just hauled into his heart / the bitter Void. / To run in the cane fields / among / the bristling of silver swords/in the sun, / to believe oneself to be a plant / to become a plant / to feel the caress of proliferating arms / There to commingle his own proliferating arms / to hear born within a music / which, having run / from horizon to horizon, / will return to die within.]

Again, as with "Summer Night," there are many places where Roumain could have read Hughes's poem, which was first published in *Crisis* under the title "Dream Variation" in July 1924; reprinted a year later in the March 25 issue of *Survey Graphic* that became the widely circulated anthology *The New Negro*; and collected in Hughes's 1926 volume *The Weary Blues*. But even if we dismiss the possibility of direct influence, the shared affinity with Laforgue and Baudelaire helps explain the rapport between Roumain and Hughes, and would no doubt have facilitated Roumain's creative adaptation of Hughes's style.

There is no question that Roumain was familiar with Hughes's "The Negro Speaks of Rivers," since Roumain quoted from this poem in his August 1931 tribute to Hughes. And in two poems Roumain published in *Haiti-Journal* that same year, "Quand bat le tam-tam" – which Hughes himself would eventually translate – and "Langston Hughes," the allusions to Hughes are unmistakable. Fowler proposes that "Quand bat le tam-tam" no longer reflects the tropicalism of Roumain's earlier work, but it would be more accurate to say that Roumain conjoins elements from Hughes's "The Negro Speaks of Rivers" with the revisionist primitivism of Hughes's "Danse africaine," a poem that first appeared in *Crisis* in August 1922, and that Piquion translated into French for publication in *La Relève* in September 1933.[126] Roumain's beating tom-tom is figuratively compared to the panting breast of a young black girl, recalling the "night-veiled girl" of "Danse africaine" who dances to the tom-tom's low, slow rhythm; and the speaker's assertions about knowledge of rivers, the river's capacity to restore continuities with remote African ancestors and cultural practices, and the river's reflection of soul, all bring to mind Hughes's "The Negro Speaks of Rivers":

> Ton coeur tremble dans l'ombre, comme
> le reflet d'un visage dans l'onde trouble.
> L'ancien mirage se lève au creux de la nuit
> Tu connais le doux sortilège du souvenir;
> Un fleuve t'emporte loin des berges,
> T'emporte vers l'ancestral paysage.
> Entends-tu ces voix: elles chantent l'amoureuse douleur
> Et dans le morne, écoute ce tam-tam haleter telle
> la gorge d'une noire jeune fille.
> Ton âme, c'est ce reflet dans l'eau murmurante
> où tes pères ont penchés [*sic*] leurs obscurs visages.
> Ses secrets mouvements te mêlent à la vague
> Et le blanc qui te fit mulâtre, c'est ce peu d'écume
> rejeté, comme un crachat, sur le rivage.[127]

Hughes would translate "When the Tom-Tom Beats" as follows:

> Your heart trembles in the shadows, like a face
>   reflected in troubled water
> The old mirage rises from the pit of the night
> You sense the sweet sorcery of the past:
> A river carries you far away from the banks,
> Carries you toward the ancestral landscape.
> Listen to those voices singing the sadness of love
> And in the mountain, hear the tom-tom

panting like the breast of a young black girl
Your soul is this image in the whispering water where
    your fathers bent their dark faces
Its hidden movements blend you with the waves
And the white that made you a mulatto is this bit
    of foam cast up, like spit, upon the shore.[128]

In "Langston Hughes," which appeared in *Haiti-Journal* in October 1931, three months after "Quand bat le tam-tam," the river imagery and echoes from Hughes's "The Negro Speaks of Rivers" are even more pronounced:

Tu connus à Lagos ces filles mélancoliques
Elles portent aux chevilles des colliers d'argent et s'offrent nues comme la nuit
    encerclée de lune.
Tu vis la France sans prononcer de paroles historiques
– Lafayette nous voici –
La Seine te parut moins belle que le Congo
. . .

Tu as promené ton coeur nomade, comme un Baedecker, de
Harlem à Dakar
La mer a prêté à tes chants un rhythme doux et rauque, et
Ses fleurs d'amertume écloses de l'écume.
Maintenant dans ce cabaret où à l'aube tu murmures:
O jouez ce blues pou' moa
Rêves-tu de palmes et de chants de pagayeurs au crépuscule?[129]

[At Lagos you knew those melancholy girls / They wear silver bracelets on their ankles and offer themselves naked like the night / encircled by the moon. / You saw France without uttering historic words / – Lafayette, here we are – / The Seine seemed less beautiful to you than the Congo / . . . / You carried your nomad heart, like a Baedecker, from / Harlem to Dakar / The sea endowed your songs with a sweet and rasping rhythm, and / Its bitter flowers opened in the spray. / Now, in this cabaret where you murmur at dawn / Oh play the blues for me / Do you dream of palms and the songs of canoe paddlers in the dusk?]

Roumain's syntax and diction ("Tu connus. . . . Tu vis . . . Tu as promené . . . tu murmures," etc.), as well as his use of American slang and reference to the blues sung in a cabaret at dawn (notably, phrased in the vernacular, "O jouez ce blues pou' moa") are all reminiscent of Hughes. This tacit homage hints at Hughes's formative influence on Roumain's style, not just in this but in other poems, and the speaker's playful expression of primitivist nostalgia and reference to "le crépuscule" intimate their shared affinity for Baudelaire. Eliot said Laforgue was the poet who first taught him how to speak, and Roumain implies that Hughes played an analogously crucial role in his own coming of age as a poet. It was Hughes, Roumain suggests, who first taught him how to value his relation to Africa, and thus to see Europe, the United States and the Caribbean with new eyes, fundamentally redefining his modernism, self-conception and sense of purpose as a poet of the Americas.

CONCLUSION

Unlike Eliot, who observed the enduring influence of Perse on the rhythms and imagery of his later work, Hughes never acknowledged any transformation of his style as a result of his experience translating Roumain's poems. "When the Tom-Tom Beats" and "Guinea" were first published in 1942, the same year as Hughes's *Shakespeare in Harlem*, a collection that marks a return to concerns and vernacular forms of the 1920s, and which, despite the cosmopolitan implications of its title poem, lacks the fervor of Hughes's transnationalism in those early years, bearing no significant reference whatsoever to the cultural scene in Paris. Still, as Michael Dash points out, "Roumain's true legacy can be located in his fertile encounter with other cultures, in the multilingual thrust of his writing, and in his emergence as a virtuoso of the polysemic text . . . His ideas represented the beginning of an epistemological break with notions of 'enracinement' and the glorification of cultural stasis," and the same holds true for Hughes's legacy.[130] In a poem written in memory of Roumain, Hughes thanks Roumain for helping him to imagine cultural communities that transcend the constraints of fixed national, racial and regional landscapes, an amalgamated, hybrid evocation of place, culture and community that Hughes himself explored in early poems such as "The Negro Speaks of Rivers" and "Negro," and which may also be found in the hybrid poetics of Eliot and Perse.

> Always
> You will be
> Man
> Finding out about
> The ever bigger world
> Before him.
> Always you will be
> . . .
>
> Hand that links
> Erzulie to the Pope
> Damballa to Lenin,
> Haiti to the universe

Bread and fish
To fisherman
To man
To me . . .[131]

Hughes's international and cross-cultural commitments during the 1940s
up through the 1960s are too numerous and varied to describe here. Suffice
to say that he worked tirelessly to foster community among artists, writers
and intellectuals throughout the world, and to criticize racial nationalism
everywhere, as he did in Dakar, a year before his death, at the First World
Festival in Negro Arts. The best writers, according to Hughes, do not aspire
blindly to whiteness or insist on being "blacker than black." The best and
most enduring will develop their sensibility and idiom regardless of race,
letting their work "leap the barriers of color, poverty, or whatever other
roadblocks to artistic truth there may be."[132]

CHAPTER 4

Signifying modernism in Wilson Harris's Eternity to Season

INTRODUCTION

In May 1964, five years after immigrating to Britain, Wilson Harris addressed the London West Indian Students' Union on the subject of "Tradition and the West Indian Novel." Over the course of his remarks, Harris observed the persisting relevance of Eliot's modernism. "The fact is," he said:

even where sincerely held, political radicalism is merely a fashionable attitude unless it is accompanied by profound insights into the experimental nature of the arts and the sciences ... There are critics who claim that the literary revolution of the first half of the twentieth century may well stem from the work of Pound and Eliot ... [H]ow is it that figures such as these, described in some quarters as conservative, remain "explosive" while many a fashionable rebel grows to be superficial and opportunistic?[1]

The dense intertextual and historical relations between Harris and Eliot are hard to miss. In 1960, the unsolicited manuscript for Harris's *Palace of the Peacock* was published in London by Faber, the firm that would subsequently publish all of Harris's novels, including a four-part series entitled *The Guyana Quartet*.[2] More than two decades ago, Bruce King remarked, "If Wilson Harris has any direct forebear it is T. S. Eliot with his meditations on time and tradition, and his fragmentation of narrative into a mosaic of dissociated images and symbols expressive of the chaos of modern culture and of the individual mind attempting to piece together an encompassing vision out of personal disorder."[3]

King contends that Harris differs starkly from Eliot, who "sought to lose himself in an impersonal tradition, salvaged from the ruins of the Old World."[4] By contrast, I hope to show that Harris is strongly indebted to Eliot's insights and experiments as a modernist poet of the Americas. Chapters 1 and 2 established Poe, Whitman and Laforgue as New World antecedents to Eliot's transnational poetics, and traced a line of development from Eliot to Perse that nourished the germination of modernism in Francophone Caribbean poetry. In chapter 3, I showed how Langston Hughes performed an analogous, pivotal role for the poetry of Jacques Roumain and other members of the Haitian Renaissance during the 1920s, as well as for the subsequent emergence of *Négritude*.

This chapter and the one following will extend the scope of my analysis to Wilson Harris and Derek Walcott, two poets whose writings confirm the presence of a modernist heritage in the Anglophone Caribbean. There is, as we shall see, a strong bond of hemispheric identification between Eliot and Anglophone Caribbean poets who came of age during the late 1940s and early 1950s, the decade leading up to independence. Charles Pollard forcefully argues that Kamau Brathwaite and Walcott were drawn to Eliot's modernism because his aesthetic clarified representational possibilities of their postcolonial experience.[5] But we have yet to recognize how this attraction to Eliot's style registers their shared history and stylistic predicament as poets of the Americas. Harris's example is critical because, as Simon Gikandi notes, he is the most acutely "self-conscious Caribbean modernist."[6]

In what follows I will examine Harris's selective engagement with four aspects of Eliot's modernism. First, Harris emphasizes the inescapable hybridity and adversarial contexts of the frontier, where Amerindian, European, Asian and African legacies are mysteriously intertwined. Second, he adapts Eliot's dialectical thinking about continuity and broad sense of tradition as a living principle. Third, Harris echoes Whitman and moves, like the late Eliot, towards sonorous incantation in poems centering on the shorescape. Last but not least, Harris draws on the mythical methods of modernism to recover an unwritten history of migratory cosmopolitanism, a "voyage between worlds" that was foundational to the development of poetry in Guyana.

Insofar as Harris perceives not just the pastness of modernism, but also its enduring applicability to present-day Caribbean experience, he shows historical self-understanding in terms that recall Eliot's. Harris is unabashed and open, about both his relation to Eliot and the challenge he poses to orthodoxies of postcolonial and postmodern theory.[7] "We know that we are nourished by the past," he once said:

but we know that the past also needs us, and that unless we can create an original role for ourselves in the present we will destroy our connections with the past ... So that this notion that the post-moderns have that there is no depth to reality is false. The post-modern movement has begun to betray creativity in my view. There is depth.

In a 1991 lecture on "Originality and Tradition," he averred, "However sophisticated a narrative may be, whatever theories of French philosophers have been associated with it, basically, once you scrape away the crust of post-modernism, what you find underneath is a pervasive and uniform despair."[8]

Situated in the context of current theoretical debates – debates where "postcolonialism" is synonymous with "postmodernism," and where modernists have been found guilty by association of all the crimes of "modernity," especially colonialism – this propinquity to Eliot threatens, absurdly, to disqualify Harris as a postcolonial writer.[9] As a corrective to this impasse, I wish to consider how Harris's poetics registers a history of migration, conquest, enslavement, hybridity, empire-building and deracination that inspired his close affinities with Eliot and other New World poets who preceded him. For Harris, as for Poe, Whitman, Laforgue, Perse and Hughes, shared diasporic history "makes a difference," as Eliot says, in fostering cross-currents of influence in the Americas.[10]

The intertextual dynamic between Harris and Eliot, Harris's constant echoing and revision of Eliot's style, fits well with Henry Louis Gates's account of "signifying" as a relation between a black text and its white discursive context: "I use the word context throughout this book to refer to the textual world that a black text echoes, mirrors, repeats, revises, or responds to in various formal ways. This process of intertextual relation I call Signifyin(g), the trope of revision, of repetition and difference, which I take from the Afro-American idiom."

Gates contends that, like Hughes and other black writers of the Americas, Harris was haunted by the widespread, longstanding belief, which originated as early as the seventeenth century, that a person of African descent cannot produce written art, has no enduring form of cultural memory, and therefore proves his innate, racial inferiority.[11] In this respect, as in others, the context of Harris's writings is strikingly different from Eliot's. At the same time that Harris's practice of signifying acknowledges a sense of kinship to Eliot that reflects their shared New World predicament, it also confirms the cultural distinctiveness of his idiom.

Thus in this chapter, as in my previous discussion of Hughes, I work to discern the distinctly local qualities of Harris's writings. Rather than assimilating the work of these black poets to a modernist project, I show how they drew on pre-modernist sources of inspiration, as well as regional and folk resources that made their poetry unique. For example, I present Harris within a complex historical contention: for Harris, American and British Romanticism represented live and rival principles, as did Amerindian,

Asian, African and Guyanese folk and oral traditions. Harris's ambivalence towards Whitman and the very notion of continuity was shaped by his responses to the nationalist fervor and violence in Guyana during the independence period. Unlike Eliot, Harris explicitly criticizes notions of cultural, racial and national coherence that would deny him the chance to draw freely on all aspects of heritage as a New World poet. Opening a fertile dialogue with the past, he emphatically rejects any and all forcibly imposed identities based on categorical abstractions that are misleadingly absolute and mutually exclusive: "The habit in the [Caribbean] region of assembling bodies of knowledge in coercive identity tends to make innovative scholarship of critical distinction and historic daring ... a rare occurrence: it is agreed, amongst sensitive scholars, that that habit contributes to impoverished dialogue with the past."[12]

Stuart Murray has argued that Harris's conception of postcoloniality is meaningless outside the framing contexts of modernity; and, further, that such continuities with Europe should not "devalue twentieth-century Caribbean political independence and the force of contemporary postcolonial articulation."[13] My analysis continues earlier attempts by scholars to resist separatist oversimplification, restore historical linkages between modernism and the colonial and postcolonial archives, and situate Harris's skeptical reassessment of modernism and signifying practices as aspects of Caribbean discourse.[14] *Eternity to Season* vividly illustrates the terms of Harris's formative, far-reaching encounter with Eliot and helps us to assess the New World legacies of modernism from a more distanced, historically perspicacious vantage point.

HYBRIDITY, FRONTIER VIOLENCE AND THE AMERINDIAN LEGACY IN "TRAIL"

Like other important New World writers – Thoreau and Melville are two who immediately come to mind – Harris studied to become a land surveyor, and his subsequent forays into the continental interior exerted a strong, lasting influence on his imagination.[15] As early as 1970, Kenneth Ramchand described how Harris's close experience with people from different cultures and classes is woven into fiction that shows "a responsiveness to the brooding landscape and the fabulous fragmented history of his native Guyana."[16] In a 1996 radio broadcast, Harris made a revealing statement about his approach to landscape, when he recalled his formative experiences as a surveyor: "I sensed ... that the landscape possessed resonance," he said; "The landscape ..., for me, is like an open book, and the alphabet ... was all around me. But it takes some time to really grasp what this alphabet is, and what the book of the living landscape is."[17]

The contours of Guyana's landscapes are also evident in Harris's second volume of poetry, *Eternity to Season*, which was privately published in 1954, and re-issued by New Beacon in 1978. It is unfortunate that *Eternity to Season* has received comparatively little attention up until now, since it usefully clarifies the significance of frontier landscapes in Harris's work. "Throughout the long and obscure history of mankind," he commented, "*a trail of silent things . . . speaks to us.*"[18] The trail in Harris's "Trail" suggests that the land, like an open book, encrypts an as yet unrecorded history of the New World. The poem opens onto an awesome panoramic view of a dense rainforest in Guyana's continental interior. Natural landmarks (river, waterfall, mountain, cliff and valley) appear in sequence, as if our eye were following the trails that lead from the bordering plateau down into a sea of mist. "Trail" dramatizes a poet's effort to interpret, integrate and order his responses to an environment that has been subject to constant, massive change. We are told, for example, that metrical "feet follow from the mountains / to seek what was once substance and is now apparition":

> Plateau that borders the river stands
> above the mighty fall: the streams flow from the mountains,
> each lonely trail is carven on rock, on pebble, on sand.
> Falls like lace in slow motion to conceal
> the perpendicular surface of earth that is hard and unrelenting.
> Turns each indifferent pebble round and round
> smooth as smooth, each grain of sand carven as carven
> suggestions in millions of shuffling feet on every plane of
> > > thought,
> flake or cliff.
>
> > The massive changes strip the mountains
> that are obliterated like shadows though they seemed
> > > unchanging.
> > The trail lasts down the falls
> and vanishes in smoke, a sea of mist, the ocean
> of time. And so the timeless feet follow from the mountains
> to seek what was once substance and is now apparition.
> It leads to a deeper valley and land. How deep that valley,
> how precipitous that skin of the earth.
> The giant flakes stand edge to edge to perfect the early traces
> > > of doom
> and remembrance, the original catastrophes of moving
> > > organisms

fish or eel dashed against the valleys of rocks. The great Fall
thunders, its body smooth as the scales
on every overhanging hill. The stream of life swells
or diminishes, cloaks its secret trail. Deep, intoxicating,
is the valley of its awareness. Beneath the vast lip of the old
                                                World
it hangs like smoke over the earth, green as promising, flashing
                                                as living,
spangled with undecipherable moss. The bottomless stream
seems to stand still
and look back to the vanished mountains.[19]

The ghostly presence of lost Amerindian civilizations is powerfully evoked by Harris's rendering of the New World frontier. The perception of the trails as "lonely" summons up an apparitional memory of "millions of shuffling feet" that, like the endless rush of water that eroded pebbles into tiny grains of sand, gradually carved the trails into the mountainside. The "vanishing" of the trails at the bottom of the falls figuratively intimates the vanishing of ancient American civilizations: they are, as Harris says, a legacy of "silent things" left by Amerindians, many of whom died of smallpox, venereal disease and the sheer exhaustion of their labor in mines run by European settlers who had migrated to the New World in search of gold.[20]

In chapter 2 I showed how, especially in the later landscape poems, Eliot tacitly commemorates the intricate intertwining of European imperial and Amerindian legacies. Amerindian places names, like the French derivation of "St. Louis," summon up the collective memory of migration and, with it, the violent encounters between European and Amerindian peoples that belie the idealized myth of the frontier. Eliot's account of tradition has often been construed in very narrow, purist, European-oriented terms, and he doubtless encouraged such an impression by referring, in his best-known and most influential essay, to the "mind of Europe."[21] But the tortuous syntax of the sentence in which this phrase occurs not only raises questions about the "country" which Eliot implicitly identifies as his own. It also insinuates the breadth and hybridity of what Eliot means by tradition. The poet, he says,

must be aware that the mind of Europe – the mind of his own country – a mind which he learns in time to be much more important than his own private mind – is a mind which changes, and that this change is a development which abandons nothing *en route*, which does not superannuate either Shakespeare, or Homer, or the rock drawing of the Magdalenian draughtsmen. That this development, refinement perhaps, complication certainly, is not, from the point of view of the artist, any improvement.[22]

The same year Eliot began writing *The Waste Land*, and only a month after the first part of "Tradition and the Individual Talent" appeared in the *Egoist*, the *Athenaeum* published "War-paint and Feathers," his review of *An Anthology of Songs and Chants from the Indians of North America*. Although the prose in Eliot's review has its moments of primitivist condescension, the piece also illustrates his questioning of evolutionary dogma.[23] Observing that "aborigines of every complexion and climate ... have arrived, each tribe pressing upon us its own claims to distinction in art and literature," Eliot concludes that the poet is "the most ready and the most able of men to learn from the savage," and "the last person to see the savage in a romantic light."[24]

This questioning of evolutionism, Eliot's claim that rock paintings by artists from the later Upper Palaeolithic cultures in western Europe are as much a part of his cultural heritage as the writings of Shakespeare or Homer, would have resonated with Harris. Furthermore, intimation of the violence that gave rise to hybrid cultural heritages in the New World in "Trail" is strikingly similar to Eliot's treatment of frontier landscapes in "The Dry Salvages" and in his translation of Perse's *Anabase*. This shared concern with what Harris calls the "adversarial contexts" of the frontier helps to explain why catastrophe is so central to the presence of the past in "Trail."[25] "Something endures," Harris writes, "at the heart of catastrophe or change which runs to meet one like a feature of unpredictable unity with and through a phenomenal nature one cannot absolutely grasp."[26] The image of fish and eel being brutally dashed against rock implies that, as a result of prolonged contact with European settler cultures in the imperial frontier's "contact zone," the Amerindian way of life was threatened with extinction.[27] The scene is one among many "traces of doom," or catastrophic annihilation, which the speaker is trying to interpret.

These adversarial contexts of transculturation in Harris's "Trail" are also the origin of creativity, since both destructive exploitation and creation coalesce in the formation of traditions. "The nature of tradition is," he writes, "in some degree, a ceaseless question about the nature of exploitation, self-exploitation, as well as the exploitation of others, the exploitation of one culture by another."[28] We see this as well in Harris's description of how the Caribs used to carve a flute out of the bones of their cannibalized Spanish enemies:

The Caribs consumed a morsel of flesh from an enemy. Then they hollowed a bone from which they had plucked that morsel and made a flute. They sought to enter the mind of their enemy, the living, the dead and the unborn. The origins of music for them lay in the bone flute. That flute was the seed of an intimate revelation of mutual spaces they shared with the enemy, mutual spaces within which to visualise the rhythm of strategy, the rhythm of attack or defence the enemy would dream to employ against them. The bone flute gave them access, as it were, to the very embryo of adversarial regime instinctive to themselves.

Earlier on, I mentioned that Eliot's recollection of frontier violence in "The Dry Salvages" involves a composite landscape technique and musical orchestration of voices that also work formally to confirm a movement towards "balance of mind" and reconciliation. In Harris's writings, the recognition of historical violence and reconciliation are similarly linked. The ritual of cannibalism invoked by the bone-flute implies that the inter-cultural possibilities of its music affirm an intimately shared "greed for ascendancy" in both the Amerindian and the Spaniard. The revelation of this and other mutual spaces inhabited by conqueror and conquered alike initiates a revolutionary, inward movement towards peaceful reconciliation, where "cannibalism begins to give ground to a deeply hidden moral compulsion to contend with innermost bias in humanity and to consume some portion of that inner rage, inner fire, associated with cruel prejudice."[29]

LANDSCAPE AND CONTINUITY IN "THE SPIRIT OF PLACE"

Eliot's confrontation with frontier violence, the Amerindian legacy and the hybridity of New World cultures occurs at the very margin of his poetic oeuvre, whereas in Harris this subject is emphatically stated and pervasive. In "Profiles of Myth and the New World," for example, Harris describes the "pitiless slogan of 'ethnic cleansing' [that] has echoed round the globe" and asserts that the vanished legacies of pre-Columbian America "may still be raised into renascent focus to assist us to see the fallacy in concepts of pathetic racial purity." Such concepts, he continues, "Signify ... the death of the imagination within frames of dogmatic identity and dogmatic homogeneity."[30] The cherished universality of tradition, which Harris identifies as the "cross-cultural psyche of humanity," would never come into being without hybridity or, for that matter, the global contexts of empire-building and conquest that wrought such violent, but fertile, comminglings of influence.[31]

Despite their difference in emphasis, both Harris and Eliot illuminate the crucial point that cross-culturalism often, if not always, involves frontier violence. Thus it is fitting that the lyric sequence in which Harris's "Trail" appears is entitled "The Spirit of Place," an allusion to the same essay by Lawrence – "Fenimore Cooper's White Novels" – that Eliot had deemed so brilliant. In Harris, as in Cooper and Eliot, the frontier setting is haunted by unappeased ghosts of dead Amerindians, a "demon of the continent" that is secreted, but nonetheless present, in the contours of landscape and poem alike.

This apparitional presence of the Amerindian past in Harris's "Trail" affirms, and extends, our understanding of "continuity" in the sense advocated by F. R. Leavis and Eliot.[32] Though Harris once castigated Leavis for possessing "no sympathy whatever for imaginative literature that fell outside of the closed world of his 'great tradition,'" in an essay called "Continuity and Discontinuity" he appears to be drawing on many of Leavis's and Eliot's ideas about continuity and the nature of a living principle.[33] "Continuity," he writes, "can be deceptive. It may seem to embalm the potential available to us. On the other hand it may assist us to perceive pressures of profoundest creativity and revisionary momentum ... Continuity cannot be seized or structured by any group and thus it should empower arts of complex originality."[34]

An important corollary follows from this. Although continuity appears to have vanished in the New World context, it is the poet's task to restore or, as Eliot says, "obtain" tradition through great labor.[35] In his 1951 essay on "Art and Criticism," Harris observed, "an objective process exists, a secret form or tradition, which yields itself, fragmentarily perhaps, but decisively as time goes on." Elsewhere, he remarked:

I am convinced that there is a tradition in depth which returns, which nourishes us even though it appears to have vanished, and that it creates a fiction in the ways in which the creative imagination comes into dialogue with clues of revisionary moment. The spectral burden of vanishing and re-appearing is at the heart of the writer's task.[36]

Eliot reasons dialectically to enlarge the significance of "tradition," insisting that timid adherence to the successes of previous generations should be discouraged; that "the past should be altered by the present as much as the present is directed by the past"; and that the poet should live "in what is not merely the present, but the present moment of the past."[37] For Harris, too, tradition involves a "profound *dialogue* with the past" that would liberate creative and critical potentialities; it requires a "re-creative rapport between old monuments and new windows upon the cosmos."[38] He fully agrees with Eliot that the most original parts of a poet's work are those in which tradition vigorously asserts its power.[39] For both poets, the essential objectivity of art resides in the creative reinterpretation of what Harris calls "the womb of tradition," where there is an "original overlap or viable frontier" between ages and cultures.[40]

Simon Gikandi has remarked Harris's use of the geographic metaphor of escarpment to represent how modernity "[divides] the moment of conquest and loss for 'the ancient American civilizations' from the temporal movements through which Europe renews and empowers itself."[41] But the metaphor also figures the central, vexed problem of continuity, as Harris himself once observed:

For the mainstream of the West Indies in my estimation possesses an enormous escarpment down which it falls, and I am thinking here of the European discovery of the New World and conquest of the ancient Amerindian civilizations which were themselves related by earlier and obscure levels of conquest ... The question is – how can one begin to reconcile the broken parts of such an enormous heritage?[42]

In "Trail," Harris's panoramic setting figuratively dramatizes an idea of continuity that extends to, and reconciles, all the ancestral cultures the New World poet is heir to. The speaker's commitment to the act of remembrance and recovery of lost traditions compels him, in the lyric's closing lines, to acknowledge a painful, but also promising and necessary, connection to the old world, the very "womb" of tradition. Shifting his gaze from the top to the bottom of the falls, dismantling the stately cadence of blank verse along the way, Harris's lyric speaker imagines that the land is like the remains of a body – a vast lip hanging over the earth. For an uncanny moment, the landscape looks like a woman's body, a mouth, or a vast unmarked grave:

> Beneath the vast lip of the old
> > World
> it hangs like smoke over the earth, green as promising, flashing
> > as living,
> spangled with undecipherable moss. The bottomless stream
> seems to stand still
> and look back to the vanished mountains.[43]

William Empson has written that in poems such as Wordsworth's *Prelude*, the mountains of Westmorland figuratively evoke the "permanent tradition of the country."[44] A more pertinent image for Harris would have been Wordsworth's portrayal of the waterfall in Gondo Gorge, in the Alps, which implies that such continuity becomes possible, and meaningful, only when there is also constant change:

> > ... downwards we hurried fast,
> And, with the half-shaped road, which we had missed,
> Entered a narrow chasm.
> > ...
> > > ... The immeasurable height
> Of woods decaying, never to be decayed,

> The stationary blasts of waterfalls,
> And in the narrow rent at every turn
> Winds thwarting winds, bewildered and forlorn,
> The torrents shooting from the clear blue sky,
> The rocks that muttered close upon our ears,
> Black drizzling crags that spake by the way-side
> As if a voice were in them, the sick sight
> And giddy prospect of the raving stream,
> The unfettered clouds and region of the Heavens,
> Tumult and peace, the darkness and the light–
> Were all like workings of one mind, the features
> Of the same face, blossoms upon one tree;
> Characters of the great Apocalypse,
> The types and symbols of Eternity,
> Of first and last, and midst, and without end.[45]

The syntactical chaos of the passage is anchored, and organized, by a simile comparing natural phenomena (that is, the decaying woods and the water-falls) to symbols of Eternity. Wordsworth's simile affirms the possibility of a shareable and continuous culture, while at the same time showing that cer-tain meanings will be irretrievably lost, as the use of particular words, types and symbols changes over time. As the passage progresses, the speaker dis-covers that his ability to draw on an inherited typology orders and interprets his encounter with nature. By willfully insisting on a meaningful correspon-dence between natural and heavenly types, Wordsworth's speaker creates an appealing configuration of symbols which – like the height of a forest that is made up of trees that will constantly be replaced by new trees, and like the stationary blasts of waterfalls – will always contain decaying traces of their old meanings, at the same time as they evoke new meanings, and are transmuted, each time they are put to a new use.

Harris's awareness of the catastrophic history suggested by the image of water falling leads him, in "Trail," to evoke reconciliation and community in terms that closely align him with Wordsworth as well as Eliot. Harris's simile, "green as promising," and his speaker's perception that the landscape is "spangled with undecipherable moss" allude to one of Wordsworth's "Elegiac Verses" for his brother. In Wordsworth's landscape, as in Harris's, the living presence of the past simultaneously horrifies and consoles:

> With multitude of purple eyes,
> Spangling a cushion green like moss ... [46]

The sheer indecipherability of Harris's style has, over the years, left impatient readers baffled and irritated.[47] Harris himself has expressed reservations about some of the poems in *Eternity to Season*, and even went so far as to request that earlier versions be omitted from a special issue of *Kyk-over-al*.[48] Although the effect of this stylistic difficulty in "Trail" is to suggest the speaker's intense isolation, the poem's poignant, pained recollection of Wordsworth also illustrates that any fear of indecipherability is mitigated by continuity.

Thus far we have seen that Harris's account of continuity with tradition draws on elements from Eliot and Leavis. But Harris's historical sense is also deeply and uniquely rooted in his own era and locality insofar as he explicitly associates blind, habitual affirmations of continuity with the racial separatism and violence perpetuated by nationalists during the struggle for independence in the region. We see this, for example, in "Laocoon," another landscape poem from "The Spirit of Place." Unlike "Trail," which centers on the continental interior as a transcultural frontier, "Laocoon" evokes the coastline, reminding us that Guyana is uniquely situated so that it literally mediates between the American continent and the island archipelago. The first two stanzas proceed imagistically, in the manner of Pound or Williams, dramatizing a dialectical tension between the parched coastland near the sea, and the fields that lie far off in the continental interior. Harris's image, "Ridges of shadow," demarcates the boundary between the first and second stanzas, in much the same way that the bush described in the poem's setting demarcates where the coast ends and the continental interior begins. These divisions figuratively evoke the parameters of the lyric speaker's composite consciousness.

> The dry earth near this salt sea
> is baked and parched
> under the sun.
>
> Ridges of shadow
> mark the distant bush
> at the far end of the fields.[49]

Harris's emphasis on orderly perception and composition in these opening stanzas makes sense when we recall that, in his view, the coastlands summon up memories of European engineers who imposed a strict, Euclidean order on the landscape.[50]

In the third stanza, however, Harris implies that such orderly distinctions and conceptual categories are as destined to fail as "ineffectual" planks in a fence. The secure ordering of landscape achieved by European engineers, and by Harris's own imagistic technique and lineation, is disrupted by the invasive sound of the sea half a mile off the coast:

> The land is bounded
> by ineffectual palings.
> The sounding sea cannonades half-a mile off the coast.[51]

It is illuminating to consider why Harris would have reworked the last line of this stanza for the 1978 edition of *Eternity to Season*, replacing "hammers" with "cannonades." Paula Burnett proposes that the revision may have been done as an *hommage* to Walcott's *Another Life*, where Walcott's phrase, "the ocean cannonading, come!" expresses the call to art.[52] This makes sense, especially given that the title of Harris's lyric, "Laocoon," recalls one of the most widely commemorated classical scenes in the history of Western art. But Harris's poem is first and foremost about the need for transnational and intercultural exchange. Laocoon, after all, was punished by the gods for warning the Trojans that the artwork given to them by the Greeks was dangerous, and for telling them not to bring it into their city. The formal and thematic disintegration of boundaries in Harris's poem evokes the inevitable, tragic failure of any effort to maintain distinctions between separate and pure national cultures. Harris's "cannonades" brings to mind not just Walcott's poem, but also the soundings of such canonical works as Arnold's "Dover Beach" and especially Thomas Hardy's "The Discovery," an uncanny prophecy of war that appeared in *Satires of Circumstance* in 1914. Like Harris's lyric speaker, the ghostly speaker in Hardy's poem wanders to a coast and hears waves breaking like cannonades:

> I wandered to a crude coast
> Like a ghost;
> Upon the hills I saw fires –
> Funeral pyres
> Seemingly – and heard breaking
> Waves like distant cannonades that set the land shaking.[53]

In the same 1990 lecture at the University of Cambridge in which he discussed Eliot's remarks on Hardy's treatment of landscape, Harris recalled how his experience as a surveyor also enriched his perception as a poet, because it taught him to enter into a dialogue with the land and, perhaps even more important, involved him in a cherished transatlantic collaboration with an English engineer, F. H. Hutchinson. Harris's transformed relations with landscape were brought about through his achieved sense of continuity, not just with Amerindian cultures, but with the cultures of Britain as well.[54] Not only does his allusive practice in the opening stanzas of "Laocoon" intimate that continuity with other national cultures is essential for the flourishing of Caribbean poetry, confirming his stated aversion to the conflicting racial nationalisms that culminated in the First World War.

Also, the poem raises a salient, ominous comparison between the violence perpetuated by racial nationalisms during both World Wars and the tragic, violent assertion of continuity and racial separatism during the struggle for independence in Harris's own era and locality:

> Versions of economic blockade in weather-charts of grain
> come near however far into a scale that measures
> what is great, commands what is small.
>
> . . .
>
> And the continuity of savage drum
> is sun's loud shadow on the television tree of the sky, continuity
> of savage spoil
> the closeness of a blossom reflected in a bloated corpse, roadside drain's
> snapshot in a glossy magazine.[55]

In an address at the University of Liège on "Originality and Tradition," Harris suggested that the tragedy of conflicting nationalisms in Europe was tragically repeating itself in the "so-called 'independent' world":

It seems to me that . . . part of the cement of Tragedy . . . lies in the so-called "independent" world. Many of the independent states in Africa, South America and elsewhere have changed nothing at all. They have simply endorsed a moribund principle in which they have framed themselves in a certain way and very often all sorts of conflicts begin to grow within that area. It has happened in Europe: the First World War, the Second World War, the conflicts between various states.[56]

Like Eliot, who insisted that "The notion of a purely self-contained European culture would be as fatal as the notion of a self-contained national culture," and like Langston Hughes, whose contribution to the rise of black internationalism was examined in the previous chapter, Harris was convinced that cross-fertilization among disparate cultures has always been, and will continue to be, an essential precondition for their growth and survival:

So if you go into some so-called Black Ghetto where you have men beating drums and claiming that they have an independent music, that is not true. They are, whether they know it or not, drawing things in from other cultures, but instead of entering the kind of situation in which the whole question could be opened up in a wholly new way, where you would penetrate the resources of enigmatic tradition, they claim a kind of independence which is a perverse cross-culturalism.[57]

MEMORIES OF WHITMAN IN HARRIS'S SHORESCAPES

Given Harris's lifelong commitment to continuity, intercultural exchange, and tradition in Eliot's broadened sense, it should not surprise us that for

Harris, as for many Caribbean poets, British and American Romanticism represents a cultural legacy that is as essential to the formation of his poetics as Amerindian, African, Asian and local folk cultures. "Creation," another landscape poem from "The Spirit of Place," evokes the difficulty, but also the necessity, of such a transnational allusive practice. Defining the poet's creative act as one of cross-culturation, "the unity of extremes that reach from one end of the world / to the other," in this poem – as in "Laocoon" – Harris juxtaposes the continental interior with a disintegrating strip of coast:

> Broods on the mud flats
> the spirit that is mild and yet severe
> painful and yet pleasurable. It is the spirit of creation. It is
> the unity of extremes that reach from one end of the world
> to the other.
>   It is
> lofty and blue living sky. It is frail skeleton
> green leaf against heaven. It is nondescript
> trunk of a tree, rugged and gnarled, weathered and shrunken:
> waiting to be reduced to dry white limbs whenever the sea
>   comes in.
> Palace and hovel,
> crumbling road, remotest village, absolute minimum
> of survival. It is
> the world that exists on different yet answering planes,
> the solitary whispering abandoned strip of land where the sea
> comes in.[58]

The sudden apparition of this coastal landscape, "whispering" like an all but abandoned line of poetry, hints at the presence of ghostly antecedents and influences, places where the sea of canonical soundings has once again come in. One such antecedent is Shelley, who memorably cast the wind's perpetual dirge in the apostrophic shape of an ode. Harris's reference to dead leaves, the dialectical relationship between the disintegration and preservation of form, and the presence of a storm which figuratively implies that even destructive impulses may be directed towards the preservation of artistic vitality – all hark back to Shelley's experiments with pastoral in "Ode to the West Wind":

>   . . . Here on this
> edge of coastland no road exists to withstand the deeps.
>
> The vast and thudding sea that sweeps unknowing and mud-
>   coloured

sullen and indifferent
is imbued with casual immensity
scorns beauty and awareness
save the beauty of its marginal desolation. Here on this
edge of coastland no road exists to withstand the deeps.

These swallow and yet preserve the iron inevitability of form,
the disintegration of matter that is never truly lost
but is in perpetual suspension, changing, melting,
tangible, intangible,
a magical undergrowth of dead leaves and surviving
roots and pillars like trees shaken by the mysterious drowned
storm of creation, creation's eternity, creation's season,
creation's extremes that exist everywhere
in the world and are here too on this distant strip of coast
in fashion and in ghost. Here as everywhere
the celebration of spirit, the discriminate fashion and wake of
                                        survival,
the surrender of an indefinable strand of experience into or out
                                        of the sea,
into body and into mind, into feature and into memory,
into life and into the strangest realisation of death.[59]

Harris's lines echo Shelley by their reference to a magical undergrowth of dead leaves and roots. They dramatize the surviving traces of "inevitability," or form, by pointing out "roots and pillars" on the coastland, and harbor a reminiscence of form through assonance (thudding/sullen); repetition; and by weaving together rhymes and near rhymes, rhythmically alternating between rhymes that are masculine (leaves/trees) and those that are feminine (changing/melting/surviving). But Harris significantly transmutes Shelley's apostrophe: the appeal, "hear, oh hear!" is replaced by a deictic, "here." Whereas in Shelley's "Ode," the speaker's yearning for transcendence and inspiration is embodied by apostrophe as a privileged Romantic trope, Harris's speaker resorts instead to a desperate affirmation of place. No Lawrencian "Spirit of Place" awakens as Harris's speaker endlessly returns to the sheer fact of his setting and predicament, "here," on the Guyana coastland.

Harris's fertile adaptation of Shelley's style is, moreover, further enriched by another self-conceiving idiom that is hemispheric, since "Creation" also recalls the shorescape setting and dirge-like laments of Whitman in *As I Ebb'd with the Ocean of Life*. Conjoining echoes from Whitman and Shelley, Harris moves to bridge the transatlantic divide between them, tacitly acknowledging how close and indebted Whitman's poem is to Shelley's.[60]

All three poems depict the shorescape as a means of evoking the demands of poetic representation; all regard, with desire and dread, the prospect of revolutionary change. But Harris's setting resembles Whitman's more than Shelley's insofar as it bears associations with the adversarial contexts and Amerindian legacy of the frontier.

We know that Harris's fascination with Whitman's frontier poetics began very early. In "Setting Sun," for example, a dramatic poem that exists only in typescript and formed the basis for *Fetish*, a collection that was privately printed three years before *Eternity to Season*, Harris opened with an epigraph taken from *Leaves of Grass*. The poem scrutinizes Whitman's first premise, the divine equality of all men, and the possibilities opened by the grandeur of Whitman's democratic mythos:

Philosophers have striven profoundly to justify the exploitation of many by man in doctrines of divine right for a privileged few.
    But all men are divine and as such have an equal share in burden and privilege in the mind of God.
    The ultimate justification or unity of man cannot be possible in other terms.
    Hierarchal or slave-king pyramid is a crumbling mould within grander moulds of the myth.[61]

For Harris and Whitman, the death-like difficulty of representation is related to the speaker's fears about his lost cultural antecedents, and the silence of the Amerindian dead who haunt the shorescape. Whitman's figurative action, in Harold Bloom's phrase, of "emptying out the self," expresses a desire to recover his lost New World legacy by "gather[ing]," and merging himself "as part of the sands and drift" where these nameless dead have been buried:

> As I wend to the shores I know not,
> As I list to the dirge, the voices of men and women wreck'd,
> As I inhale the impalpable breezes that set in upon me,
> As the ocean so mysteriously rolls toward me closer and closer,
> I too but signify at the utmost a little wash'd-up drift,
> A few sands and dead leaves to gather,
> Gather, and merge myself as part of the sands and drift.[62]

Similarly, in "Creation" Harris presents a speaker who inconsolably laments the dead and perceives traces of vanished civilizations, mounds on the shorescape that recall Amerindian peoples who buried their dead by the sea.[63] There are, however, a number of telling differences between Whitman's poem and Harris's. Whereas Whitman's end-stopped lines cohere by their focus on the speaker's actions, positions or perceptions, Harris fragments his syntax and employs confusing enjambments to disturb the reader's complacent expectation of closure. In contrast to Whitman's fervent anaphora, Harris generally uses repetition to highlight the danger it poses to sense. In Harris, repetition borders on the brink of "pure" poetry or nonsense, especially when it involves abstractions such as, in this case, the word "creation": "roots and pillars like trees shaken by the mysterious drowned / storm of *creation, creation's* eternity, *creation's* season, / *creation's* extremes that exist everywhere" (emphasis added).

Harris's recollection of Whitman and movement towards sonorous incantation in "Creation" bring his poetics into close alignment with Eliot's. In "Cape Ann," as we have seen, the musical, nonsense aspects of Eliot's lyric obliquely refer to the history of transculturation in the Americas, as well as the sustained conflict and cross-cultural exchange that took place between British settlers and the Agawam Indian nation in the New World during the seventeenth century. In "The Dry Salvages," a war poem composed during a time when he was carefully reassessing Whitman's poetics of the frontier, Eliot draws extensively on the coastal imagery and antiphonal design in Whitman's *Sea Drift* lyrics. But although Harris's "Creation" resembles Eliot's "The Dry Salvages" through its remembrance of Whitman's sea dirge for vanished Amerindians, "voices of men and women wreck'd," and the birth of poetic sensibility on Paumanok's shores, Harris's relation to Whitman also reflects circumstances that are distinctly local. In contrast with Eliot, whose eventual rapprochement with Whitman was brought about in the context of World War, Harris's ambivalence towards Whitman's nationalistic poems about the frontier is best understood in light of his response to nationalist violence during the independence struggle in Guyana. In "The Name of Liberty," an essay which first appeared in a special issue of *Third Text* in 1990, Harris recalled the political chaos that was brought about during the 1950s, when Whitman's ideas about freedom had been used to inspire nationalism and incite a leftist revolution in the region. Throughout his poetry, Harris's steady ambivalence towards the "heady, chaotic love affair with Liberty" which Whitman inspired in Guyana is evident in the many ways he uses landscape to resist and transmute Whitman's nationalistic poetics of the American frontier:

I was reminded of scenes I witnessed as a young man on the streets of Georgetown, British Guiana, in the mid-twentieth-century when processions of ordinary people, trade unionists, sugar estate workers, etc., etc., paraded carrying banners adorned with pictures of Stalin, Lenin, Thomas Paine, Karl Marx, Walt Whitman, and Trotsky. It was a heady, chaotic love affair with Liberty that was to have its tragic consequences.[64]

"The Dry Salvages" also anticipates Harris's lyric practice, not just in "Creation" but throughout *Eternity to Season*, insofar as Eliot's setting is a composite landscape, conjoining two frontiers – the Mississippi River in St. Louis and the land's edge off the New England coast. In Eliot, as in Harris, river and shorescape are juxtaposed to suggest the paradoxical convergence of eternity and time's endless flow. Harris's "Home," for example, part of the "*Cumberland*" sequence, works to combine river and shorescape in a single trope, the "river of ocean," that marks a liberating, redemptive meeting place of flux and the immutable:

> Freedom is not this timeless mask to wear.
> Freedom is an architecture of movement
> down the river of ocean . . .
> . . .
>   . . . Making time
> in the boat men steer and ride down the river of ocean
> through still banks on the farthest shore where no time is.[65]

But whereas in Eliot the composite landscape establishes a coherence of places and cultural perspectives that in his earlier writings were portrayed as separate, painfully conflicting and irreconcilable, in Harris the image refers to the distinctive geography and local culture of Guyana and, in doing so, acquires figurative connotations that are unique to his Caribbean locality. Consider the dramatic poem "Canje," which opens with an explanatory prose headnote not unlike Eliot's in "The Dry Salvages."[66] Drawing on the imagery of folk legend, Harris implies that, like a freshwater river that meets the ocean but withstands inroads of salt, the New World poet must retain a sense of his uniqueness, and avoid being reduced to sterile mimicry, but draw nonetheless on a rich and strange array of cultural resources:

There is a legend that a great lake of fresh water feeds the Canje River and is still to dry up. The known facts are that the Canje River is part of a natural flood basin influenced by the ocean tides and successful so far in withstanding long inroads of salt from the sea. It is the source of irrigation for the big estates between the Canje and Corentyne Rivers of Guiana. Cumberland, already featured in these series of poems, is one of the villages at the mouth of the Canje River. These villages are subject to salt water in every dry season, and the inhabitants have to resort to fishing for a livelihood, wood-cutting in the Upper Canje, or field labour on the big sugar estates.[67]

In "The Golden Age," a shorescape poem that concludes "The Spirit of Place," Harris alludes once again to the legendary flood basin, and to Eliot's ideal of impersonality, when his lyric speaker mentions the importance of "self-surrender to every alien tide." The idioms and forms that constitute traces of the "alien" cultural legacy of European conquest in the Americas are compared to fishing boats that have been washed up with all the other debris on the coast. Like an intelligent beachcomber, Harris's speaker reflects upon, values and tries but always fails to order the fragments of culture that have been washed to the frontiers of consciousness:

> Fishing boats
> lie on their side, empty shells high and discarded. This debris
> of the coast is eloquent witness that wherever someone comes
> value orders and reflects a procession of built-up acts
> of self-surrender to every alien tide. Grounds
> what is in turn invaluable and trivial. Something passes,
> something remains.[68]

Here, as in "Creation," Harris's shorescape is both a figurative frontier of consciousness and a literal, geographical frontier where different cultures may be encountered, compared and artfully juxtaposed. The curious inter-twinement of Caribbean cultures with those from other parts of the world has, by necessity, prompted a perspective in Harris's poetry that is, like Eliot's, laboriously and restlessly comparative. For these and other reasons, both "Creation" and "The Golden Age" allude to Eliot's coastal setting in "Marina," where the rediscovery of an old boat inspires a rededication to the creation of new forms. But where "Marina" hints that even a flawed poem is offered in the hope that its words will be of use to those who need them in the future, Harris's "The Golden Age" suggests that the poet's work consists not so much in remembering what he himself has made, as in learning to record the experience of surrendering himself to diverse influences. The rhythmic contour of "Marina," as well as Eliot's nightmarish figuration of transatlanticism, deracination and self-division in "The Love Song of J. Alfred Prufrock" – "a pair of ragged claws / Scuttling across the floors of silent seas" – are both present in "Creation":

> What then exists, what plant or beast lives, what seed
> or what soul endures, what crab scuttles,
> clothes its soft and yielding flesh with a shell.[69]

The shorescape of "Marina" reaches towards islands, an effect Harris would have found appealing. But in "Creation" Harris's allusive practice also self-reflexively dramatizes his affinity with Eliot as a Prufrockian New World antecedent. The crab-like action of "scuttling" between national cultures in search of a style to call home is suspended in verbal architec-ture that is poised between declarative statement and a question that is simultaneously direct and indirect. The phrasing itself foregrounds what Paul Gilroy, following Edouard Glissant, calls the "rhizomorphic" quality of diasporic formations, where globalization and hybridity have challenged the ideal of organic attachment to national communities.[70]

MIGRATION, MYTHICAL METHOD AND THE VOID OF HISTORY IN "BEHRING STRAITS"

The shorescape summons up historical, literary and figurative associations that are fundamentally different from those borne by the jungle interior in Harris's poetry. In "Trail," as we have seen, the interior commemorates the hybridity and adversarial contexts of transculturation in Guyana, establishing cherished continuity with Amerindian cultural legacies as well as Wordsworth's Romantic style. The shorescape, by contrast, discloses Harris's affinities with Whitman and Eliot, affinities that are rooted in shared New World history. These two evocations of landscape in *Eternity to Season* reflect two very different conceptions of Harris's Caribbean identity. The continental interior figures relations that are largely transatlantic and colonial or postcolonial, inscribed within the geopolitical scope of the British empire and Commonwealth. The shorescape, by contrast, places Harris in a context that is hemispheric and neo-imperialist.

The steady friction between these distinct geographical idioms implies that both categories, the transatlantic and the hemispheric, define Harris's work in terms that are equally laden with troubling preconceptions, equally partial and limited. Nonetheless, as frontiers of culture both are essential to Harris's formation as a poet. We cannot fathom the symbolic resonance of Harris's landscapes without also recognizing the consequences of globalization wrought by imperialism and its aftermath, or Harris's fidelity to modernism's cosmopolitan ideal. The importance of these interwoven global contexts for the emergence of Caribbean poetry is a subject Harris revisits throughout his career.[71] In a 1996 BBC broadcast, he observed:

Guyana is a remarkable wilderness. It has known Spanish settlers, then French and Dutch rule but became a British colony in the early nineteenth century.

Its population is less than a million but encompasses peoples from every corner of the globe, Africa, India, China, Portugal ...

Amerindians such as the Macusis, the Wapishanas, the Arawaks ... are still to be found in Guyana and South America ... Feather from a wing and eager fish were united, it seemed, into an orchestra of species and a sacrament of subsistence they (these ancient peoples) had long cultivated since their ancestors emigrated twelve thousand years ago from Asia across the Bering Straits into the continent we now call America.[72]

In "Behring Straits," one of the most important and difficult poems in *Eternity to Season*, a mythic voyage juxtaposes three distinct historical phases of migration: first, the successive waves of European migration (Spanish, Dutch, English and so on) since the discovery of the New World in the fifteenth century; second, the Middle Passage of Africans who were brought over to the Americas as slaves; and finally, the prehistoric migration of Asian peoples 12,000 years ago.

> The tremendous voyage between two worlds
> is contained in every hollow shell, in every name that echoes
> a nameless bell,
> in tree-trunk or cave
> or sound: in drowned Asia's bones:
> a log-book in the clouds
> names the straits of eternity: the marbles
> of ocean and indomitable tides.
>
> So life discovers the remotest beaches in time
> that are always present in action: the interior walls of being
> open like a mirrorless pool, the ocean's nostalgia
> and the stormy communication of truth turn still deeply
> like settlement and root.
>
> Untangled the trees mount to the sky
> and the silence is filled with a different wave like sound
> that alters dimension. The cool cave of a ship
> is sudden beached with sun
> is drowned in a fluid ecstasy that devours and is devoured in
> > turn
> external still profound.
>
> The voyage between two worlds
> is fraught with this grandeur and this anonymity. Who blazes
> > a trail
> is overtaken by a labyrinth
> leading to many conclusions.
> > The valleys of ocean
> are spent
> and the mountains stand cloudlike and august, solid and bent
> to the sailor on his round. Until they figuratively drown
> in an overwhelming sea or a spiritual
> mound. So the incomplete discovery of the world
> in the blueness of its delicacy
> is broken on the beach of its lofty ground.

Like a wave that meets resistance and must rise unerringly
into an outline or alienation or history
into a bond that both strengthens and severs in the movement of life:

since heaven deepens the immortal sea
like eternity that disguises
a wound.
But earth waits for the continual voyager
who dances on mortal ground.[73]

Here, as in many of Harris's shorescape poems, the echoes of Eliot are
pervasive and unmistakable. Like Eliot, Harris dramatizes how, despite the
inexorable decay and fragmentation of meanings as cultures are brought
from the Old World to the New, some measure of continuity remains: the
bell, tree-trunk and description of drowned bones recall Eliot's allusion in
The Waste Land to Shakespeare's island music and vivid imagining of a
New World in *The Tempest*. Another image, "hollow shell[s]," brings to
mind Eliot's transmutation of Conradian hollowness, "The Hollow Men,"
a poem we examined in chapter 2. But, in contrast with Eliot's poem, which
centers on the debasement and spiritual despair of lost, violent souls who
are unable to love, in Harris's "Behring Straits" hollowness depicts loss,
spiritual despair and violence in an explicitly evoked New World context,
where the poet–speaker's words are unmoored from tradition and thus, at
times, virtually incomprehensible. Every word, every name, is like a hollow
shell that contains unspeakable memories of migration to the Americas.

It is true, as Paula Burnett avers, that the arrival of the first people in the
Americas across the Behring Straits, and the recovery of cultural memory
before the European conquest, are central to the meaning of Harris's poem
as a whole. But Harris's pained, oblique rendering of the adversarial contexts
of transculturation, like his allusion to Eliot's hollowness, and his account of
how the Caribs carved flutes out of the bones of their cannibalized Spanish
enemies, all belie Burnett's contention that Harris is "staging ... an innocent origin for the present-day peoples of the Americas, uncontaminated
by the barbarism of post-Columbian conquest."[74]

Rather than presenting a unified, coherent narrative of pure and innocent
origins, "Behring Straits" records a mosaic of the fragmented, diverse perspectives that tenuously compose New World history. The experiences of
conquerors and settlers from Europe are rendered, as well as the anonymous
histories of Amerindians and African slaves. Harris's "log-book," for example, metonymically commemorates European voyages, and "a nameless
bell" obliquely refers to namelessness as one consequence of slavery by

substituting "nameless" for the word "slave" in what would otherwise be a "slave bell." Together, the haunting memory of slaves lost at sea during the Middle Passage, the presence of Amerindian mounds on the beaches of Guyana, and the adjective "cloudlike" call into question the "solidity" of values embodied by the Wordsworthian image of "august" mountains, and mourn the moral and human costs of improving the shorescape.

Observing Harris's allusion to Eliot's portrayal of history's cunning passages and contrived corridors in "Gerontion," Michael Gilkes perceptively notes that, in "Behring Straits," "The pioneer, like the visionary, is always in danger of being caught up in the web of historical time: of being overtaken by 'a labyrinth leading to many conclusions.'"[75] For Harris, as for Eliot, history is dangerous, not least because it imprisons us in a misleadingly simplified, logical, self-serving and cunningly contrived point of view. "I believe," Harris once said, "the possibility exists for us to become involved in perspectives of renascence which can bring into play a figurative meaning beyond an apparently real world or prison of history."[76]

The fractured syntax, prosodic disfigurement and obscure diction of "Behring Straits" all suggest the shortcomings of conventional historiography where, as Harris contends, biases are often obscured by overriding claims to narrative coherence, logical causality and reason.[77] At the same time that Harris's speaker in "Behring Straits" acknowledges the "grandeur" of European conquest and discovery through his own act of writing, he is not blindly triumphant, since he also acknowledges the "incomplete[ness]" and partiality of all historical narratives, and his imaginative trailblazing on the frontier ends in a bewildering labyrinth of logical possibilities. As in Eliot's "Gerontion," history seduces, deceives and proliferates contradictory perspectives.

Derek Walcott, whose work we will consider in the next and last chapter of this book, may well have been recalling Harris's "Behring Straits" when he composed these lines from *Another Life*:

> A child without history, without knowledge of its pre-world,
> . . .
>
> That child who puts the shell's howl to his ear,
> hears nothing, hears everything
> that the historian cannot hear, the howls
> of all the races that crossed the water,
> the howls of the grandfathers drowned
> in that intricately swivelled Babel,
> hears the fellaheen, the Madrasi, the Mandingo, the Ashanti . . .
> . . .

In the shallop of the shell,
in the round prayer,
in the palate of the conch,
in the dead sail of the almond leaf
are all of the voyages.[78]

The many similarities between Harris's poem and Walcott's are suggestive. For Walcott, as for Harris, the cultural legacy of the Americas is
contained in each shell. Both poets, confronted by the "apparent historylessness" of the New World, rely on the powers of imaginative intuition,
learning to question historical narratives that are organized by their misleading reference to a logically coherent but partial point of view. Both
poems ambivalently commemorate the intricate intertwining of historical
legacies in the Americas, and recall how the assurance of recorded history
is questioned by Eliot's speaker in "The Dry Salvages" (II):

> ... I have said before
> That the past experience revived in the meaning
> Is not the experience of one life only
> But of many generations – not forgetting
> Something that is probably quite ineffable:
> The backward look behind the assurance
> Of recorded history, the backward half-look
> Over the shoulder, towards the primitive terror.[79]

Both poems examine the dangerous inaccuracy, but also the necessity, of
frontier mythologies, rehearsing Krishna's admonition about the dangers
of triumphalism: "Not fare well, / But fare forward, voyagers."[80]

In contrast to Harris, however, Walcott does not explicitly mention a
prehistoric migration that gave rise to Amerindian civilizations in the New
World, though he would detail the "obliteration" of Amerindians in "Over
Colorado," a lyric that appeared in his 1976 volume *Sea Grapes*, published
three years after *Another Life*. The emphasis on post-Columbian histories,
as well as his reliance on Eliot's "howl" (a howl attributed to persons and
not, as in Eliot, to the sea), suggest that Walcott was far more ambivalent
than Harris about the non-European aspects of his American heritage.

The memory of Eliot's engagement with frontier mythology, and Harris's
reference to a mythic "voyage between worlds" in "Behring Straits" bring us
to a final point about Harris's signifying relation to modernism – namely,
his development of a mythical method. Eliot argued for the importance of
myth as early as 1923, when he said that "In using the myth, in manipulating a continuous parallel between contemporaneity and antiquity," Joyce
discovered a means of conferring "a shape and significance to the immense

panorama of futility and anarchy which is contemporary history." Noting that the significance of myth had been overlooked by early critics of Joyce's work, Eliot singled out Valery Larbaud – a poet and critic who was a mutual friend of both Perse and Joyce, and who worked to have fragments of *Ulysses* translated into French and published in *Commerce* – as the first "to appreciate the significance of the method employed."[81] Writing almost six decades after Eliot, Harris commemorated the centrality of myth as a crucial facet of the modernist legacy, a method he finds in Joyce, Perse, Eliot and others. He observed:

> Writers as varied as James Joyce, St John Perse ... T. S. Eliot ... Ralph Ellison ... D. H. Lawrence, Pablo Neruda – to give outstanding examples – have employed myth with deliberation, but in order to ask new questions, so to speak, of untamable reality. Yet even here – however self-conscious the equilibrium between artist and myth – unconscious variables secrete themselves in the live tapestry of word and image whose enigmatic manifestation lies in the future ... Thus even the self-conscious usage of myth ... involves a descent into unconscious variables whose manifestation affects the future.[82]

It is clear that Harris learned a great deal from Eliot's mythical method. For Harris, as for Eliot, myth represents a crucial resource for modern artists, because it organizes refractory, "untamable" fragments of history. Searching for mythic, "epic stratagems available to Caribbean man in the dilemmas of history which surround him," in "Behring Straits" Harris employs myth to elucidate, through poetic retrospection, the enigmatic manifestation of events, giving shape to history.[83] In addition, for both Eliot and Harris, myth imparts a heightened awareness of, and clarifying perspective on, the limitations, and contingent contexts, of contemporary values, teaching them about the nature of historiography.[84] Poised between dogmatic conviction and doubt, Harris's speaker expresses an ambivalent relation to history, acknowledging the necessity of purposeful action and belief in the reality of events, at the same time that he skeptically exposes the partiality of historical narratives.

There are, moreover, a number of telling differences between Harris and Eliot in their use of myth. Whereas Eliot describes history's "immense panorama," in "Behring Straits" Harris emphasizes what he calls the "Caribbean complex situation of apparent 'historylessness'": images of mountainous waves that "figuratively drown" and disappear, like the vanished civilizations on the shorescape, suggest the disappearance of history into a void. For Harris, the reliance on myth is necessary, insofar as it allows his imagination to fill the "apparent void of history which haunts the black man."[85] Eliot intimates, but does not emphasize, his skepticism about evolutionists' claims about "higher" and "lower" degrees of culture. Harris, by contrast, adamantly rejects the idea that one civilization is superior to any other. A "gateway complex," in Harris's lexicon, is a place where contemporary experience meets up with a mythical past. By encouraging the exchange of ideas and influences across cultural frontiers, it restores continuities between past and present, and between individuals and communities, and inspires creative translation and imaginative recovery of vanished civilizations in the Americas.[86]

Harris's method involves a whole array of media, ranging from orally transmitted legends, to folk dances, to written documents such as poems or translations. Whereas Eliot drew largely on Hindu and Buddhist mythology, and European and ancient classical sources, Harris's gateway complex also derives from sources that are African, Amerindian and regionally distinctive.

Finally, for Harris myths are, in his words, "re-born within the flesh of many cultures," implying a conception of "racelessness" that does not so much stifle diversity, as affirm Harris's "daring theorem of native universality."[87] A good example of Harris's comparativist use of myth may be found in a lyric sequence set in an old coastal village, "Cumberland," which is visited by a character named Odysseus. Throughout this sequence, and in many other poems in *Eternity to Season*, Harris apprentices himself to the technique of using archetypal speech masks or personae. The reader is introduced to a series of "archetypal characters" who live in the village of Cumberland: Tiresias (the seer), Heracles (the slave), Achilles (the great runner) and Anticlei (the mother). The sequence opens with an epigraph from Pound's *A Draft of XXX Cantos*. The passage, which is taken from Canto one, Pound's loose translation of the Renaissance Latinist Andreas Divus's 1538 reworking of Homer's *Odyssey*, literally "trans-lates," or carries, the text of Pound's translation into the Guyana colonies:

> "Poured we libations unto each the dead,
> First mead and sweet wine, mixed with white flour.
> Then prayed I many a prayer to the sickly death's heads;"
> (Ezra Pound-Canto 1)[88]

By manipulating a parallel between classical antiquity, Pound's mythical method in the *Cantos*, and his own recollection of the accumulated versions and translations of the Odyssean voyage, Harris illustrates his need for dialogue with the past.[89] The "Cumberland" sequence stages his recuperation of traditions that would otherwise have been entirely lost, or seemed totally irrelevant to his own experience, "at the edge of the world," on the Guyana coastlands. In "Profiles of Myth in the New World," Harris comments on his effort to extend the expressive range of English as a "living language": "Is it possible for an imaginative writer to work in a language he does not love? I love the English language deeply. It is my native language. I was born in Guyana, South America. Such are the proportions, extensions, extremities, of a living language."[90] For Harris, the ritual libation to the dead invoked by Pound's speaker in Canto one, and the suggestive image of mixing mead and wine with white flour, figuratively acknowledge this ever-changing, strangely hybridized, much beloved New World language he shared with Pound.

Harris's epigraph also implies that shared history in the New World enhances the possibility of exchange across cultural frontiers. Consider, for example, these lines from "Tiresias," the poem which opens the "Cumberland" sequence, where Harris reminds us that African slaves were originally taken to the Americas by European settlers:

> The subtle links of time
> bind this dark village: the old slave lanes, the broken road,
> ancient trees,
> time past and gone. Gone so swift
> the clouds hang
> their momentary, quick, cosmic
> print of rain.
> Chains of fever in bone and bark
> rattle,
> rising to wing every hallucinated perspective.
> Freedom is a dusty passage
> from sunrise to sunset impregnated with endless
> particles that bloom and stress
> the visions that are nearest or far
> complexity. They unbind master and slave,
> owner, ownerless.[91]

Recalling Eliot's note about Tiresias in *The Waste Land* – "although a mere spectator and not indeed a 'character' ... yet the most important personage in the poem, uniting all the rest" – Harris confers a meaningful shape on the chaotic panorama of contemporary Caribbean history.[92] Images such as the slave lanes, the road and the "passage" recall that, as the Guyanese historian Walter Rodney has shown, by the late nineteenth century, "the vast majority of inhabitants ... were a product of migration and transplant over the previous two centuries."[93] In the wake of emancipation, in order to meet a perceived demand for labor, and in response to a series of labor strikes organized by Afro-Guyanese workers, immigrants from Africa, Portugal, China and British India were brought over by the colonial government as indentured laborers. To give some sense of the scale of these migrations, we should note that between 1838 and 1917, about 240,000 indentured workers migrated from the Indian subcontinent.[94] Whereas in most other Commonwealth Caribbean societies, most people have, on average, made two major moves in the course of their lifetimes, in Guyana most people have migrated three times.[95]

At the same time that Harris relies on the ordering potential of myth, however, his gateway method also resists this impulse towards organic totality by calling attention to the subjective, and projective, nature of historical understanding. In "Tiresias," as in "Behring Straits," Harris's difficult syntax, his description of clouds that quickly come and go, and the obliquity of his reference to the Middle Passage all serve to remind us of the displaced speaker's "hallucinated perspective," a disoriented point of view whose surreality exposes the inchoate contingencies that disrupt any picturesque familiarity of place. Mythical method in Harris's poem does not so much entail a withdrawal into the timeless realm of triumphalism, as require his disconcerting confrontation with a welter of innumerable details. As a "gateway between civilizations," Harris's use of myth juxtaposes a wide and various range of cultures and eras, and this comparativist method in turn allows him to assess and question the accuracy of any given claim to historical knowledge.

Despite their differences, for both Harris and Eliot mythical method is a means of unlocking us from our imprisonment in a single cultural perspective. Harris contends that racelessness, in his sense, does not promote global uniformity of the human race but rather invites us to forge links between cultures, a comparative method that would, in his view, mitigate the impulse to violence that arises when we imprison ourselves within limited categories of race and nation. In a 1990 lecture at the University of Cambridge, Harris spoke of the knowledge of tradition and intellectual bravery required to forge comparative connections between cultures, a view he shared with Eliot:

We have to take a step into making connections and links between cultures which we tend not to make, which we fear to make. The balance, the creative and re-creative balance between cultures, requires an enormous penetration of tradition. It is a penetration of tradition which lays open tradition in a totally new way ... There are these ways in which we can read this rhythm, these connections, so that we begin to sense this ceaseless balance between cultures. This is not an easy task.[96]

For Harris, as for Eliot, the critique of myth is contrapuntal: one form of belief is used to read the other, and vice versa. By helping to open a gateway to unfamiliar cultural perspectives, both poets hope that fervent believers in nationalistic myths of progress will learn to apprehend their irreducible contingency. Conjoining Asian, African and European migrations in the single image of voyaging, Harris's "Behring Straits" questions the perception of European discovery as progress; summons up the brutal history of slavery and colonialism; and resists historiographic certitudes. Like Eliot's Krishna, whose advice about faring forward is only meaningful in contradistinction to the progressive ideal embodied by the voyage, Harris's speaker does not pretend to stand entirely outside of myth; he only suggests that the activity of belief should be, as he puts it, "fraught."

I have dwelt at length on Harris's close, signifying relationships to Eliot and Pound in *Eternity to Season*, because this volume marks a crucial turning point in the emergence of modernist styles in the Anglophone Caribbean, and because Harris's poetry has been comparatively neglected up to this point. But no account of transnational modernism in the New World would be complete without Walcott, whose work I will consider in the next and final chapter, and whose dedication to modernist technique fostered creative continuity with his Caribbean roots, while freeing him from the habit of nationalist feeling.

CHAPTER 5

Beyond apprenticeship: Derek Walcott's passage to the Americas

INTRODUCTION

In 1985, Derek Walcott recalled Eliot's importance for his own coming of age as a poet. "I used to write every day in an exercise book," he said, "and when I first wrote I wrote with great originality. I just wrote as hard and as well as I felt. I remember the great elation and release I felt, a sort of hooking on to a thing, when I read . . . Eliot, and everyone."[1] Like Harris, whose New World modernism demands self-surrender to every possible current of intercultural influence, Walcott spoke of his "complete apprenticeship, a complete surrender" to the impersonality of modernist craft.[2]

One reason Walcott's apprenticeship to American poetry has been neglected is that many of the works that illustrate this phase of his career were not included in selected and collected volumes. Early critics and reviewers, while sympathetic to Walcott's predicament as a young colonial poet, tended to dismiss the poems of apprenticeship to Eliot as derivative of "European literary models."[3] As a corrective to this, pathbreaking studies by Rei Terada and John Thieme called attention to the significance of Walcott's American influences and, more recently, Charles Pollard, Laurence Breiner and Paula Burnett have examined Walcott's selective reshaping of Eliot's poetics.[4] But none of these critics explains in detail how Walcott's relations with American antecedents from Poe to St.-John Perse figure in his emerging self-conception as a New World poet.

More than Harris or Hughes, Walcott is explicitly concerned with Perse's influential role in the development of black poetry in the Americas. But, like them, in claiming Perse's legacy he emphatically rejects nostalgic, vengeful fictions of purity raised by any and all who would fatally impoverish his sense of tradition, confining it within the bounds of region, nation or race.[5] As we shall see, the ideal of "craft" informs Walcott's transnational apprenticeship to American modernism, helping him to inventively collocate a hybrid New World heritage in at least four ways. First, craft involves poetic principles elaborated by Pound, Eliot and other American descendants of Poe. At the same time, however, as we shall see, Walcott's notion exacts a plain, figuratively unadorned, conversational style that is reminiscent of Whitman's, and the friction between these two competing expressions of craft in Walcott's poetry instantiates the intertwining of divergent, starkly opposed hemispheric identities. Third, craft connotes a local, hidden dimension of Walcott's New World heritage, aligning him with a regional legacy of Caribbean artisans and his own father. Finally, the "craft of words" is a cherished metaphor that dramatizes Walcott's aspiration to a modernist, integrative, cosmopolitan lyric practice that disturbs the nationalist idea of American literature as a culturally homogeneous field.

HYBRIDITY AND THE LIMITS OF COMPLICATION IN "HART CRANE" (1951)

Walcott's prosodic development shows him simultaneously attracted to two very different styles: complication and plainness.[6] This symbiosis, which lies at the heart of Walcott's poetics, reflects the sustained interplay between two very different connotations of craftsmanship, and facilitates his revisionary encounter with the hybrid, transnational idioms discussed in previous chapters of this book. A plain style, in Walcott's view, suggests a definition of the craftsman as an artisan. We see this, for example, when in an interview Walcott figuratively compared his formal aspirations with the carpenter's craft of making frames.

There's also a very strong sense of carpentry in Protestantism, in making things simply and in a utilitarian way. At this period of my life and work, I think of myself in a way as a carpenter, as one making frames, simply and well. I'm working a lot in quatrains, or I have been, and I feel that there is something in them that is very ordinary, you know, without any mystique. I'm trying to get rid of the mystique as much as possible. And so I find myself wanting to write very simply cut, very contracted, very speakable and very challenging quatrains in rhymes. Any other shape seems ornate, an elaboration on that essential cube that is really the poem. So we can then say the craft is as ritualistic as that of a carpenter putting down his plane and measuring his stanzas and setting them squarely.[7]

Like Eliot and Hughes, following Gautier, Walcott focuses on the technique of crafting quatrains. But in his account, the concern with plainness may partly come from his childhood experiences as a Methodist in an island society that was overwhelmingly Roman Catholic.[8] His mother, Alix, was headmistress of the Methodist Infant School and, as Walcott recalled years later in *The Bounty*, as a result of her influence he was drawn to the clear, conversational sound and perfectly rhymed quatrains of Protestant hymns.

At the same time that Walcott associates craftsmanship with forms that are as plain, ordinary and simply cut as an artisan's wood frame, he also contends that, even as a very young child growing up in the Caribbean, he had been drawn to a style that is complicated, wrought and densely figurative. This attraction to complication also issues out of the distinct contingencies of Walcott's milieu, contingencies that vividly register the diasporic, multilingual consequences of imperialism in the region. St Lucia, where Walcott was born in 1930, is a tiny volcanic island located in the southeastern Caribbean Sea, between Martinique and Saint Vincent. Fifty years after the arrival of a French buccaneer, François le Clerc, in the mid sixteenth century, the Dutch arrived to settle the island.[9] But they eventually sold it to the French West India Company and the first successful colony was established there by the French in 1635. Despite the fact that the British were interested in the island as well, and sent over a number of colonists, by the mid eighteenth century all the major settlements, towns and sugar plantations were French. England and France were constantly warring over possession of the island, and it changed hands several times during the eighteenth century before finally being ceded to the British in 1814.

The language situation that emerged in St Lucia is thus one that would have encouraged complication. As Walcott recalls:

I grew up in two languages, Creole and French. And, of course, tonal English with a Creolized inflection. So there were actually three languages or even four. There was French, which was not spoken too much on the island, French Creole, English and then French accent. Writing in Creole was much more exciting than writing down English, but at the same time I was trying to learn the craft of English verse as well as I could.[10]

The island was officially designated as "English speaking" and, as a student in colonial schools and colleges, Walcott was given a solid grounding in English literature as his natural inheritance.[11] However, as in other parts of the Caribbean, any simple classification obscures the multilingual reality of everyday life on the island. Although English is St Lucia's official language, most everyday interactions among urban and rural people are conducted in a French-based creole, and when English is used it is spoken with a creolized inflection.[12]

The elaborate entanglement of diasporic histories, and the shared cultural memory of settlement and empire-building inscribed in Walcott's frontier landscapes, point up Walcott's affinity with the hybrid poetics of

Eliot and Perse. For Walcott, as for Eliot, the inescapable frontier legacy of hybridity is acknowledged through figures of paradox, formal division and dualism; like Perse, Walcott focuses his sights on the possibilities of metropolitan language. But in contrast with Perse, who altogether avoided the use of French-based creole words in *Pour fêter une enfance*, Walcott explictly confronts his nostalgic yearning to express himself in French creole, at the same time that he celebrates the craft of English verse. In "Cul de Sac Valley," for example, Walcott examines the beauty and expressive possibilities of a dimeter quatrain (which his speaker aptly describes as both a figurative and literal "settlement"), only to discover the incommensurability of such a highly structured, simplifying and symmetrical frame with the chaotic welter of conflicting, overlapping cultural traditions evoked by the geography of the Caribbean landscape:

> A panel of sunrise
> on a hillside shop
> gave these stanzas
> their stilted shape.
>
> If my craft is blest;
> if this hand is as
> accurate, as honest
> as their carpenters,
>
> every frame, intent
> on its angles, would
> echo this settlement
> of unpainted wood
>
> as consonants scroll
> off my shaving plane
> in the fragrant Creole
> of their native grain;
>
> from a trestle bench
> they'd curl at my foot,
> C's, R's, with a French
> or West African root
>
> from a dialect throng-
> ing, its leaves unread
> yet light on the tongue
> of their native road;
>
> but drawing towards
> my pegged-out twine
> with beveled boards
> of unpainted pine,

> like muttering shale
> exhaling trees refresh
> memory with their smell:
> *bois canot, bois campêche,*
>
> hissing: *What you wish
> from us will never be,
> your words is English,
> is a different tree.*[13]

Walcott's attraction to densely compounded figures of speech and frequent recourse to an incantatory style are also reminiscent of the "pure" poetry rendered by Perse and Eliot; and he would, like them, be aware that the ideal of *la poésie pure*, first raised in Poe's "The Poetic Principle," was elaborated by Baudelaire, Mallarmé and Valéry. Still, for Walcott this notion also has uniquely local contexts and significances. In his view, the stylistic complications he finds in Trinidadian handicraft represent a wood-worked analogy to *la poésie pure*, where each figure looks "like an involved drawing of itself": "The finest silhouettes of Port of Spain are idealizations of the craftsman's handiwork, not of concrete and glass, but of baroque woodwork, each fantasy looking more like an involved drawing of itself than the actual building . . . That is what I have read around me from boyhood, from the beginnings of poetry, the grace of effort."[14]

Although Eliot grasped the representational significance of musicality and formal complication, he only advocated it under certain conditions. He argued that in Henry James, for example, syntactical complication is generally justified, since James aims at precision, and realizes that any simplification would distort his rendering of the "real intricacies and by-paths of mental movement." But there are many other, wholly unwarranted instances of "active complication," when a poet ends up complicating an abstract thought he had already put to himself in a much simpler way, so as to produce a more musical sound.[15] This produces "rhetoric," threatening the historical life of the language as a whole.[16] Pound, by contrast, was a far less equivocal advocate of complication: poetry was, as he put it, "a very complex art."[17] He defined the poet's craft as a complicated verbal "entanglement" that "can be read or heard without yawning."[18]

Walcott's awareness of the risks as well as the necessity of "crafty" complication, in Pound's sense, informs his early, fertile encounters with modernist style, and would foster his self-awareness as a New World poet.[19] Rather than adapting the densely figurative, incantatory complications of Perse, however, he turned instead to the example of Hart Crane, a poet whose close ties to Cuba shaped many of his best-known works.[20] In "Hart Crane," an *hommage* that appeared in the 1951 collection, *Poems*, Walcott examines the consequences of complication in works by Crane, who evidently paid little heed to Eliot's warning against the effects of rhetoric. In his opening lines, Walcott invokes Crane's guiding, multifaceted symbol, the Brooklyn Bridge. After comparing Crane's idiom, first to a bridge, and then to a steel harp suspended over a running wound, his lyric speaker concludes that Crane must have ultimately rejected his own skillful feats of verbal architecture, seeing them for what they were, as Crane's inward acknowledgment of despair:

> He walked a bridge where
> Gull's wings brush wires and sound
> A harp of steel in air,
> Above the river's running wound.
> Natural and architectural despair.
> Life was a package in his restless hand,
> Traffic of barges below, while wind
> Rumpled his hair like an affectionate teacher.[21]

Walcott's speaker is clearly drawn to Crane's complication. He imagines what must have been Crane's mental state, just before he drowned in the Gulf of Mexico, during a boat trip to the United States in 1933. But rather than foreground the transcendent, apocalyptic and visionary (if often tortuously self-parodic) lyricism of Crane's poet–speaker in *The Bridge*, Walcott's speaker assumes the stance of Crane's suicidal bedlamite, imagining how terror at the lonely anonymity of life in urban America would have driven the aspiring poet to suicide. Turning away from the stone canyons of Brooklyn, his speaker gazes inwardly at a mesmerizing whirlpool of consciousness, and wishes for death:

> Bye, bye to Brooklyn,
> The bay's lace collar of puritan America
> And bye, bye, the steel thin
> Bridges over barges, the wharf's hysteria,
> The canyons of stone.
> The whirlpool smiled – "Knowledge is death alone."[22]

In part, Walcott's attraction to the complications inherent in Crane's transnational poetics had the added benefit of bringing Walcott closer to his Caribbean roots, since oral theatre, the tradition of storytelling, Calypso, Carnival and other aspects of popular culture in the Caribbean often involve what Walcott describes as the "enjoyment of rhetoric."[23] "I come from a place that likes grandeur," Walcott has said; "It likes large gestures; it is not inhibited by flourish; it is a rhetorical society; it is a society of physical performance; it is a society of style. The highest achievement of style is rhetoric, as it is in speech and performance. It isn't a modest society . . . Modesty is not possible in performance in the Caribbean, and that's wonderful."[24] But, as he noted in an interview, despite the fact that complication may be necessary and liberating, when taken to extremes it also poses serious risks: "When I look at work which I have influenced in the Caribbean, I find myself horrified that people choose to glorify my worst vices. There is an excess of metaphor, a diffuse but gnarled kind of poem which people imitate. If that is the sound I'm supposed to make, then it's distressing."[25]

Early critics of Crane such as Blackmur have suggested that there is a causal relation between Crane's style and suicide.[26] In the final stanza of "Hart Crane," Walcott's speaker speculates that figurative complication may have served Crane as a necessary "asylum" – that is, as a place both of refuge and of intolerable confinement. But, in the end, he tacitly concurs with Blackmur, calling attention to the dangerous limits of Crane's style, and hinting that such consolations should be avoided at all costs:

> The sea was only ritual, he had
> Already seen complexity go mad
> In the asylum, metaphor. He stood
> From Brooklyn, on the brink
> Of being, a straw doll blown
> From Manhattan to Mexico to sink
> Into that sea where vast deliriums drown.[27]

At the same time that Walcott's poem commemorates Crane's experimental effort to forge an idiomatic bridge extending "from Manhattan to Mexico," it also carries a self-reflexive admonition: that rhetorical complication, in Eliot's sense, may lure the poet away from craft and sense into a state of deliberately unfathomable (and, worse, ephemeral) verbal obscurity. As in Harris, in early poems such as "Hart Crane" the difficult obscurity of Walcott's style suggests the predicament of isolation he shared with Crane, but the poem's very act of remembering Crane also illustrates that any fear of indecipherability is mitigated by continuity with tradition.

WHITMAN'S NATIONALIST POETICS: PLAINNESS AND THE CRAFTSMAN IDEAL

In 1958, Walcott departed from Crane's verbal complication, seeking instead an effect of "plainness." He remarked, "What I have been trying to do with [my poems] over the last five years is to get a certain factual, biographical plainness about them . . . The idea is the same as in prose . . . Say nothing, but cut the bronze medallion and present it to the normal poetry reader."[28] This aspiration to plainness, in turn, prompted Walcott's confrontation with Whitman's nationalist poetics.

Like Walcott, Whitman believed that a poem should be completely without figurative adornment, as unfinished as a carpenter's handicraft: "The art of art," he said, "and the sunshine of the light of letters is simplicity. Nothing is better than simplicity . . . nothing can make up for excess or for the lack of definiteness."[29] But where Walcott tacitly laments the insufficiency and cultural losses incurred by formal simplification, in Whitman simplicity is fervently desired, because it confirms Whitman's egalitarian faith in "the unyielding principle of the average," the timeless commonality of all human experience.[30] For Walcott, craft necessarily entails starkly differentiated levels of ability. He insists:

Art is not democratic, art is hierarchical, and all artists know that. They know that it takes all your life to achieve some level where you can be among your peers. But if immediately your peers are made to be the illiterate, or the people who feel education is restricted entirely to self-expression without craft, then society is in danger. It is in more danger than it is from terrorists and revolutionaries.[31]

For this and other reasons, like his Caribbean contemporary Wilson Harris, and like Eliot and Perse, Walcott's attitude towards Whitman is one of steady, fruitful ambivalence. Although he once criticized Whitman's passion for cataloguing as "paternalistic," at other times Walcott has felt called upon to defend Whitman's vision of a democratic vista.[32] In an essay published in 1989, he observed that Whitman:

proclaims a new form, a new breadth for his new country, in a line as long as its new horizons, opening up poetry in the same way that his pioneers were opening up America. But broad as this poetry appeared to be, it also had, at its centre, a narrow didactic passion, a presumption of inevitability in its evangelism, its proclamations that for American poets this was the only way to see and therefore to write.[33]

We have already observed Harris's mixed feelings towards Whitman, and the "heady, chaotic love affair with Liberty" which culminated in tragic nationalist violence during Guyana's independence struggle. For Walcott, too, ambivalence towards the nationalist implications of Whitman's prosody peaked during the late 1960s and 1970s, a period when Walcott repeatedly faced the difficult task of writing elegies that would record his responses to independence movements and nationalist violence throughout the Americas. "Elegy," composed on June 6, 1968, and published the following year in *The Gulf and Other Poems*, is an elegy in which Walcott resorts to

anti-Whitmanian, tortuous complication, in an effort to record the growing stridency and violence of the Black Power Movement in the United
States.

> Some splintered arrowhead lodged in her brain
> sets the black singer howling in his bear trap,
> shines young eyes with the brightness of the mad,
> tires the old with her residual sadness;
> and yearly lilacs in her dooryards bloom,
> and the cherry orchard's surf
> blinds Washington and whispers
> to the assassin in his furnished room
> of an ideal America, whose flickering screens
> show, in slow herds, the ghosts of the Cheyennes
> scuffling across the staked and wired plains
> with whispering, rag-bound feet,
>
> while the farm-couple framed in their Gothic door
> like Calvin's saints, waspish, pragmatic, poor,
> gripping the devil's pitchfork
> stare rigidly toward the immortal wheat.[34]

Bruce King vividly reports how the subsequent spread of Black Power to
Port of Spain and elsewhere in the Caribbean – a long period of marches
and near-revolution – made Walcott angry, fearful and depressed. In 1970,
demonstrations and marches that began during Carnival quickly escalated
into violent riots, complete with fire bombs and looting. Since the common justification for violence was habitually phrased in racial terms, light-
skinned people like Walcott were increasingly subjected to insults and threat
on the part of protesters. "Years later," King writes,

in the drafts of his unpublished autobiography Walcott would try to express his
conflicting feelings about the 1970 revolt. At Woodford Square he listened to the
orators screaming for power over their microphones and proclaiming that only
pure black would be allowed to survive. He felt threatened and worried about
his children's future in Trinidad. His first priority was the safety of his house, to
which he returned by taxi. The driver warned him that the placard bearers, who
were holding up traffic, were dangerous. Hearing shouts of "black is beautiful"
Walcott thought about the implications; did it mean that he and his children were
ugly?[35]

Walcott's allusion to Whitman's Civil War elegy suggests that Whitman's "self-expression without craft" had contributed to the rise of such
narrow didacticism and nationalist rhetoric, and, in doing so, had deprived
people throughout the New World of an enduring idiom of mourning.

Furthermore, as a cosmopolite poised between cultures, Walcott found himself on the horns of a hemispheric dilemma: at the same time that he admired the verbal openness of Whitman's America, and even felt "influenced . . . into becoming some kind of American," he also realized the importance of retaining a distinct Caribbean cultural identity.

Once, when asked to discuss his prose work-in-progress, *American without America*, Walcott said, "Broadly speaking, it is autobiographical, but it is also about our current West Indian . . . fear of being absorbed into American culture. We're trying to retain our identity."[36] Paradoxically, Walcott is concerned to discover continuities throughout the New World that would allow him to flourish as a poet, but if he were to altogether lose the idiom, intonation, accent and cadences of his original way of speaking, the conditions that make transnational comparison and idiomatic exchanges possible and meaningful would no longer hold.

Walcott takes up Whitman's threat to individuality as a theme in "Over Colorado," which appeared in Walcott's 1976 collection, *Sea Grapes*. In this poem, the poet–speaker is flying in an airplane over Colorado. He looks down, and imagines the "obliteration" of Native Americans, who were being "removed" at about the same time Whitman was declaiming about America's democratic vistas. The opening line, written in pentameter, recalls Frost's sonnet "Once by the Pacific," and implicitly contrasts Frost's formal constraints and technical discipline with Whitman's verbal expansiveness. After rolling out this first line, in the rest of the poem Walcott proceeds imagistically, mainly limiting himself to trimeter tercets:

> When Whitman's beard unrolled like the Pacific,
> when he quit talking
> to prophesy the great waggons [*sic*]
>
> the dream began to lumber to delirium.
> Once, flying over Colorado
> its starved palomino mountains
>
> I saw, like ants, a staggering file
> of Indians enter a cloud's beard;
> then the cloud broke on
>
> a frozen brave, his fossil
> a fern-print on the spine of rock
> his snow-soft whisper
>
> Colorado, rust and white;
> the snow his praise, the snow
> his obliterator.

That was years ago,
in a jet crossing to Los Angeles,
I don't know why it comes now,

or why I see only this
through those democratic vistas
parting your leaves of grass.[37]

The first sentence spills over into the second stanza, proudly mocking Whitman's formlessness, but the next image, a line of starving Indians staggering like ants, suggests the frailty, and painful privacy, of Walcott's own idiom. The speaker imagines a "frozen brave" whose unique existence – embodied by his fossil, "a fern-print on the spine of rock" – has been virtually obliterated. Taken as a whole, the lyric evokes Walcott's "fear of being absorbed into American culture," where absorption means not being remembered, or known, in a society whose prosaic idiom is cold and white as Colorado snow, and endless as Whitman's grassy vistas.

Perhaps Walcott's growing involvement with the USA during the 1970s, as well as his enhanced self-consciousness as a poet of the Americas, prompted him to assert his affiliation with Whitman with a greater sense of urgency. But the task of coming to terms with Whitman's nationalist poetic actually began as early as the 1940s.[38] In "The Yellow Cemetery," a poem of mourning that appeared in Walcott's very first, self-published volume, *25 Poems* (1948), yellow is symbolically associated with Whitman and "the degeneration of technique," or the "yellowing" of poetic language into polemic.[39] In an epigraph taken from *Song of Myself*, Walcott emphasizes Whitman's use of prairie-grass as a biblical symbol of hopeful communion ("They are alive and well somewhere, / The smallest sprout shows that there is really no death"). But throughout his poem Walcott draws on this same frontier imagery – imagery that recurs, as we have seen, in poems such as Eliot's "Difficulties of a Statesman" and Perse's *Anabase* – while echoing Milton's indignation at the corrupt clergy in *Lycidas*. In implicit condemnation of Whitman, Walcott's speaker rails against the "low populations of the democratic dead" who lie buried in grasshair tombs, robbed of their cherished individuality:

Do not talk of dying, you say, but all men dead or sick,
In the brain and rib-hollow rooms
The candles of the eye burn and shorten, and how quick
The fine girl sleeps in her grave of hair, the grasshair tombs.
O look at the sane low populations of the democratic dead,
How all are doomed to a dome of mud, all brought to book,
Believing in a world for the perverse saint and the holy crook.[40]

Of all the American poets whom Walcott was reading during the late 1940s, his stance towards Whitman most closely resembles Pound's.[41] Thus it is fitting that, in *Epitaph for the Young, Another Life* and elsewhere, he deliberately borrows from Pound as a means of deflecting Whitman's influence. In section 12 of "Homage to Gregorias," for example, Walcott adapts Whitman's description of a carpenter dressing his plank in *Song of Myself*, but disrupts the mythic illusion of Whitman's transparency by calling attention to the hexameter's physical extension on the page:

> I watched the vowels curl from the tongue of the carpenter's
> /plane
>
> resinous, fragrant
> labials of our forests,
> over the plain wood
> the back crouched,
> the vine-muscled wrist,
> like a man rowing,
> sweat-fleck on blond cedar.[42]

Remembering Pound, Hemingway and the avant-gardes in Paris during the twenties, Walcott pays homage to the same milieu that so critically shaped, as we have seen, the poetry of Hughes, Eliot and Perse:

> It was still Paris.
> The twenties. Montparnasse.
> Paris, and now its crepuscule
> sets in Pound's eye, now as I watch
> this twinkling hoar-frost photograph
> of the silvery old man bundled, silent, ice-glint
> of frozen fire before the enemy,
> *faits vos hommages*,
> as the tongues of shavings coil from the moving pen,
> to a Paris of plane trees,
> to the peeled ease of Hemingway's early prose,
> *faites vos hommages*,
> to the hills stippled with violet
> as if they had seen Pissaro.[43]

Decades earlier, in Canto 10 of *Epitaph for the Young*, an uncollected poem published in 1949, Walcott alludes extensively to Pound:

> A Chinese boy, now in the class, alien traditions, oddments
> Of alien culture.
> Li Po, my friend, you will remember
> How time took under his sleeve the cicada's song,

And left the cockroach to describe circles in our dry brains,
On the day that you abandoned the wine glass of Rihaku
For the chamber pots of reason.
I am with tired loins in a dry country,
The wind blows the last white prayers from my head,
I believe I will give up the goose quill for a laundry
In far Hao.
A mixture of faces, damp faces torn like paper by the black wind,
Their fathers' sons, an epitaph for the young.
Lord, send my roots rain.[44]

Echoing Eliot's *The Waste Land* and "Gerontion," Walcott also brings to
mind Pound's "faces in the crowd; / Petals on a wet, black bough" from
the haiku-inspired "In a Station of the Metro."[45] More important, and less
obvious, he also recalls Pound's "Epitaphs," from the 1916 volume *Lustra*,
where Pound's second epitaph is for the eighth-century Chinese poet, Li
T'ai Po:

And Li Po also died drunk.
He tried to embrace a moon
In the Yellow River.[46]

This allusion, like others, intimates the seeming impossibility, and miracle,
of poetic emergence in the New World. The speaker is, as both Walcott
and Pound must have been at early points in their careers, bewildered and
entranced by the hybridity of classrooms on the frontiers of empire.

Elsewhere, in Canto 7 of *Epitaph*, Walcott refers ironically to Whitman's
"Pioneers! O Pioneers!" situating Whitman's hybrid idiom and grandiose
"yawp" within the historical contexts of imperialism and frontier violence:

Pioneers, O Pioneers.
. . .

Vivas to you camerados,
I do not tell again the tale of the Alamo,
With yawps and whoops I tell of
Wastebaskets of crushed plans breathing in small rooms,
Professor Eunich,
The critics praised them, read the early reviews,
Horizon and dollar beckoned, they made bad habits
Of all their virtues and bored their admirers yearly.[47]

We have seen that in "Difficulties of a Statesman" Eliot conjoins echoes of
Whitman's "Pioneers! O Pioneers!" with Perse's adaptation of the Whitmanian frontier setting in *Anabase*. Both poets, like Harris, stress the violence

of transculturation on the frontier and the destruction of Amerindian civilizations, evoking aspects of empire-building that Whitman neatly elides. By contrast, in *Epitaph*, Walcott is less centrally concerned about frontier history than he is about the burdens of his own coming of age as a poet. Whitman's personality and illusory egalitarianism are observed through the corrective lens of Pound's impersonality, a technique where, as Kenner shrewdly noted, any "personal accidents of the perceiving medium" have been effaced. In Pound, the parody of the poet–aesthete helped to distance Pound the person from an unsavory (but entirely possible) interpretation of himself – a figure, as Kenner says, "with whom Pound is anxious not to be confounded."[48] In *Epitaph*, by contrast, we witness the poet's double recoiling from two equally unacceptable extremes – both the whooping New World barbarian and the repressed, narrow-minded aesthete – as clichéd stereotypes of the American poet.

MODERNIST RETICENCE AND MONUMENTALITY IN "FOR ALL CRAFTSMEN" (1953)

When Eliot, quoting Dante, named Pound as the "better craftsman" (*il miglio fabbro*) in his dedication of *The Waste Land*, he was asserting a definitive tenet of the modernist movement in American poetry – namely, the commitment to craftsmanship as a necessary enhancement of sensibility. The term "craftsmanship," in this by now familiar sense of the word, refers to the idea that poems owe their vitality to the technique shown in composition. Both Eliot and Pound contend that technique, "the only gauge and test of a man's lasting sincerity," fulfills an essential obligation to tradition.[49] Although a given style may be distinct, it should not reflect the personality of the individual craftsman, achieving instead an effect of "reticence," without any explicit self-revelation.[50]

Walcott's early work indicates that he was deeply affected by these principles of craft. In 1965, for instance, he praised New World poets for drawing their strength, "like . . . all dedicated craftsmen," from a paradoxically fertile desert of cultural rubble in the Americas.[51] By 1974, his notion of the craftsman had subtly changed, at the same that it assumed an even greater centrality to his self-conception as a poet of the Americas:

The stripped and naked man, however abused, however disabused of old beliefs, instinctually, even desperately begins again as craftsman. In the indication of the slightest necessary gesture of ordering the world around him, of losing his old name and rechristening himself, in the arduous enunciation of a dimmed alphabet, in the shaping of tools, pen or spade, is the whole, profound sigh of human optimism, of what we in the archipelago still believe in: work and hope. It is out of this that the New World, or the Third World, should begin.[52]

Walcott's adaptation of the Crusoe archetype, which may well have been the result of Perse's influence, illustrates a key aspect of craft, as well as his difference from Perse. For both poets, Crusoe examplifies the figure of the modern artist as exile. But whereas the Crusoe archetype of Perse's *Éloges* dreams longingly for a lost tropical childhood, Walcott's Crusoe poems dramatize, first and foremost, how craft allows a poet to come face-to-face with the harsh realities of island life. Crusoe is, in Walcott's work, the person who begins with nothing, who has to build everything he needs, a figure of the artist as craftsman. "You can only create something you hope can be a work of art," he once said about "The Castaway":

Alone, and in this case, it's set in the Caribbean, I imagine. But it's also the image of Crusoe as someone who has to begin again with whatever tools are around – and the tools may be a piece of paper or a pencil, or something, or canvas, or a brush – but I think that's what it's about, the isolation that is part of creativity.[53]

"For All Craftsmen," an uncollected lyric that appeared in a 1953 issue of *Bim*, anticipates poems such as "The Castaway," "Crusoe's Journal" and "Crusoe's Island," and vividly illustrates how much Walcott learned from Eliot and Pound about the poet's craft. The opening stanzas exhibit a style that embodies the primary features of Pound's reticence. Walcott's speaker self-reflexively elaborates a sculptural metaphor, chiseling away unnecessary words, so that his syntax pushes at the bounds of comprehensibility. Each end-stopped line begins and ends just at the points of grammatical articulation, so that what was a natural, prosaic speaking voice is now like a cultivated landscape, or a sculpted form:

> And when they shall ask "Has it come to nothing?"
> Of who sculpted a phrase with a chisel,
> Or taught his grief
> To bend with the wind, for there can be grace in secession,
> As somebody asked Phidias, or some charwoman Gautier
> "Has it come to nothing?"
> No one shall answer but the phrase itself;
> The sculptured line be quiet as these hills,
> The phrase, ephemeral as the spider grass,
> When the dew makes itself five emeralds long.
>
> . . .
>
> This is what Flaubert meant, Gautier and Phidias,
> All the true ones

Not chanticleers of rhetoric,
The 'unacknowledged legislators'
Dust on their haloes.[54]

For Walcott, as for Eliot and Pound, this sculptural analogy explains how reticence orders and distinguishes poetic language from colloquial expression without craft, helping the poet to make a "quiet statement" that reconciles his desire for monumentality with his aversion to publicity.[55] "Colloquial poetry," according to Pound, "is to the real art as the barber's wax dummy is to sculpture"; in his view, a poem's meaning should be impenetrable to some, but easily read by all.[56] In *Homage to Sextus Propertius*, for example, Pound acknowledges the differences that divide him from the majority of his reading public, self-consciously retreating into reticent allusion, and rendering his lyric in terms that are public but nonetheless cryptic:

God's aid, let not my bones lie in a public location
With crowds too assiduous in their crossing of it;
For thus are tombs of lovers most desecrated.

May a woody and sequestered place cover me with its foliage
Or may I inter beneath the hummock
          of some as yet uncatalogued sand;
At any rate I shall not have my epitaph in a high road.[57]

Likewise, in "For All Craftsmen," the dense proliferation of allusions also impedes comprehension. Ironically alluding to Shelley's 1821 *Defense of Poetry*, Walcott questions his idealization of the poet's heroic social role; referring to the crafted, rational understatement of Phidias, Gautier and Flaubert (who once described himself as aspiring to a style "as rhythmical as verse, [and] as precise as the language of science"), he implicitly distances himself from Shelley's emotional and rhetorical intensity.[58]

Walcott's yearning for monuments, his awareness of the historical absence of ruins in the Americas, initially attracted him to the modernist ideal of the craftsman as the maker of durable monuments. In a 1990 interview, he observed:

Nothing can be put down in the sea. You can't plant on it, you can't live on it, you can't walk on it . . . You feel that first of all, that if you weren't there you wouldn't be missed. If you are on land looking at ruins, the ruins commemorate you. They more commemorate than lament the achievement of man. They may contain a moral lesson but underneath there is still praise of the tyrant or hero. There is still awe at the immensity of the ruin. And that's what the ruins of any great cultures do. In a way they commemorate decay . . . The sea is not elegiac in that way. The sea does not have anything on it that is a memento of man.[59]

The protectively allusion-laden, cryptic style of Walcott's opening in "For All Craftsmen" modulates to a more transparent, conversational idiom, as his speaker reflects on his purpose, and duties, as a craftsman. In contrast, however, to such thinkers as Hannah Arendt, who distinguishes the durable, monumental creations of the craftsman from the ephemeral objects made by the common laborer or slave, Walcott expands his definition of craft and discovers a close sense of identification with the humble artisans and slaves of the Caribbean.[60] Describing the poet's gesture of laying down his poem alongside the artisan's tools, he poignantly commemorates the countless, invisible labors of nameless artisans who did not leave enduring monuments, and thereby acknowledges the history and consequences of slavery in the Americas:

> We shall lay down our work alongside the chisel
> Of the stonecutter, with the fisherman's cutlass,
> Wanting no more than honesty in labour,
> That what we loved were not ashamed to worship,
> To carve and perpetuate some grace
> That came in the light, between daylight and nightfall,
> That what we made was more to us than error,
> Frailer than alabaster in its firmness,
> Was more to us than love in its fragility.[61]

The poet–speaker's identification with the artisan reflects a desire for "honesty" that recalls Gerontion's "I would meet you upon this honestly," and confirms Pound's claim that "There are several kinds of honest work. There is the thing that will out. There is the conscientious formulation, a thing of infinitely greater labour."[62] But Walcott also implies such honesty will only be possible when the poet has learned to acknowledge all aspects of his hybrid New World heritage; to "worship" what he loves without shame.[63]

The stylistic consequences of shame are evident in the painfully awkward phrasing of "For All Craftsmen" – when, for example, Walcott drops the pronoun "we" in an effort to compress the statement into the conventional pentameter of blank verse ("that what we loved were not ashamed to worship"). They recall the tortuous indirection, discussed in chapter 2, of works such as Eliot's suppressed "Ode on Independence Day, July 4th, 1918," as well as Pound's wise, unforgettable admonition in *The Pisan Cantos*:

What thou lovest well remains,
                            the rest is dross
What thou lov'st well shall not be reft from thee
What thou lov'st well is thy true heritage.[64]

In "For All Craftsmen," Walcott insightfully places the admonition against vanity and dishonesty in poetry within the panoramic context of New World slavery and the absence of monuments as sources of paralyzing shame. By expressing love for craftsmen such as the stonecutter and fisherman, his poem ministers to what Jahan Ramazani calls the "wound of history," an affliction that would otherwise fester, shamefully untended.[65] The speaker concludes with the hope that, despite his weakness for Gerontion-like rhetorical windiness, a measure of precious truth, well loved, remains:

> That somewhere, the mind, being touched, hardens to marble,
> Lasts and survives the windy palaces
> In the revolving twilight of the truth,
> Outlasting its own loveliness, being truth:
> Though we were none, were torn, were beaten, broken
> In the white praise or contumely of a wave,
> The light shone in that instant and became
> Life for an instant, all and part of life,
> And in its transience remains unaltered,
> Its own discovery and its own self surpassing
> As we have seen the green wave curl to glass in
> Stiffening light,
> And the wild duck transfixed, with winter passing.[66]

Comparing his poem to a curling wave that "glass[es] in" light just before it reaches a breaking point, Walcott evokes a style that recalls the figurative complication of "Hart Crane," but whose prosaic reticence promises another kind of protective privacy. The wild duck is a symbol "we" all see, but it is privately cryptic, implying much more than the poem plainly says. The symbol resurfaces, transmuted to a blue-winged teal, a migratory duck whose range extends throughout the United States to Central and South America, in Walcott's *Another Life*. The bird appears in a watercolor by the poet's father, Warwick, who died when Walcott was a year old:

> Maman,
> you sat folded in silence,
> as if your husband might walk up the street,
> while in the forests the cicadas pedalled their machines
> and silence, a black maid in white,

> barefooted, polished and repolished
> the glass across his fading water-colours,
> the dumb Victrola cabinet,
> the panels and the gleam of blue-winged teal
> beating the mirror's lake.[67]

Throughout his childhood, Walcott was intensely aware of his father's creative avocations: in addition to being a poet, Warwick Walcott had also done meticulous copies of Millet's *The Gleaners*, an original of gulls tossed in a sea of pluming breakers called *Riders of the Storm*, a miniature oil portrait of Walcott's mother, and a self-portrait in watercolor. The effect of these details is to suggest, as Walcott himself has observed, that the death of his father was a decisive factor in Walcott's own decision to become a poet. Walcott used to copy, in watercolor, a number of paintings by old masters, just as his father had copied Millet; thus his father's paintings and watercolors had given him a vital impetus, and a sense of continuity, in pursuing his own craft as a poet of the Americas.[68] "These objects had established my vocation," he recalls, "and made it as inevitable as that of any craftsman's son, for I felt that my father's work, however minor, was unfinished."[69] Again, in *Omeros*, as in *Another Life*, memories of the poet–speaker's dead father summon up the painful absence of historical monuments as a consequence of Caribbean slavery. In a scene where the poet–speaker meets his father's ghost, the ghost relates the humiliations of his given and family names:

> In the printery's noise, and as we went downstairs
> in that now familiar and unfamiliar house,
> he said, in an accent of polished weariness,
>
> "I was raised in this obscure Caribbean port,
> where my bastard father christened me for his shire:
> Warwick. The Bard's county. But never felt part
>
> of the foreign machinery known as Literature.
> I preferred verse to fame, but I wrote with the heart
> of an amateur. It's that Will you inherit.[70]

"For All Craftsmen" lacks the technical mastery, prosaic exactitude and clarity of *Another Life* and *Omeros*. But all three poems affirm a modernist aspiration to monumentality, while at the same time commemorating what would otherwise be a forgotten legacy of craftsmanship left to Walcott by island artisans and his own father.

MIGRATION BY METHOD: WALCOTT'S PASSAGE TO
THE AMERICAS

Like his Anglophone Caribbean contemporary, Wilson Harris, and like all the New World poets discussed in previous chapters, Walcott's poetics discloses how the diasporic consequences of imperialism have configured close, surprising affinities among poets and cultures of the Americas. "We share this part of the world," he once observed, "and have shared it for centuries now" – New World history has been "salted with the bitter memory of migration."[71] As for Harris, the importance of Odysseus – a mythic embodiment of diasporic history – for Walcott's mythical method is well known, and his epic influences have been so exhaustively discussed, that by now even journalists familiarly describe him as a "Homer of the West Indies."[72]

As a migratory trope, craft expresses Walcott's aspiration to a modernist, cosmopolitan lyric practice that crosses frontiers of culture, era and race. "Steersman, My Brother," an elegy from *In A Green Night*, vividly illustrates the terms of his transnational apprenticeship to American poetry. The lyric's guiding metaphor is a "proudly ribbed endeavour" like the ill-fated *Pequod* in Melville's *Moby-Dick*, or the white whale itself, and intimates Walcott's own effort to migrate by method, inventively collocating a hybrid New World heritage by drawing, in part, on the integrative modernist techniques of Eliot, Pound, Crane and others:

> We "write on water" if our souls are drowned
> Within the origin of all life, the sea.
> Yet Queequeg's coffin rose and Ishmael found
> Those prows a compass to eternity.
> And several, rooted visionaries think
> If flesh is mortal, love is infinite;
> That though our proudly ribbed endeavours sink
> In dirt, or swirling sea,
> Our souls, like plants, yearn for the shores of light.
>
> But now such simple sermons are like sand
> Dispersed in wind, like lanterns crackled out,
> Since he lies buried in a strange land.[73]

Over thirty years after the publication of "Steersman, My Brother," Walcott remarked:

we must read further, especially with American masters. We must read as far as the white whale draws us, beyond the tight, calendar hamlets and harbors of New England and its chapels with their harpoon spires, to a wider and more terrifying space, the elemental ocean, beyond provinciality, history, race . . . We must follow

Moby Dick, the huge ribbed metaphor of the white whale carrying the freight of the republic's sins as the republic perishes in the whirlpool with a sole survivor . . . who is, despite Melville's convictions of racial superiority, a poet.[74]

Walcott's interest in Melville may have been partly inspired by C. L. R. James, a Trinidadian writer whom he greatly admired, and who interpreted Queequeg's rising coffin as an ambiguously hopeful sign, in what was otherwise a devastatingly pessimistic critique of national narrative composed on the brink of Civil War.[75] "While Melville sees no solution to the problem of society," James wrote, "he does not say that there is none. *He* can see none."[76] Like James's treatise *Mariners, Renegades and Castaways*, composed on Ellis Island, Walcott's poem evokes a record of his existence under conditions of extreme isolation, where national identity and the sheer capacity for speech and social recognition have all but fallen away. Like Melville and James, Walcott's poet–speaker ambivalently desires, at the same time that he questions the possibility of, peaceful collaboration and exchange among different nationalities and races in the Americas. Dashing the naïve hopes of "rooted visionaries" who cherish the illusion of pure cultures and origins, the poem's opening lines cryptically evoke a culturally hybrid New World society hurtling towards inevitable doom. The opening quotation, "write on water," takes up Crane's theme of millennial and delayed triumph.[77] Having raised Ahab's maddeningly unanswerable question of cultural origins, Walcott's poet–speaker projects himself grandiosely, as a Messiah, resorting to dense, figurative complication and cryptic allegory that set him apart and above others in his society.

Recalling the shorescape and allusion to Milton's *Lycidas* in "The Yellow Cemetery," in "Steersman, My Brother" Walcott's elegist mourns not just the death of the nameless steersman, but also the loss of faith, cultural continuity, ritual and significant formality that would make this death, and any other leave-taking, meaningfully memorable:

> Not for his bones, anchored in dirt, I write
> This elegy, nor for his spirit given
> As he believed up to the fishing Christ,
> Those shoals of martyrs in the nets of heaven;
> But where a wailing autumn strips the year
> And drives the rootless, ageing leaves for miles,
> I weep for hearts like mine, continually driven
> As these lost leaves across earth's barren ground.
> Those whom yearspring, dayspring and heartbreak rain
> Cannot renew, whose noon is a white night,
> Those twilight intellects on the edge of light.[78]

Like Harris's "Creation," Walcott's poem is haunted by the ghostly presence of Shelley's "Ode," and his title brings to mind Whitman's Civil War elegies. In contrast to Whitman, however, and unlike James, who regarded the transnational, migratory harpooners in Melville's novel as the true heroes of *Moby-Dick*, Walcott's speaker mourns the fate of disillusioned, rootless "hearts like mine," scattered like leaves in the autumn wind.[79] Echoing the vacuity of lost passion in "Gerontion," he suggests that the faith of such "twilight intellects" will never be renewed. Instead, they are imprisoned, like Gerontion, in history's endlessly predictable cycles of hope and despair:

> Motion is all our truth, a whirling sphere
> Of change, decay and ebb, the augurs
> Or halcyons of the turning year,
> The Crab and fishes draw the dozen zones;
> Yearly the cyclic hope renews its round,
> The things of sand and water creep and fly,
> And draw the axle of the groaning year,
> Yet in this ash of energy, the foam,
> Where is the soul of my lost helmsman found?
> Where, in such waste, must man find his long home?[80]

As in "For All Craftsmen," however, Walcott's sudden reference to craft marks a dramatic turning point in his poem. Modulating to a more transparent and conversational idiom, linking imperfect rhyme ("thirst" / "trust") with an ominously perfect rhyme ("trust" / "dust"), Walcott momentarily echoes the dimeters and trimeters of Protestant hymnody, as his speaker tentatively discovers faith in technique, "a mere craft / Of words," to bear him through such dark, violent times. The perfectly rhymed juxtaposition of two terms, "craft" and "raft," whose neat chime belies the vast difference in their meanings, suggests that Walcott's figurative complication contains, at the same time it evolved out of, his earlier experience of a much plainer religious idiom:

> I had such faith as yours, but the tides
> Of bitterness broke over me, and the raft
> Of my saved cargoes perished. Now, what rides
> The violent waters of my life, is a mere craft
> Of words, and thirst
> For those fresh springs of grace, which, as I write,
> Mourning my faith's death in your death, derides
> That earlier, steady trust
> That there are harbours, there are fields of light,
> But vision cannot see them for time's dust.[81]

In this early instance, the metaphor of craft recalls the conditions that initially prompted Walcott to search, as Eliot says, "for refreshment and influence" through the lyric practices of modernism, satisfying his thirst for words he can believe in.[82]

Given the metaphor's connotative range and importance, it is striking that, after 1962, craft appears so rarely in Walcott's oeuvre, disappearing until, four decades later, in *Tiepolo's Hound*, Walcott figuratively reconfirms his faith in technique. Whereas, in "For All Craftsmen," Walcott implicitly aligned himself with island artisans but omitted clear mention of his own father, in *Tiepolo's Hound* he commemorates his father's legacy with tenderness and clarity. The conversational immediacy, understatement and exactitude of Walcott's alternately rhymed pentameter couplets are reminiscent of the firmness, delicacy and light precision of his father's pencil studies and watercolors; these, in turn, are situated transnationally in relation to a longstanding tradition of English craftsmanship:

> From my father's cabinet I trace his predecessors
> in a small blue book: *The English Topographical Draughtsmen*,
>
> his pencil studies, delicately firm as theirs,
> the lyrical, light precision of these craftsmen –
>
> Girtin, Sandby, and Cotman, Peter De Wint,
> meadows with needle spires in monochrome,
>
> locks and canals with enormous clouds that went
> rolling over England, postcards from home,
>
> his namesake's county, Warwickshire . . .
>
> . . .
>
> Without ever knowing my father it seems to me now
> (I thought I saw him pause in the parenthesis
>
> of our stairs once), from the blank unfurrowed brow
> of his self-portrait, that he embodied the tenderness
>
> of water, his preferred medium.[83]

Eliot once observed that craft involves the transmission not just of techniques, but of a whole way of seeing and living:

the apprentice (ideally, at least) did not merely serve his master, and did not merely learn from him as one would learn at a technical school – he became assimilated into a way of life which went with that particular trade or craft; and perhaps the lost secret of the craft is this, that not merely a skill but an entire way of life was transmitted.[84]

In *Tiepolo's Hound*, Walcott slows his steady pace, calling attention to the significance of physical perception and response as a measure of technique. For him craft involves education, in Eliot's terms, that has been not just sensual or intellectual, but sensuous:

> And here is where my narrative must pause,
> my couplets rest, at what remains between us,
>
> not Paris's privilege or clouds over Pontoise,
> nor the white hulls and flags of the marinas,
>
> but the same reflections that, from a tree's noise,
> arrested him, or as he stared at them,
>
> wavering memories. Again I lift the oars
> of this couplet, my craft resumes its theme.[85]

The pause is not just an act of reflection. It is also a physical place ("*here*") that brings separate worlds together, helping us to acknowledge, as we question, boundaries that lie between us. Dramatizing both the stakes, and the risks, of his effort to navigate beyond cultural frontiers, Walcott's craft not only brings ordered continuity to his lifelong search for an adequately hybrid style. It is also a perpetual source of interest, making the entire pursuit of poetry worthwhile.

Epilogue

Throughout this book, I have tried to question prevailing assumptions about the regional, national and ethnic subdivisions of American literature; to explain how, and why, modernist forms appealed so strongly to black poets in the Americas; to discern the intricate, peculiar filigree of New World cultures; to uncover analogous contexts, surprising comparisons and unexamined areas of textual study; and to demonstrate that Caribbean poetry, like African-American poetry, needs to be understood within the larger contexts of transamerican modernism and the multilingual, diasporic, New World contexts of imperialism. The dense intertextual relations among Eliot, Perse and Laforgue – relations, as we have seen, that helped inspire the first stirrings of poetic modernism in the Francophone Caribbean – were fostered by their common history and cultural predicament as New World poets, and their shared, abiding and, at times, ambivalent attraction to Poe and Whitman.

My consideration of Hughes's cosmopolitan ethos, involvement with French modernism and pervasive influence in the Francophone Caribbean raises important complementarities between Hughes and Eliot. By disclosing key parallels in their lines of stylistic development, I question the widely held view that Hughes was part of a literary movement that starkly opposed and rivaled Eliot's modernism. Both Eliot and Hughes were vitally concerned that poetry should provide a cherished medium of exchange in the New World, and their amply documented influence on the formation of modernist styles in the Caribbean is strong indication of their success in this regard.

In my analysis of Anglophone Caribbean writers such as Harris and Walcott, the debt to Eliot's modernism is much more clear-cut and explicit than it is in Hughes's writing. But like Hughes, and like many of their Francophone Caribbean antecedents and contemporaries, Harris and Walcott drew on local resources that helped them to resist assimilation to Eliot's modernist project. Signifying on the varied formal repertoire of modernist forms, they recovered, and realized, an unwritten history of migratory cosmopolitanism in the region.

My own passage to the wider Americas, traversed in these pages, is only a preliminary investigation of how such a relational, intercultural, transnational poetics came to be. Much has been omitted, and much is left to be done. I have said nothing at all, for example, about cross-currents of influence among modernists in the USA and in Spanish America, or between Hughes and Guillén, Walcott and Neruda. Restricting the regional contours of my own study, I occlude many transatlantic connections that are essential for any historical account of literary emergence in the Caribbean, such as the influence of Yeats or Joyce on Walcott, Conrad's role in the formation of Harris's modernism, and other key findings.[1]

Future studies will clarify the global scope of Eliot's influence in Africa, Asia, the Middle East and elsewhere, well beyond the boundaries I establish here. But, despite these and other limitations, as one possible perspective among many, my hemispheric, comparative, transnational approach has much to offer. Moving beyond the safely circumscribed terrain of nationalist feeling, we stand to learn something new, even about the poets we think we know best.

Notes

INTRODUCTION. TOWARDS A COMPARATIVE AMERICAN POETICS

1. T. S. Eliot, *Notes Towards the Definition of Culture* (1948) (London: Faber and Faber Ltd., 1962), 114.
2. James Clifford, *Routes: Travel and Translation in the Late Twentieth Century* (Cambridge, MA: Harvard University Press, 1997), 4–5.
3. Amy Kaplan, *The Anarchy of Empire in the Making of U.S. Culture* (Cambridge, MA: Harvard University Press, 2005); Betsy Erkkila, "The Poetics of Whiteness: Poe and the Racial Imaginary," *Romancing the Shadow: Poe and Race*, ed. J. Kennedy and L. Weissberg (New York: Oxford University Press, 2001), 41–74; Anna Brickhouse, *Transamerican Literary Relations and the Nineteenth-Century Public Sphere* (Cambridge: Cambridge University Press, 2004); Lawrence Buell, "Circling the Spheres: A Dialogue," *American Literature* 70 (1998); Paul Giles, *Transatlantic Insurrections: British Culture and the Formation of American Literature, 1730–1860* (Philadelphia: University of Pennsylvania Press, 2001) and *Virtual Americas: Transnational Fiction and the Transatlantic Imaginary* (Durham, NC: Duke University Press, 2002); John Carlos Rowe, *Literary Culture and U.S. Imperialism: From the Revolution to World War II* (Oxford: Oxford University Press, 2000); Robert Weisbuch, *Atlantic Double-Cross: American Literature and British Influence in the Age of Emerson* (Chicago: University of Chicago Press, 1986); Myra Jehlen and Michael Warner, eds., *The English Literatures of America, 1500–1800* (New York: Routledge, 1997); Wai-Chee Dimock, *Empire for Liberty: Melville and the Poetics of Individualism* (Princeton: Princeton University Press, 1989).
4. Linda Basch, Nina Glick Schiller and Cristina Szanton Blanc, eds., *Nations Unbound: Transnational Projects, Postcolonial Predicaments, and Deterritorialized Nation-States* (New York: Gordon and Breach, 1994); Arjun Appadurai, *Modernity at Large: Cultural Dimensions of Globalization* (Minneapolis: University of Minnesota Press, 1996); Nina Glick Schiller, "Transmigrants and Nation-States: Something Old and Something New in the Immigrant Experience," *The Handbook of International Migration: The American Experience*, ed. Charles Hirshman, Josh Dewind and Philip Kasinitz (New York: Russell Sage Foundation, 1999); Liliana R. Goldin, "Transnational Identities: The Search for

186

Analytic Tools," *Identities on the Move: Transnational Processes in North America and the Caribbean Basin*, ed. Liliana R. Goldin (Albany, NY: Institute for Mesoamerican Studies, 1999), 1–11.

5. Paul Gilroy, *The Black Atlantic: Modernity and Double Consciousness* (Cambridge, MA: Harvard University Press, 1993), 6–7.

6. Amritjit Singh and Peter Schmidt, "Introduction," *Postcolonial Theory and the United States: Race, Ethnicity, and Literature*, ed. A. Singh and P. Schmidt (Jackson: University Press of Mississippi, 2000), viii, 17.

7. Edward Said, *Culture and Imperialism* (New York: Knopf, 1993), 43.

8. For an account of "vernacular" cosmopolitanism that facilitates salutary, transformative acts of cultural translation, see Homi Bhabha, "Unsatisfied: Notes on Vernacular Cosmopolitanism," *Text and Nation: Cross-Disciplinary Essays on Cultural and National Identities*, ed. Laura Garcia-Moreno and Peter Pfeiffer (Columbia, SC: Camden House, 1996), 191–207.

9. John Carlos Rowe, "Nineteenth-Century United States Literary Culture and Transnationality," *PMLA* 118.1 (January 2003), 79.

10. See, for example, Bernard Bailyn and Philip Morgan, eds., *Strangers Within the Realism: Cultural Margins of the First British Empire* (Chapel Hill: University of North Carolina Press, 1991); Oscar Handlin, *The Uprooted* (Boston, MA: Little, Brown, 1952); and Maldwyn Allen Jones, *American Immigration* (Chicago, IL: University of Chicago Press, 1960).

11. Anthony Giddens, *The Consequences of Modernity* (Stanford: Stanford University Press, 1990), 108–109.

12. Raymond Williams, *The Politics of Modernism: Against the New Conformists* (London: Verso, 1989), 77.

13. Henry James, *The American Scene*, in *Collected Travel Writings: Great Britain and America* (New York: Library of America, 1993), 459.

14. A. James Arnold, *Modernism and Negritude: The Poetry and Poetics of Aimé Césaire* (Cambridge, MA: Harvard University Press, 1981); J. Michael Dash, *The Other America: Caribbean Literature in a New World Context* (Charlottesville: University Press of Virginia, 1998).

15. See, for example, Christopher Ricks, *T. S. Eliot and Prejudice* (Berkeley: University of California Press, 1988); Anthony Julius, *T. S. Eliot, Anti-Semitism, and Literary Form* (Cambridge: Cambridge University Press, 1995); Louis Menand, "T. S. Eliot and the Jews," *American Studies* (New York: Farrar, Straus and Giroux, 2002), 54–75; and Ronald Schuchard, "Burbank with a Baedecker, Eliot with a Cigar: American Intellectuals, Anti-Semitism, and the Idea of Culture," *Modernism/Modernity* 10.1 (January 2003), 1–56.

16. Richard Slotkin, *Regeneration Through Violence: The Mythology of the American Frontier, 1600–1860* (Middletown, CT: Wesleyan University Press, 1973).

17. Edouard Glissant, *Caribbean Discourse: Selected Essays*, trans. J. Michael Dash (Charlottesville: University Press of Virginia, 1989), 226.

18. Herbert Klein, ed., *The Middle Passage: Comparative Studies in the Atlantic Slave Trade* (Princeton: Princeton University Press, 1978); Nicolas Lemann, *The Promised Land: The Great Black Migration and How It Changed*

America (New York: Knopf, 1991); Carol Marks, *Farewell, We're Good and Gone* (Bloomington: Indiana University Press, 1989); James Grossman, *Land of Hope* (Chicago: University of Chicago Press, 1989). For an analysis of the shaping effect of migration on African-American fiction, see Farrah Griffin, *Who Set You Flowing?* (New York: Oxford University Press, 1995), and Charles Scruggs, *Sweet Home: Invisible Cities in the Afro-American Novel* (Baltimore, MD: Johns Hopkins University Press, 1993).

19. Langston Hughes, "Jazz as Communication," *The Collected Works of Langston Hughes*, vol. IX: *Esssays on Art, Race, Politics, and World Affairs*, ed. Christopher de Santis (Columbia: University of Missouri Press, 2002), 370.

20. Michael North, *The Dialect of Modernism: Race, Language, and Twentieth-Century Literature* (New York: Oxford University Press, 1994); Ross Posnock, *Color and Culture: Black Writers and the Making of the Modern Intellectual* (Cambridge, MA: Harvard University Press, 1998); Werner Sollors, *Beyond Ethnicity: Consent and Descent in American Culture* (New York: Oxford University Press, 1986); Ann Douglas, *Terrible Honesty: Mongrel Manhattan in the 1920s* (New York: The Noonday Press, 1995); George Hutchinson, *The Harlem Renaissance in Black and White* (Cambridge, MA: Harvard University Press, 1995); Gilroy, *Black Atlantic*; Anita Patterson, *From Emerson to King: Democracy, Race, and the Politics of Protest* (New York: Oxford University Press, 1997).

21. See, for example, Walton Look Lai, *Indentured Labor, Caribbean Sugar: Chinese and Indian Migrants to the British West Indies, 1838–1918* (Baltimore, MD: Johns Hopkins University Press, 2004), and M. J. Proudfoot, *Population Movements in the Caribbean* (Port of Spain, Trinidad: Kent House, 1950).

22. Ceri Peach, *West Indian Migration to Britain: A Social Geography* (London: Oxford University Press, 1968); Saskia Sassen, *The Mobility of Labor and Capital* (Cambridge: Cambridge University Press, 1988), 56.

23. Derek Walcott, "Reflections on Omeros," *South Atlantic Quarterly* 29.2 (Spring 1997), 243.

24. J. Michael Dash, *The Other America*; Simon Gikandi, *Writing in Limbo: Modernism and Caribbean Literature* (Ithaca: Cornell University Press, 1992); Jahan Ramazani, *The Hybrid Muse: Postcolonial Poetry in English* (Chicago: University of Chicago Press, 2001) and "A Transnational Poetics," *American Literary History* 18.2 (Summer 2006), 332–359; Charles Pollard, *New World Modernisms: T. S. Eliot, Derek Walcott, and Kamau Brathwaite* (Charlottesville: University of Virginia Press, 2004); George Handley, *New World Poetics: Nature and the Adamic Imagination in Whitman, Neruda, and Walcott* (Athens: University of Georgia Press, 2007).

25. Stephen Spender, *The Struggle of the Modern* (London: Hamish Hamilton, 1963), 71.

26. Simon During, "Waiting for the Post: Some Relations between Modernity, Colonization, and Writing," *Ariel* 20.4 (October 1989), 31–61.

27. Silvio Torres-Saillant, *Caribbean Poetics: Toward an Aesthetic of West Indian Literature* (Cambridge: Cambridge University Press, 1997), 24, 29.

28. Torres-Saillant, *Caribbean Poetics*, 17, 29.

29. Torres-Saillant, *Caribbean Poetics*, 1, 22.
30. Helen Vendler, *The Given and the Made: Strategies of Poetic Redefinition* (Cambridge, MA: Harvard University Press, 1995), 3–4.
31. Robert Pinsky, *Democracy, Culture and the Voice of Poetry* (Princeton: Princeton University Press, 2002), 18; T. S. Eliot, "Tradition and the Individual Talent," *Selected Essays* (New York: Harcourt, Brace and World, 1950), 4.
32. Paul de Man, "Form and Intent in the American New Criticism," *Blindness and Insight: Essays in the Rhetoric of Contemporary Criticism* (2nd edn., Minneapolis: University of Minnesota Press, 1983), 20–21.
33. Henry Louis Gates, *Figures in Black* (New York: Oxford University Press, 1987), xxxi.
34. See, for example, John Carlos Rowe, ed., *Post-Nationalist American Studies* (Berkeley: University of California Press, 2000), 23–39; Michael Levenson, *A Genealogy of Modernism* (Cambridge: Cambridge University Press, 1984); Sanford Schwartz, *The Matrix of Modernism: Pound, Eliot, and Early Twentieth-Century Thought* (Princeton: Princeton University Press, 1985); James Longenbach, *Modernist Poetics of History* (Princeton: Princeton University Press, 1987); Frank Lentricchia, *Modernist Quartet* (Cambridge: Cambridge University Press, 1994); Kenneth Asher, *T. S. Eliot and Ideology* (Cambridge: Cambridge University Press, 1995); Stan Smith, *The Origins of Modernism: Eliot, Pound, Yeats and the Rhetorics of Renewal* (New York: Harvester, 1994); and William Chace, *The Political Identities of Ezra Pound and T. S. Eliot* (Stanford: Stanford University Press, 1973).
35. Albert Gelpi, *A Coherent Splendor: The American Poetic Renaissance, 1910–1950* (New York: Cambridge University Press, 1987), 2–5, 114.
36. See, for example, Aldon Lynn Nielsen, *Reading Race: White American Poets and Racial Discourse in the Twentieth Century* (Athens: University of Georgia Press, 1988), 49–101.

1 TRANSNATIONAL TOPOGRAPHIES IN POE, ELIOT AND ST.-JOHN PERSE

1. T. S. Eliot, "From Poe to Valéry," *To Criticize the Critic and Other Writings* (1965) (reprint, Lincoln: University of Nebraska Press, 1991), 27.
2. T. S. Eliot, "'A Dream within a Dream': T. S. Eliot on Edgar Allan Poe," *Listener* 29 (Feb. 25, 1943), 243–244.
3. Matthiessen, *American Renaissance: Art and Expression in the Age of Emerson and Whitman* (London: Oxford University Press, 1941), 578–579.
4. Matthiessen, *American Renaissance*, 579.
5. T. S. Eliot, review of *Israfel*, by Hervey Allen, *Nation and Athenaeum* 41 (May 21, 1927), 219.
6. T. S. Eliot, "American Literature," *Athenaeum* 4643 (April 25, 1919), 236–237.
7. Edgar Allan Poe, *Essays and Reviews*, ed. G. R. Thompson (New York: Library of America, 1984), 1025.
8. Eliot, "American Literature," 236.

9. James Russell Lowell, "Edgar Allan Poe" (1850), *Edgar Allan Poe: Critical Assessments*, ed. Graham Clarke, vol. II (Mountfield, East Sussex: Helm Information, 1991), I, 9.
10. Terence Whalen, *Edgar Allan Poe and the Masses: The Political Economy of Literature in Antebellum America* (Princeton: Princeton University Press, 1999).
11. Poe, *Essays and Reviews*, 1065, 1027, 1076.
12. Giles, *Transatlantic Insurrections*, 190; Jonathan Elmer, *Reading at the Social Limit: Affect, Mass Culture, and Edgar Allan Poe* (Stanford: Stanford University Press, 1995), 26.
13. Meredith McGill, "Poe, Literary Nationalism, and Authorial Identity," *The American Face of Edgar Allan Poe*, ed. S. Rosenheim and S. Rachman (Baltimore, MD: Johns Hopkins University Press, 1995), 275.
14. Quoted in Sir Herbert Read, "T. S E. – a Memoir," in *T. S. Eliot: The Man and His Work*, ed. Allen Tate (London: Chatto and Windus, 1967), 15.
15. John Soldo, *The Tempering of T. S. Eliot* (Ann Arbor: UMI Research Press, 1983), 67.
16. T. S. Eliot, "The Three Provincialities" (1922), reprinted in *Essays in Criticism* 1.1 (January 1951), 39–40.
17. Eliot, "American Literature," 237.
18. T. S. Eliot, "American Literature and the American Language," *To Criticize*, 55.
19. Eliot, "American Literature and the American Language," 59.
20. Arthur Symons, *The Symbolist Movement in Literature* (1908) (revised and enlarged edn. New York: Haskell House, 1971), 114.
21. T. S. Eliot, Foreword to *Symbolisme from Poe to Mallarmé: The Growth of a Myth*, by Joseph Chiari (London: Rockliff, 1956), v–vi.
22. Charles Baudelaire, *Baudelaire on Poe: Critical Papers*, ed. and trans. L. and F. Hyslop (State College, PA: Bald Eagle Press, 1952), 100–101.
23. Lois Hyslop and Francis E. Hyslop, Jr., "Introduction" to Baudelaire, *Baudelaire on Poe*, 31; Paul Valéry, "Situation de Baudelaire," *Variété*, vol. II (Paris: Librairie Gallimard, 1930).
24. Edmund Wilson, *Axel's Castle: A Study in the Imaginative Literature of 1870–1930* (New York: Scribner's, 1931), 19; Stéphane Mallarmé, "Le Tombeau d'Edgar Poe," *Poésies* (Paris: Flammarion, 1989), 99.
25. T. S. Eliot, "From Poe to Valéry," *To Criticize*, 40.
26. Walter Benjamin, *Charles Baudelaire: A Lyric Poet in the Era of High Capitalism*, trans. Harry Zohn (London: Verso, 1985); Benjamin, "Surrealism – The Last Snapshot of the European Intelligensia," *Selected Writings*, vol. II, ed. M. Jennings (Cambridge, MA: Harvard University Press, 1999); James Lawler, "Demons of the Intellect: The Symbolists and Poe," *Critical Inquiry* 14.1 (Autumn 1987), 109–110; Jonathan Culler, "Baudelaire and Poe," *Zeitschrift für Französische Sprache* 100 (1990), 61–73.
27. Baudelaire, *Baudelaire on Poe*, 67, 92–93, 143, 155.
28. Baudelaire, *Baudelaire on Poe*, 13, 125, 133; Peter Michael Wetherill, *Charles Baudelaire et la poésie d'Edgar Allan Poe* (Paris: A. G. Nizet, 1962), 35; S. A.

Rhodes, *The Cult of Beauty in Charles Baudelaire* (New York: Institute of French Studies at Columbia University, 1929), 339–40.

29. Célestin Pierre Cambiare, "The Influence of Edgar Allan Poe in France" (1927), *Edgar Allan Poe*, ed. Clarke, II, 303, 30; Charles Baudelaire, "Poe: His Life and Works" (1852), *Baudelaire on Poe*, 67; Peter Wetherill, *Charles Baudelaire*, 55–56.

30. Eliot, "From Poe to Valéry," *To Criticize*, 36–37.

31. Hyslop and Hyslop, "Introduction" to Baudelaire, *Baudelaire on Poe*, II–12.

32. Charles Baudelaire, *Correspondance*, vol. II (Paris: Gallimard, "Pléiade," 1973), 386.

33. Andreas Wetzel, "Poe/Baudelaire: Poetics in Translation," *Cincinnati Romance Review* 6 (1987), 61–62.

34. Wilson, *Axel's Castle*; F. O. Matthiessen, *The Achievement of T. S. Eliot* (Boston, MA: Houghton Mifflin, 1935), 40–42; Grover Smith, *T. S. Eliot and the Use of Memory* (Lewisburg: Bucknell University Press, 1996); Helen Vendler, *Coming of Age as a Poet* (Cambridge, MA: Harvard University Press, 2003), 85, 89, 91, 97, 100, 107.

35. Edward Cutler, *Recovering the New: Transatlantic Roots of Modernism* (Hanover, NH: University Press of New England, 2003), 12.

36. Grover Smith, *T. S. Eliot and the Use of Memory*, 40–41, 43–44, 49; Lee Oser, *T. S. Eliot and American Poetry* (Columbia: University of Missouri Press, 1998), 24.

37. Hugh Kenner, *The Invisible Poet: T. S. Eliot* (New York: McDowell, Obolensky, 1959), 136–137.

38. A. David Moody, *Thomas Stearns Eliot: Poet* (2nd edn., Cambridge: Cambridge University Press, 1994), 67.

39. Christopher Ricks, "A l'envers ou à Anvers?," *Times Literary Supplement* (March 14, 1997).

40. John Paul Riquelme, *Harmony of Dissonances: T. S. Eliot, Romanticism, and Imagination* (Baltimore, MD: Johns Hopkins University Press, 1991), 157.

41. T. S. Eliot, "Gerontion," *The Complete Poems and Plays, 1909–1950* (New York: Harcourt Brace, 1952), 21.

42. Eliot, "Gerontion," *Complete Poems*, 21–22.

43. Matthiessen, *The Achievement of T. S. Eliot*, 73; Henry Adams, *The Education of Henry Adams* (New York: Oxford University Press, 1999), 226.

44. T. S. Eliot, "A Sceptical Patrician," review of *The Education of Henry Adams*, *Athenaeum* 4647 (May 23, 1919), 361–362; Ronald Bush, *T. S. Eliot: A Study in Character and Style* (New York: Oxford University Press, 1984), 32.

45. Henry Adams, *The Education*, 22.

46. Henry Adams, *The Education*, 66.

47. Eliot, "Gerontion," *Complete Poems*, 23.

48. *The Oxford English Dictionary, Compact Edition*, vol. II (Oxford: Oxford University Press, 1971), 2296.

49. Eloise Knapp Hay, *T. S. Eliot's Negative Way* (Cambridge, MA: Harvard University Press, 1982), 34.

50. T. S. Eliot, "A Commentary," *Criterion* (April 1931), 484; Eliot, *After Strange Gods: A Primer of Modern Heresy* (New York: Harcourt Brace, 1934), 16; Eric Sigg, *The American T. S. Eliot: A Study of the Early Writings* (Cambridge: Cambridge University Press, 1989), 177–178.
51. Eliot, "American Literature," 237; Eliot, "A Sceptical Patrician," 361–362.
52. Edgar Allan Poe, "Ulalume," *Complete Poems*, ed. T. O. Mabbott (Urbana: University of Illinois Press, 2000), 416, lines 1–19. The poem first appeared in the December 1847 issue of *American Review*, and this version is from a September 1849 manuscript written for Susan Ingram.
53. Poe, *Complete Poems*, ed. Mabbott, 420 n.6.
54. T. O. Mabbott, "Poe's 'Ulalume,'" *Explicator* 6 (February 1948); Lewis Leary, "Poe's 'Ulalume,'" *Explicator* 6 (February 1948).
55. Poe, *Complete Poems*, ed. Mabbott, 421 nn.16–19.
56. James E. Miller, "'Ulalume' Resurrected," *Philological Quarterly* 34 (April 1955), 203; J. O. Bailey, "The Geography of Poe's 'Dream-Land' and 'Ulalume,'" *Studies in Philology* 48 (July 1948), 518–520; Victoria Nelson, "Symmes Hole, or the South Polar Romance," *Raritan* 17 (Fall 1997), 136.
57. Richard Kopley and Kevin J. Hayes, in "Two Verse Masterworks: 'The Raven' and 'Ulalume,'" *The Cambridge Companion to Edgar Allan Poe*, ed. Kevin Hayes (Cambridge: Cambridge University Press, 2002), 199.
58. Quoted in Poe, *Complete Poems*, ed. Mabbott, 189.
59. Edgar Allan Poe, "The Valley Nis" (1831), *Complete Poems*, ed. Mabbott, 191–192, lines 1–16.
60. Poe, *Complete Poems*, ed. Mabbott, 193–194.
61. Poe, "The Valley Nis," *Complete Poems*, ed. Mabbott, 192, lines 27–37.
62. Poe, *Complete Poems*, ed. Mabbott, 190.
63. Poe, *Complete Poems*, ed. Mabbott, 191.
64. Poe, *Complete Poems*, ed. Mabbott, 190.
65. Wallace Fowlie, "Baudelaire and Eliot: Interpreters of Their Age," *Sewannee Review*, ed. Allen Tate, 74.1 (January–March 1966), 293–309; William Chapman Sharpe, *Unreal Cities: Urban Figuration in Wordsworth, Baudelaire, Whitman, Eliot, and Williams* (Baltimore, MD: Johns Hopkins University Press, 1990), 40–45: Vendler, *Coming of Age as a Poet*.
66. T. S. Eliot, "What Dante Means to Me" (1950), *To Criticize*, 126–127.
67. T. S. Eliot, "Baudelaire" (1930), *Selected Essays*, 377.
68. Fowlie, "Baudelaire and Eliot: Interpreters of Their Age," 307–308.
69. Charles Baudelaire, *Le Voyage* (IV), *Les Fleurs du mal* (Paris: Gallimard, 1999), 254.
70. Poe, "The City in the Sea" (1850), *Complete Poems*, 201–202, lines 12–15, 21–23.
71. Jacques Salvan, "Le Sens de la chute dans l'œuvre de Baudelaire," *French Review* 34.2 (December 1960), 132–133.
72. André Salmon, "Anvers," *Créances: 1905–1910* (Paris: Gallimard, 1926), 225; Baudelaire, *Le Voyage* (II), 253.

73. Baudelaire, *Un Voyage à Cythère*, in *Les Fleurs du mal*, 226; T. S. Eliot, "Embarquement pour Cythère," *Inventions of the March Hare*, ed. Christopher Ricks (New York: Harcourt Brace, 1996), 27, 151–152.
74. Kenner, *The Invisible Poet*, 14.
75. Denis Donoghue, *Being Modern Together* (Atlanta, GA: Scholars Press, 1991), 9, 12–13, 16–17, 20.
76. Oser, *T. S. Eliot and American Poetry*, 6; Conrad Aiken, "Prefatory Note" to "Anatomy of Melancholy" (1958), *T. S. Eliot: The Man and His Work*, ed. Allen Tate (New York: Dell, 1966), 196.
77. Henry M. Belden, "Poe's 'The City in the Sea' and Dante's City of Dis," *American Literature* 7 (November 1935), 332–334.
78. Oser, *T. S. Eliot and American Poetry*, 4–5.
79. Poe, *Complete Poems*, ed. Mabbott, 197.
80. Poe, *Complete Poems*, ed. Mabbott, 197.
81. Edgar Allan Poe, *Al Aaraaf* (1829), *Complete Poems*, ed. Mabbott, Part II, lines 11–12, 20–43. I have expanded Mabbott's text, based on the 1845 version, published in *The Raven and Other Poems*, by replacing lines 37–39 with the seven-line extract published in the *Yankee and Boston Literary Gazette* (December 1829).
82. Poe, *Complete Poems*, ed. Mabbott, 95.
83. T. S. Eliot, *The Waste Land* (II), *Complete Poems*, 39, lines 77–85.
84. Grover Smith, *T. S. Eliot and the Use of Memory*, 40; T. S. Eliot, "Prose and Verse," *Poetry and Prose: Three Essays by T. S. Eliot, Frederic Manning [and] Richard Aldington* (London: The Poetry Bookshop, 1921).
85. Betsy Erkkila, "The Poetics of Whiteness: Poe and the Racial Imaginary," *Romancing the Shadow: Poe and Race*, ed. J. Kennedy and L. Weissberg (New York: Oxford University Press, 2001), 48; John Carlos Rowe, "Edgar Allan Poe's Imperial Fantasy and the American Frontier," *Romancing the Shadow: Poe and Race*, 75–105.
86. Bush, *T. S. Eliot*, 77.
87. Eliot, "From Poe to Valéry," *To Criticize*, 31.
88. Bush, *T. S. Eliot*, 124; Richard Abel, "The Influence of St.-John Perse on T. S. Eliot," *Contemporary Literature* 14.2 (Spring 1973), 213–239; C. E. Nelson, "Saint-John Perse and T. S. Eliot," *Western Humanities Review* 17.2 (Spring 1963), 163–171; Roger Little, "T. S. Eliot and Saint-John Perse," *Arlington Quarterly* 2.2 (Autumn 1969), 5–17.
89. Archibald MacLeish, Preface to *Éloges and Other Poems by St.-John Perse*, trans. Louis Varèse (New York: Norton, 1944), 10; T. S. Eliot, Preface to *This American World* by Edgar Ansel Mowrer (London: Faber and Gwyer, 1928), xiii–xiv.
90. Erika Ostrovsky, *Under the Sign of Ambiguity: Saint-John Perse / Alexis Leger* (New York: New York University Press, 1985), 25–26, 62; Bush, *T. S. Eliot*, 17; Lyndall Gordon, *Eliot's Early Years* (London: Oxford University Press, 1977), 38.
91. Eliot, Preface to *This American World*, xiii–xiv.

92. Ostrovsky, *Under the Sign of Ambiguity*, 38.

93. Ostrovsky, *Under the Sign of Ambiguity*, 55; Arthur Knodel, *Saint John Perse: A Study of His Poetry* (Edinburgh: University Press Edinburgh, 1966), 32.

94. Carol Rigolot, *Forged Genealogies: Saint-John Perse's Conversations with Culture* (Chapel Hill: University of North Carolina Press, 2001), 34–35.

95. St.-John Perse, *Letters*, trans. and ed. Arthur Knodel (Princeton: Princeton University Press, 1979), 44–45; Rigolot, *Forged Genealogies*, 36.

96. Derek Walcott, "The Muse of History," *What the Twilight Says* (New York: Farrar, Straus and Giroux, 1998), 38, 49–50.

97. Edouard Glissant, "Saint-John Perse and the Caribbean," *Caribbean Discourse*, 228.

98. Saintléger Léger [Perse], *Pour fêter une enfance* (IV), *La Nouvelle Revue Française* 16 (April 1, 1910), 443.

99. Eliot, "American Literature and the American Language," *To Criticize*, 54.

100. Dash, *The Other America*, 59.

101. Glissant, "Saint-John Perse and the Caribbean," *Caribbean Discourse*, 230.

102. Poe, "A Dream Within A Dream" (1850), *Complete Poems*, ed. Mabbott, 452, lines 19–22.

103. Stéphane Mallarmé, *Oeuvres complètes* (Paris: Gallimard, 1945), 237.

104. Rigolot, *Forged Genealogies*, 38.

105. St.-John Perse, "Les Cloches," *Collected Poems*, trans. W. H. Auden, Hugh Chisholm, Denis Devlin, T. S. Eliot, Robert Fitzgerald, Wallace Fowlie, Richard Howard, Louis Varèse (Princeton: Princeton University Press, 1971), 58.

106. Poe, "The Philosophy of Composition," *Essays and Reviews*, 25.

107. Perse, "Le Mur," *Collected Poems*, 58.

108. Knodel, *Saint-John Perse*, 12–13.

109. Rigolot, *Forged Genealogies*, 29–30; Eliot, "From Poe to Valéry," *To Criticize*, 34.

110. Régis Antoine, *Les écrivains français et les Antilles* (Paris: Maisonneuve et Larose, 1978), 331.

111. Perse, *Pour fêter une enfance* (I, III), *Collected Poems*, 20, 22.

112. Walcott, "The Muse of History," *What the Twilight Says*, 40–41.

113. Henry Bangou, "Allocution d'ouverture du colloque," *Saint-John Perse: Antillanité et universalité*, ed. H. Levillain and M. Sacotte (Paris: Editions Caribéennes, 1988), 11.

114. Régis Antoine, "Une Echappée magnifiante sur la Guadeloupe," *Saint-John Perse: Antillanité et universalité*, 28.

115. Henriette Levillain and Mireille Sacotte, "Presentation," *Saint-John Perse: Antillanité et universalité*, 20.

116. Perse, *Pour fêter une enfance* (II), *Collected Poems*, 22.

117. Perse, *Pour fêter une enfance* (III), *Collected Poems*, 24.

118. Yves Bernabé, "Parole et pouvoir dans la poésie de Saint-John Perse," *Saint-John Perse: Antillanité et universalité*, ed. Levillain and Sacotte, 34, 37.

119. Perse, *Pour fêter une enfance* (VI), *Collected Poems*, 32.

120. Saint-John Perse, *Éloges* (XII), *Collected Poems*, 46, 48.

121. Yves Bernabé, "Parole et pouvoir," *Saint-John Perse: Antillanité et universalité*, ed. Levillain and Sacotte, 41.

122. Abel, "The Influence of St.-John Perse on T. S. Eliot," 216 n.9.

123. Sophie Levie, *Commerce, 1924–1932: une revue internationale moderniste* (Rome: Fondazione Camillo Caetani, 1989), 205 n.1.

124. Ostrovsky, *Under the Sign of Ambiguity*, 61–64.

125. Rigolot, *Forged Genealogies*, 157.

126. Bush, *T. S. Eliot*, 86; Ricks, *T. S. Eliot and Prejudice*, 208.

127. T. S. Eliot, "A Brief Introduction to the Method of Paul Valéry," *Le Serpent* by Paul Valéry, trans. Mark Wardle (London: R. Cobden-Sanderson, 1924), 15.

128. Eliot, "American Literature and the American Language," *To Criticize*, 56.

129. St.-John Perse, "En homage à T. S. Eliot: traduction d'un poème," *Oeuvres complètes* (Paris: Gallimard, 1982), 465.

130. Grover Smith, *T. S. Eliot's Poetry and Plays: A Study in Sources and Meaning* (Chicago: University of Chicago Press, 1956), 102; Eliot, "A Brief Introduction," 8. For an account of Perse's admiration for Laforgue and Conrad, see Ostrovsky, *Under the Sign of Ambiguity*, 55, 97.

131. Celso de Oliveira, "A Note on Eliot and Baudelaire," *American Literature* 55.1 (March 1983), 81.

132. Ostrovsky, *Under the Sign of Ambiguity*, 97.

133. Ostrovsky, *Under the Sign of Ambiguity*, 117.

134. T. S. Eliot, "Un feuillet unique," *Saint-John Perse: Hommage international des "Cahiers de la Pléiade"* (Paris: Boivin, 1950), 8.

135. G. Smith, *T. S. Eliot's Poetry and Plays*, 123; Abel, "The Influence of St.-John Perse on T. S. Eliot," 217–222; Bush, *T. S. Eliot*, 127, 130, 147, 133.

136. G. Smith, *T. S. Eliot's Poetry and Plays*, 140; Levie, *Commerce*, 170.

137. Levie, *Commerce*, 170.

2 HYBRIDITY AND THE NEW WORLD: LAFORGUE, ELIOT AND THE WHITMANIAN POETICS OF THE FRONTIER

1. T. S. Eliot, Introduction to *Ezra Pound: Selected Poems* (London: Faber and Faber, 1928), viii–ix, xi.

2. Donald Gallup, "Mr. Eliot at the Churchill Club," *Southern Review* 21.4 (October 1985), 970, 971.

3. Eliot, "American Literature and Language" (1953), *To Criticize*, 53.

4. Eliot, "American Literature and Language," *To Criticize*, 56.

5. Matthiessen, *American Renaissance*, 579; Yvor Winters, *In Defense of Reason* (New York: The Swallows Press, 1947), 91, 93, 588–589.

6. Roy Harvey Pearce, *The Continuity of American Poetry* (Middletown, CT: Wesleyan University Press, 1987), 304; Donald Pease, "Blake, Crane, Whitman, and Modernism: A Poetics of Pure Possibility," *PMLA* 96.1

(January 1981), 76; Richard Poirier, *The Renewal of Literature: Emersonian Reflections* (New York: Random House, 1987), 100.

7. D. H. Lawrence, *Studies in Classic American Literature* (New York: Thomas Seltzer, 1923), 243.

8. T. S. Eliot, "Reflections on Vers Libre" (1917), *To Criticize*, 187.

9. Sydney Musgrove, *T. S. Eliot and Walt Whitman* (Wellington: New Zealand University Press, 1952); interview with T. S. Eliot, *Writers at Work* ed. George Plimpton (New York: Penguin, 1977), 110; Sigg, *The American T. S. Eliot*; Lyndall Gordon, "The American Eliot and 'The Dry Salvages,'" *Words in Time: New Essays on Eliot's Four Quartets*, ed. E. Lobb (Ann Arbor: University of Michigan Press, 1993), 38–51; Ronald Bush, "Nathaniel Hawthorne and T. S. Eliot's American Connection," *Southern Review* 21 (October 1985), 924–933; Ronald Bush, "T. S. Eliot: Singing the Emerson Blues," *Emerson: Prospect and Retrospect*, ed. J. Porte (Cambridge, MA: Harvard University Press, 1982), 179–197; A. David Moody, "The American Strain," *The Placing of T. S. Eliot*, ed. J. S. Brooker (Columbia: University of Missouri Press, 1991), 77–89; Lentricchia, *Modernist Quartet*.

10. Wilson, *Axel's Castle*, 12; Matthiessen, *American Renaissance*, 57, 268, 575.

11. Matthiessen, *The Achievement of T. S. Eliot*, 6; Musgrove, *T. S. Eliot and Walt Whitman*, 64–77; Charles Feidelson, *Symbolism and American Literature* (Chicago: University of Chicago Press, 1953), 213, 217; Gregory Jay, *T. S. Eliot and the Poetics of Literary History* (Baton Rouge: Louisiana State University Press, 1983), 168–171; Cleo McNelly Kearns, "Eliot, Russell, and Whitman: Realism, Politics, and Literary Persona in *The Waste Land*," *T. S. Eliot's The Waste Land*, ed. Harold Bloom (New York: Chelsea House, 1986), 137–152; Harold Bloom, "Introduction," *T. S. Eliot's The Waste Land*, 1–7; John Lynen, *Design of the Present: Essays on Time and Form in American Literature* (New Haven: Yale University Press, 1969), 342–343; Philip Hobsbaum, "Eliot, Whitman, and the American Tradition," *Journal of American Studies* 3 (1969), 239–264; and James Miller, *The American Quest for a Supreme Fiction* (Chicago: University of Chicago Press, 1979), 101–125.

12. Allen Trachtenberg, "Walt Whitman: Precipitant of the Modern," *The Cambridge Companion to Whitman*, ed. E. Greenspan (New York: Cambridge University Press, 1995), 195.

13. Slotkin, *Regeneration Through Violence*.

14. Nancy Duvall Hargrove, *Landscape as Symbol in the Poetry of T. S. Eliot* (Jackson: University Press of Mississippi, 1978); Marshall McLuhan, "The Aesthetic Moment in Landscape Poetry," *English Institute Essays*, ed. Alan Downer (New York: Columbia University Press, 1952); McLuhan, "Tennyson and Picturesque Poetry," *Essays in Criticism* 1 (July 1951), 262–282; Elizabeth Drew, *T. S. Eliot: The Design of His Poetry* (New York: Charles Scribner's Sons, 1949), 98.

15. Eliot, "Un Feuillet unique," 8.

16. Mary Louise Pratt, *Imperial Eyes: Travel Writing and Transculturation* (London: Routledge, 1992), 6; Ron Carter, "A Question of Interpretation: An Overview of

Some Recent Developments in Stylistics," *Linguistics and the Study of Literature*, ed. Theo D'haen (Amsterdam, 1986), 7–26.

17. Homi Bhabha, *The Location of Culture* (London: Routledge, 1994), 38; Jahan Ramazani, *The Hybrid Muse: Postcolonial Poetry in English*, 183. Edouard Glissant, "Cross-Cultural Poetics," *Caribbean Discourse*, 140–141; Wilson Harris, "Creoleness: The Crossroads of a Civilization?" *The Unfinished Genesis of the Imagination. Selected Essays of Wilson Harris*, ed. Andrew Bundy (London: Routledge, 1999), 237–247; Gloria Anzaldua, *Borderlands / La Frontera* (2nd edn., San Francisco: Aunt Lute Books, 1999).

18. Cleanth Brooks, "The Waste Land: Critique of the Myth," *Modern Poetry and the Tradition* (1939) (rpt., New York: Oxford University Press, 1965), 136–172; Ronald Bush, "T. S. Eliot and Modernism at the Present Time: A Provocation," *T. S. Eliot: The Modernist in History*, ed. Ronald Bush (Cambridge: Cambridge University Press, 1991), 191–204; Terry Eagleton, *Criticism and Ideology* (1976) (rpt., London: Verso, 1985), 145–151.

19. T. S. Eliot, "War-paint and Feathers," review of *An Anthology of Songs and Chants from the Indians of North America*, *Athenaeum* 4668 (October 17, 1919), 1036.

20. Ronald Bush, "The Presence of the Past: Ethnographic Thinking / Literary Politics," *Prehistories of the Future: The Primitivist Project and the Culture of Modernism*, ed. Ronald Bush and Elazar Barkan (Stanford: Stanford University Press, 1995), 23–41.

21. Edward Watts, *Writing and Postcolonialism in the Early Republic* (Charlottesville: University Press of Virginia, 1998), 2, 17–18.

22. T. S. Eliot, *Notes Towards the Definition of Culture*, 63–64.

23. Edward Greene, *T. S. Eliot et la France* (Paris: Boivin, 1951); Warren Ramsey, *Jules Laforgue and the Ironic Inheritance* (New York: Oxford University Press, 1953); Kenner, *The Invisible Poet*, 13–39; T. S. Eliot, *Inventions of the March Hare: Poems, 1909–1917*, ed. Christopher Ricks (New York: Harcourt Brace, 1996), 399–410; Ronald Schuchard, *Eliot's Dark Angel: Intersections of Life and Art* (New York: Oxford University Press, 1999), 70–86; Vendler, *Coming of Age as a Poet*.

24. Eliot, "What Dante Means to Me," *To Criticize*, 126.

25. Symons, *The Symbolist Movement in Literature*, 296.

26. David Arkell, *Looking for Laforgue: An Informal Biography* (Manchester: Carcanet Press, 1979), 15.

27. Eliot, "From Poe to Valéry," *To Criticize*, 32, 34; Mallarmé, *Oeuvres complètes*, 241.

28. Arkell, *Looking for Laforgue*, 152; Jules Laforgue, "Complainte du Roi de Thulé," *Poems*, trans. Peter Dale (London: Anvil Press, 2007), 128.

29. Musgrove, *T. S. Eliot and Walt Whitman*, 31; Betsy Erkkila, *Walt Whitman Among the French: Poet and Myth* (Princeton: Princeton University Press, 1980), 69–70; Jay, *T. S. Eliot and the Poetics of Literary History*, 168; Oser, *T. S. Eliot and American Poetry*, 17.

30. Emile Blemont, "La Poésie en Angleterre et aux États-Unis, III, Walt Whitman," *La Renaissance Artistique et Littéraire* 7 (June 1872), 54–56; 11 (July 1872), 86–87, 90–91; and Therese Bentzon, "Un Poète américain, Walt Whitman: 'Muscle and Pluck Forever,'" *Revue des Deux Mondes* 42 (June 1872), 565–582.

31. Jules Laforgue, "*Les Brins d'herbe*: traduit de l'étonnant poète américain, Walt Whitman," *La Vogue* 1.10 (June 1886), 325–328; 1.11 (July 1886), 388–390; 2.3 (Aug. 1886), 73–76.

32. Anne Holmes, *Jules Laforgue and Poetic Innovation* (Oxford: Clarendon Press, 1993), 95, 99; Jules Laforgue, *Lettres à un ami (1880–6)*, ed. G. Jean-Aubry (Paris: Mercure de France, 1941), 193.

33. Erkkila, *Walt Whitman Among the French*, 69–70.

34. Walt Whitman, "Starting from Paumanok" (III, x), *Complete Poetry and Collected Prose*, ed. J. Kaplan (New York: Library of America, 1982), 177, 181.

35. Walt Whitman, "Night on the Prairies," *Complete Poetry and Collected Prose*, 566.

36. Matthiessen, *American Renaissance*, 529–530.

37. Vendler, *The Given and the Made*, 3.

38. Walt Whitman, "Prairie Analogies – The Tree Question," *Specimen Days*, in *Complete Poetry and Collected Prose*, 865.

39. Michael Collie, *Jules Laforgue* (London: Athlone Press, 1977), 2.

40. Jules Laforgue, "Albums," *Poésies complètes*, vol. II, ed. Pascal Pia (Paris: Gallimard, 1979), 110.

41. Jules Laforgue, "Cythère," *Poems*, 296.

42. Holmes, *Jules Laforgue and Poetic Innovation*, 82–94.

43. T. S. Eliot, "Lune de miel," *Complete Poems and Plays, 1909–1950* (New York: Harcourt Brace, 1971), 29; Grover Smith, *T. S. Eliot's Poetry and Plays* (Chicago: University of Chicago Press, 1956), 35.

44. Quoted in Hargrove, *Landscape as Symbol*, 168.

45. Lyndall Gordon, *T. S. Eliot: An Imperfect Life* (New York: Norton, 1998), 46–47.

46. Eric Sigg, "Eliot as a Product of America," *The Cambridge Companion to T. S. Eliot*, ed. D. Moody (Cambridge: Cambridge University Press, 1994), 28.

47. Sir Herbert Read, "T. S E. – a Memoir," in *T. S. Eliot: The Man and His Work*, ed. Tate, 15.

48. T. S. Eliot, "The Music of Poetry," *On Poetry and Poets* (London: Faber and Faber, 1957), 31; Eliot, "La Musique de la poésie," trans. Rachel Bespalof, *Fontaine* (Algiers), 27/28 (June/July 1943), 17–32.

49. Eliot, "The Music of Poetry," *On Poetry and Poets*, 31.

50. T. S. Eliot, "Mélange adultère de tout," *Complete Poems*, 28.

51. Eliot, "Mélange adultère de tout," *Complete Poems*, 29.

52. North, *Dialect of Modernism*, 9, 84, 77–79.

53. North, *Dialect of Modernism*, 83; Grover Smith, *T. S. Eliot's Poetry and Plays*, 35.

54. Feidelson, *Symbolism and American Literature*, 19; James Miller, *A Critical Guide to Leaves of Grass* (Chicago: University of Chicago Press, 1957), 155; Matthiessen, *American Renaissance*, 518, 519.

55. Henry Wadsworth Longfellow, *Complete Works*, vol. II (Boston: Houghton Mifflin, 1904), 117; E. C. Ross, "Whitman's Verse," *Modern Language Notes* (June 1930), 364.

56. Walt Whitman, "Pioneers! O Pioneers!," *Complete Poetry and Collected Prose*, 371–372, 374.

57. Gay Wilson Allen, *American Prosody* (New York: Farrar, Straus and Giroux, 1978), 173–174.

58. Autrey Nell Wiley, "Reiterative Devices in Leaves of Grass," *American Literature* 1.2 (May 1929), 163.

59. Robert Sayre, *Thoreau and the American Indians* (Princeton: Princeton University Press, 1977), 128.

60. T. S. Eliot, "Burbank with a Baedeker: Bleistein with a Cigar," *Complete Poems*, 24.

61. Musgrove, *T. S. Eliot and Walt Whitman*, 49–50; Oser, *T. S. Eliot and American Poetry*, 23.

62. T. S. Eliot, Chorus IX from *The Rock*, in *Complete Poems*, 111.

63. Ronald Bush, "The Presence of the Past: Ethnographic Thinking / Literary Politics," *Prehistories of the Future*, ed. Bush and Barkan, 33.

64. T. S. Eliot, *The Idea of a Christian Society* (1939), rpt. with *Notes Towards the Definition of Culture*, in *Christianity and Culture* (San Diego: Harcourt Brace Jovanovich, 1977), 49.

65. T. S. Eliot, "Ode on Independence Day, July 4th, 1918," *Inventions of the March Hare*, 383.

66. Grover Smith, *T. S. Eliot's Poetry and Plays*, 37.

67. Bloom, "Introduction," *T. S. Eliot's The Waste Land*, 1; McNelly Kearns, "Eliot, Russell, and Whitman," *T. S. Eliot's The Waste Land*, ed. Bloom, 144; Gordon, *T. S. Eliot: An Imperfect Life*, 124–125.

68. Hargrove, *Landscape as Symbol*, 121–123.

69. Robert Martin, *The Homosexual Tradition in American Poetry* (Iowa City: University of Iowa Press, 1998), 47–89; Joseph Cady, "Not Happy in the Capitol: Homosexuality and the Calamus Poems," *American Studies* 19 (Fall 1978), 5–22; James Miller, *A Critical Guide to Leaves of Grass*, 52–79; Betsy Erkkila, *Whitman: The Political Poet* (New York: Oxford University Press, 1989), 155–189.

70. Quoted in James Miller, *A Critical Guide to Leaves of Grass*, 71.

71. Bloom, "Introduction," *T. S. Eliot's The Waste Land*, 1; Gordon, *T. S. Eliot: An Imperfect Life*, 124–125; Walt Whitman, "O Hymen! O Hymenee," *Complete Poetry and Collected Prose*, 265.

72. Eliot, "American Literature and Language," *To Criticize*, 46.

73. Eliot, "The Music of Poetry," *On Poetry and Poets*, 35.

74. Eliot, "The Music of Poetry," *On Poetry and Poets*, 28.

75. Eliot, "The Music of Poetry," *On Poetry and Poets*, 29.

76. Oser, *T. S. Eliot and American Poetry*, 20.

77. Quoted in F. O. Matthiessen, "The 'Quartets,'" *Four Quartets: A Casebook*, ed. Bernard Bergonzi (London: Macmilllan, 1969), 96.

78. T. S. Eliot, "Note to the Third Edition," in Perse, *Anabasis: A Poem by St.-J. Perse*, trans. T. S. Eliot (3rd edn., London: Faber and Faber, 1959), 15.

79. T. S. Eliot, "Preface" (1930) to Perse, *Anabasis: A Poem by St.-J. Perse*, trans. T. S. Eliot (1st edn., London: Faber and Faber, 1930), 11.

80. Letter from T. S. Eliot to A. Léger (January 15, 1927), in Perse, *Honneur à Saint-John Perse* (Paris: Gallimard, 1965), 419; Eliot, "Preface" (1930), to Perse, *Anabasis*, 10.

81. Interview with Perse, *Le Figaro littéraire* (November 5, 1960).

82. Perse, *Anabasis* (3rd edn.), Canto 8, 50, 52.

83. T. S. Eliot, "Tradition and the Individual Talent," *The Sacred Wood* (London: Methuen, 1928), 59.

84. T. S. Eliot, "Note to Revised Edition" (1949) in Perse, *Anabasis* (3rd edn.), 13; Perse, *Anabasis* (3rd edn.), Canto 8.

85. T. S. Eliot, "A Commentary: That Poetry is Made with Words," *New English Weekly* 15.2 (April 27, 1939), 27–28.

86. Musgrove, *T. S. Eliot and Walt Whitman*, 10.

87. T. S. Eliot, "Difficulties of a Statesman," *Complete Poems*, 87.

88. Abel, "The Influence of St.-John Perse on T. S. Eliot," 223; Perse, *Anabasis* (3rd edn.), Canto 10, 60.

89. Eliot, "Difficulties of a Statesman," *Complete Poems*, 87–88.

90. Ricks, *T. S. Eliot and Prejudice*, 248.

91. Eliot, "Difficulties of a Statesman," *Complete Poems*, 87–88.

92. Valery Larbaud, "Éloges," in Perse, *Oeuvres complètes*, 1227.

93. Derek Walcott, "The Muse of History," *What the Twilight Says*, 50.

94. Erkkila, *Walt Whitman Among the French*, 217.

95. Arthur Knodel, *Saint-John Perse*, 46.

96. Edouard Glissant, "Saint-John Perse and the Caribbean," *Caribbean Discourse*, 226.

97. Perse, *Oeuvres complètes*, 922.

98. Perse, *Oeuvres complètes*, 640.

99. Rigolot, *Forged Genealogies*, 146–161.

100. Eliot, "Difficulties of a Statesman," *Complete Poems*, 88–89.

101. Bush, *T. S. Eliot*, 153, 128; Grover Smith, *T. S. Eliot's Poetry and Plays*, 160; Greene, *T. S. Eliot et la France*, 136 n.1; Abel, "The Influence of St.-John Perse on T. S. Eliot," 217–222.

102. Eliot, "Difficulties of a Statesman," *Complete Poems*, 88.

103. Abel, "The Influence of St.-John Perse on T. S. Eliot," 230.

104. T. S. Eliot, *Ash-Wednesday* (I), *Complete Poems*, 60.

105. Helen Gardner, *The Composition of "Four Quartets"* (London: Faber and Faber, 1978), 35; T. S. Eliot, *Burnt Norton*, IV, *Complete Poems*, 121.

106. Eliot may have known that most of the hybrids were created in Britain, France, Belgium and Germany, working with plants from Japan and China, during the mid to late nineteenth century.

107. Levie, *Commerce*, 170.

108. Elizabeth Cameron, "Alexis Saint-Léger Léger," *The Diplomats, 1919–1939*, ed. Gordon Craig and Felix Gilbert (Princeton: Princeton University Press, 1953), 382.

109. Cameron, "Alexis Saint-Léger Léger," 395.

110. For an account of Perse's American exile, see Jeffrey Mehlman, *Émigré New York: French Intellectuals in Wartime Manhattan, 1940–1944* (Baltimore, MD: Johns Hopkins University Press, 2000), 165–180.

111. Quoted in Cameron, "Alexis Saint-Léger Léger," 393–394.

112. Cameron, "Alexis Saint-Léger Léger," 384, 394, 405.

113. Cameron, "Alexis Saint-Léger Léger," 381.

114. Perse, *Oeuvres complètes*, 1231.

115. Perse, *Anabasis* (3rd edn.), Canto 6, 40, 42.

116. Saint-John Perse, *Anabasis*, trans. T. S. Eliot (New York: Harcourt Brace, 1938), 43, 45.

117. T. S. Eliot, "Note sur Mallarmé et Poe," trans. Roman Fernandez, *La Nouvelle Revue Française* (November 1, 1926), 525; Walt Whitman, "Starting from Paumanok" (VII), *Complete Poetry and Collected Prose*, 180.

118. Hugo Von Hofmannsthal, "Preface," trans. James Stern, in Perse, *Anabasis: A Poem by St.-J. Perse*, trans. T. S. Eliot (2nd edn., London: Faber and Faber, 1949), 86.

119. Slotkin, *Regeneration Through Violence*, 4.

120. Larbaud, "Éloges," in Perse, *Oeuvres complètes*, 1231.

121. Rigolot, *Forged Genealogies*, 145.

122. Whitman, "Starting from Paumanok" (XVI), 186.

123. Perse, Lettre à Adrienne Monnier (26 mars 1948), *Oeuvres complètes*, 553.

124. Perse, *Collected Poems*, 321.

125. Arthur Knodel, "Towards an Understanding of *Anabase*," *PMLA* 79.3 (June 1964), 330.

126. Knodel, "Towards an Understanding of *Anabase*," 336.

127. Eliot, "Preface" (1930), to Perse, *Anabasis*, 7–8; Knodel, "Towards an Understanding of *Anabase*," 330.

128. Rigolot, *Forged Genealogies*, 66.

129. Knodel, *Saint-John Perse*, 47–48.

130. Rigolot, *Forged Genealogies*, 108, 93.

131. Ostrovsky, *Under the Sign of Ambiguity*, 107.

132. Quoted in André Gide, "Don d'un arbre," *Les Cahiers de la Pléiade* (été–automne 1950), 26.

133. This ambiguity is compounded by the fact that another species of bird, *Parus cristatus*, is also called "crested tit," and is widely distributed throughout the Iberian Peninsula, France and Scotland, and across Europe and western Russia to the Ural Mountains.

134. Bush, *T. S. Eliot*, 126.

135. Albert Henry, *Anabase de Saint-John Perse* (Paris: Gallimard, 1983), 62.

136. Rigolot, *Forged Genealogies*, 86.

137. St.-John Perse, *Lettres d'Alexis Léger à Gabriel Frizeau*, ed. Albert Henry (Brussels: Académie Royale de Belgique, 1993), 171, 165.
138. Bhabha, *The Location of Culture*, 38.
139. Knodel, *Saint-John Perse*, 48.
140. Knodel, "Towards an Understanding of *Anabase*," 335.
141. Glissant, "Saint-John Perse and the Caribbean," *Caribbean Discourse*, 226.
142. Glissant, "Saint-John Perse and the Caribbean," *Caribbean Discourse*, 226.
143. See, for example, James Nolan, *Poet-Chief: The Native American Poetics of Walt Whitman and Pablo Neruda* (Albuquerque: University of New Mexico Press, 1994); Sylvia Molloy, "His America Our America: José Martí Reads Whitman," *Breaking Bounds: Whitman and American Cultural Studies*, ed. Betsy Erkkila and Jay Grossman (New York: Oxford University Press, 1996), 83–91.
144. Gordon, *T. S. Eliot: An Imperfect Life*, 240.
145. Grover Smith, *T. S. Eliot's Poetry and Plays*, 134; Gordon, *T. S. Eliot: An Imperfect Life*, 241.
146. T. S. Eliot, "Marina," *Complete Poems*, 72.
147. T. S. Eliot, "v. Cape Ann," *Landscapes*, in *Complete Poems*, 95.
148. T. S. Eliot, "The Influence of Landscape upon the Poet," *Daedalus* 89.2 (Spring, 1960), 421–422. The compound names of these sparrows, as well as the water thrush, are generally spelled without the hyphen.
149. T. S. Eliot, Preface to *This American World*, xiii–xiv.
150. The Northern Bobwhite, *Colinus virginianus*, is more common south of Cape Cod, but some are found farther north. Blackburnian warblers and water thrushes, members of the same family of Wood Warblers, *Parulidae*, are also found in New England but their distribution also extends farther south, to Georgia.
151. *The Oxford English Dictionary, Compact Edition*, II, 2057.
152. Eliot, "The Music of Poetry," *On Poetry and Poets*, 21; Eliot, "From Poe to Valéry," *To Criticize*, 38–39.
153. Hargrove, *Landscape as Symbol*, 113.
154. In 1700, Masconomo, the sagamore of the Agawam Indian nation, was paid £3/19s for all land rights to Manchester-by-the-Sea.
155. T. S. Eliot, "The Dry Salvages" (I), *Complete Poems*, 130–131.
156. Eliot, "The Influence of Landscape upon the Poet."
157. Gardner, *The Composition of "Four Quartets,"* 120.
158. Gardner, *The Composition of "Four Quartets,"* 53.
159. Gordon, *T. S. Eliot: An Imperfect Life*, 358.
160. Eliot, "American Literature and Language," *To Criticize*, 52.
161. Eliot, "American Literature and Language," *To Criticize*, 52; D. H. Lawrence, "Fenimore Cooper's White Novels," *Studies in Classic American Literature*, 51.
162. Helen Gardner, *The Art of T. S. Eliot* (New York: E. P. Dutton, 1950), 35.
163. Eliot, "The Influence of Landscape upon the Poet," 422.

164. T. S. Eliot, "Reflections on Vers Libre" (1917), *Selected Prose of T. S. Eliot*, ed. F. Kermode (New York: Harcourt Brace, 1975), 34.

165. Eliot, "A Commentary," 27; Eliot, "The Music of Poetry," *On Poetry and Poets*, 30.

166. T. S. Eliot, "Introduction" to *The Adventures of Huckleberry Finn* (1950), in *Huckleberry Finn* by Mark Twain (New York: Norton Critical Edition, 1998), 351–352, 354.

167. Eliot, "Preface" (1930), to Perse, *Anabase*, 10–11; T. S. Eliot, Introduction to *Ezra Pound: Selected Poems*, xi.

168. Kenner, *The Invisible Poet*, 315.

169. Ricks, *T. S. Eliot and Prejudice*, 275.

170. Gardner, *The Art of T. S. Eliot*, 49–50.

171. Eliot, "The Dry Salvages" (I), *Complete Poems*, 130–131.

172. T. S. Eliot, *The Waste Land: A Facsimile and Transcript of the Original Drafts*, ed. Valerie Eliot (New York: Harcourt Brace Jovanovich, 1971), 55, 57, 129 n.1.

173. Walt Whitman, *Sea Drift*, in *Complete Poetry and Collected Prose*, 388, 394, 398.

174. Walt Whitman, *Specimen Days*, *Prose Works 1892*, vol. I, ed. Floyd Stovall (New York: New York University Press, 1963), 138.

175. Kerry Larsen, *Whitman's Drama of Consensus* (Chicago: University of Chicago Press, 1988), 189; Kenner, *The Invisible Poet*, 305.

176. Gardner, *The Art of T. S. Eliot*, 123; Moody, "The American Strain," 80; Gordon, "The American Eliot," 44; Oser, *T. S. Eliot and American Poetry*, 117; Feidelson, *Symbolism and American Literature*, 213, 217; Jay, *T. S. Eliot and the Poetics of Literary History*, 168–171; Kearns, "Eliot, Russell, and Whitman," *T. S. Eliot's The Waste Land*, ed. Bloom, 137–152; Bloom, "Introduction," *T. S. Eliot's The Waste Land*, 1–7.

177. T. S. Eliot, "Whitman and Tennyson," *Nation and Athenaeum* (December 18, 1926), 426.

178. Gallup, "Mr. Eliot at the Churchill Club," 971.

179. Walt Whitman, *Song of Myself*, section 35, *Complete Poetry and Collected Prose*, 227–228.

180. Walt Whitman, *Song of Myself*, sections 35–36, *Complete Poetry and Collected Prose*, 229–230.

181. Moody, *Thomas Stearns Eliot*, 238.

182. Eliot, "A Commentary," *Criterion*, 289–290.

183. Ricks, *T. S. Eliot and Prejudice*, 207, 257, 258; Eliot, "Whitman and Tennyson," 426.

184. Abel, "The Influence of St.-John Perse on T. S. Eliot," 232–233.

185. Eric Sigg, "Eliot as a Product of America," *The Cambridge Companion to T. S. Eliot*, ed. Moody, 24.

186. Ricks, *T. S. Eliot and Prejudice*, 266–267.

187. Moody, "The American Strain," 87.

188. Helen Gardner, "The Landscapes of Eliot's Poetry," *Critical Quarterly* 10 (Winter 1968), 330.

3 FROM HARLEM TO HAITI: LANGSTON HUGHES, JACQUES ROUMAIN AND THE AVANT-GARDES

1. Langston Hughes, "Langston Hughes on Writing" (1961), *Essays*, 388.
2. Ezra Pound, "Harold Monro," *Polite Essays* (Norfolk, CT: New Directions, 1939), 14.
3. Langston Hughes, "The Ceaseless Rings of Walt Whitman" (1946), *Essays*, 482; Langston Hughes, "These Bad New Negroes: A Critique on Critics" (1927), *Essays*, 40.
4. Hutchinson, *The Harlem Renaissance in Black and White*, 96–97; Craig Werner, "Blues for T. S. Eliot and Langston Hughes: The Afro-Modernist Aesthetic of Harlem Gallery," *Black American Literature Forum* 24.3 (Fall 1990), 454; Arnold Rampersad, *The Life of Langston Hughes*, vol. 1 (New York: Oxford University Press, 1986), 29, 102–103; Arnold Rampersad, "Langston Hughes and Approaches to Modernism in the Harlem Renaissance," *The Harlem Renaissance: Revaluations*, ed. A. Singh, W. Shiver and S. Brodwin (New York: Garland, 1989), 52.
5. Steven Tracy, *Langston Hughes and the Blues* (Urbana: University of Illinois Press, 1988); James Emanuel, *Langston Hughes* (New York: Twayne, 1967); Richard Barksdale, *Langston Hughes: The Poet and His Critics* (Chicago: American Library Association, 1977); R. Baxter Miller, *The Art and Imagination of Langston Hughes* (Lexington: University Press of Kentucky, 1989); Onwuchekwa Jemie, *Langston Hughes: An Introduction to the Poetry* (New York: Columbia University Press, 1976).
6. T. J. Clark, *Farewell to an Idea: Episodes from a History of Modernism* (New Haven: Yale University Press, 1999); Wanda Corn, *The Great American Thing: Modern Art and National Identity, 1915–1935* (Berkeley: University of California Press, 1999); Walter Benn Michaels, *Our America: Nativism, Modernism, and Pluralism* (Durham, NC: Duke University Press, 1995).
7. Rampersad, *The Life*; Faith Berry, *Langston Hughes: Before and Beyond Harlem* (Westport, CT: Lawrence Hill, 1983); Edward J. Mullen, *Langston Hughes in the Hispanic World and Haiti* (Hemden, CT: Arcon, 1977).
8. David Roessel, "'A Racial Act': The Letters of Langston Hughes and Ezra Pound," *Ezra Pound and African American Modernism*, ed. Michael Coyle (Orono, ME: National Poetry Foundation, 2001), 214.
9. Langston Hughes, "Jazz as Communication," *Essays*, 370.
10. Henry James, "Paris Revisited," *Galaxy* 24.1 (January 1878), 6; Malcom Cowley, *Exile's Return: A Literary Odyssey of the 1920s* (New York: Viking, 1956), 102.
11. Langston Hughes, *The Big Sea* (New York: Hill and Wang, 1993), 163–164.
12. Letter from Langston Hughes to Alain Locke, April 6, 1923, quoted in Berry, *Langston Hughes*, 52.
13. Frederick Douglass, "Letter from Paris" (November 19, 1887), *Americans in Paris: A Literary Anthology*, ed. Adam Gopnik (New York: Library of America, 2004), 167.

14. James Weldon Johnson, *Along This Way* (New York: Viking Press, 1933), 209.

15. Michel Fabre, *From Harlem to Paris: Black American Writers in France, 1840–1980* (Urbana: University of Illinois Press, 1993), 70.

16. Hughes, *The Big Sea*, 62.

17. Alfred J. Guillaume, "And Bid Him Translate: Langston Hughes's Translations of Poetry from French," *Langston Hughes Review* 4.2 (Fall 1985), 1–2.

18. Hughes, *The Big Sea*, 144, 140.

19. Hughes, *The Big Sea*, 33–34.

20. Langston Hughes, "Jazzonia," *The Collected Poems of Langston Hughes*, ed. A. Rampersad (New York: Knopf, 1994), 34.

21. Langston Hughes, "Negro Dancers," *Collected Poems*, 44, 617. The poem was first published in *Crisis* (March 1925), and reprinted in *The Weary Blues*. As Rampersad notes, lines 3, 6 and 15 were subsequently changed for publication in the volume *The Dream Keeper*, to "Two mo' ways to do de Charleston."

22. Fabre, *From Harlem to Paris*, 66.

23. Rampersad, *The Life*, 344.

24. Langston Hughes, *I Wonder as I Wander* (1956) (rpt. New York: Hill and Wang, 1964), 400.

25. Tristan Tzara, "Dada Manifesto" [1918] and "Lecture on Dada" [1922], *Dada Painters and Poets*, ed. Robert Motherwell (Cambridge, MA: Belknap Press, 2005), 78–79, 81, 246–251.

26. Douglas Clayton, *Pierrot in Petrograd: The Commedia dell'Art / Balagan in Twentieth Century Russian Theatre and Drama* (Montreal: McGill-Queen's University Press, 1993).

27. Quoted in Kenner, *The Invisible Poet*, 84.

28. Langston Hughes, *The American Negro Reference Book*, ed. John P. Davis (Englewood Cliffs, NJ: Prentice-Hall, 1966), 832.

29. Louis Aragon, "Magnitogorsk," trans. Langston Hughes, *Littérature internationale* 4 (1933–1934), 82–83.

30. Berry, *Langston Hughes*, 257; Rampersad, *The Life*, 339; Fabre, *From Harlem to Paris*, 72.

31. Hughes, *I Wonder As I Wander*, 318; Fabre, *From Harlem to Paris*, 73.

32. Langston Hughes, "The Alliance of Antifascist Intellectuals, Madrid," *Essays*, 151.

33. Rampersad, "Langston Hughes and Approaches to Modernism," 63.

34. Ezra Pound, "Irony, Laforgue and Some Satire," *Literary Essays of Ezra Pound*, ed. T. S. Eliot (Norfolk, CT: New Directions, 1954), 283–284, 282.

35. Adriane Despot, "Jean-Gaspard Deburau and the Pantomime at the Théâtre des Funambules," *Education Theater Journal* 27.3 (October 1975), 364–376; Martin Green and John Swan, *The Triumph of Pierrot: The Commedia dell'Arte and the Modern Imagination* (University Park: Pennsylvania State University Press, 1986), 11.

36. Holmes, *Jules Laforgue and Poetic Innovation*, 31, 34–35.

37. Michael Collie and J. M. L'Heureux, Introduction to Jules Laforgue, *Derniers Vers* (Toronto: University of Toronto Press, 1965), 5.
38. Langston Hughes, "March Moon," *Collected Poems*, 93.
39. Langston Hughes, "Pierrot," *Collected Poems*, 95–96.
40. Madhuri Deshmukh, "Langston Hughes as Black Pierrot: A Transatlantic Game of Masks," *Langston Hughes Review* 18 (Fall 2004), 4.
41. Holmes, *Jules Laforgue and Poetic Innovation*, 53.
42. Anita Patterson, "Jazz, Realism, and the Modernist Lyric: The Poetry of Langston Hughes," *Modern Language Quarterly* 61.4 (December 2000), 651–682.
43. Langston Hughes, "The Black Pierrot," *Collected Poems*, 31.
44. Charles Baudelaire, "De L'Essence du Rire" (1855), quoted in Malcom McIntosh, "Baudelaire's Caricature Essays," *Modern Language Notes* 71.7 (November 1956), 504.
45. Langston Hughes, "The Fascination of Cities," *Essays*, 31.
46. Louis Aragon, "Magnitogorsk," *Hourra l'Oural* (Paris: Denoel 35 Steele, 1934); Aragon, "Magnitogorsk," trans. Hughes, 82.
47. Aragon, "Magnitogorsk," trans. Hughes, 82–83.
48. Dash, *The Other America*, 30.
49. Elazar Barkan, "Introduction," *Prehistories of the Future*, ed. Barkan and Bush, 13.
50. Charles Baudelaire, "Les Ténèbres" and "Le Crépuscule du soir," *Les Fleurs du mal*, 76–77, 180.
51. Charles Baudelaire, "La Fin de la journée," *Les Fleurs du mal*, 250–251.
52. Langston Hughes, "Dream Variations," *Collected Poems*, 40.
53. Jules Laforgue, "Complainte des nostalgies préhistoriques," *Poems of Jules Laforgue*, trans. Peter Dale (London: Anvil Press, 1986), 86.
54. Langston Hughes, "My Poems and Myself" (July 12, 1945), *Essays*, 255–256.
55. Walter Farrell and Patricia Johnson, "Poetic Interpretations of Urban Black Folk Culture: Langston Hughes and the 'Bebop' Era," *MELUS* 8.3 (1981), 61; Steven Tracy, *Langston Hughes and the Blues*, 224–225; Robert O'Brien Hokanson, "Jazzing It Up: The Be-bop Modernism of Langston Hughes," *Mosaic* 31.4 (December 1998), 64–65, 70.
56. David Chinitz, *T. S. Eliot and the Cultural Divide* (Chicago: University of Chicago Press, 2003), 37.
57. In *Figures in Black*, Gates remarks, "We are forced to wonder aloud where in dialect poetry, with the notable exception of Sterling Brown, a black poet used his medium as effectively as did Eliot in *Sweeney Agonistes*" (289 n.17).
58. Brent Edwards, *The Practice of Diaspora: Literature, Translation, and the Rise of Black Internationalism* (Cambridge, MA: Harvard University Press, 2003), 65.
59. Langston Hughes, "Jazz Band in a Parisian Cabaret," *Collected Poems*, 60.
60. Edwards, *The Practice of Diaspora*, 66; Fabre, *From Harlem to Paris*, 66.
61. T. S. Eliot, "Marie Lloyd," *Selected Essays*, 405–408.
62. Hughes, "Jazz Band in a Parisian Cabaret," 60.
63. Chinitz, *T. S. Eliot and the Cultural Divide*, 33–34.

64. T. S. Eliot, "Suite Clownesque" (111), *Inventions of the March Hare*, 35.

65. T. S. Eliot, "The smoke that gathers blue and sinks," *Inventions of the March Hare*, 70.

66. Langston Hughes, "Trumpet Player," *Collected Poems*, 338, 657.

67. Hughes, "Trumpet Player," 338.

68. Quoted in Robert Farnsworth, *Melvin Tolson, 1898–1966: Plain Talk and Poetic Prophecy* (Columbia: University of Missouri Press, 1984), 141–142.

69. T. S. Eliot, "Conclusion," *The Use of Poetry and the Use of Criticism* (1933) (rpt., Cambridge, MA: Harvard University Press, 1964), 151; Langston Hughes, "Dream Boogie," *Collected Poems*, 388.

70. Chinitz, *T. S. Eliot and the Cultural Divide*, 28; Douglas, *Terrible Honesty*, 354; Howard Rye, "Fearsome Means of Discord: Early Encounters with Black Jazz," *Black Music in Britain*, ed. Paul Oliver (Philadelphia: Open University Press, 1990), 45.

71. North, *Dialect of Modernism*, 10; Chinitz, *T. S. Eliot and the Cultural Divide*.

72. Eliot, "From Poe to Valéry," *To Criticize*, 32.

73. Eliot, "The Music of Poetry," *On Poetry and Poets*, 22.

74. Langston Hughes, "The Roots of Jazz" (1958?), *Essays*, 370–371.

75. Rampersad, "Langston Hughes and Approaches to Modernism," 52, 61.

76. Langston Hughes, "Concerning Nicolás Guillén" (September 29, 1948), *Essays*, 485; Mullen, *Langston Hughes in the Hispanic World and Haiti*.

77. Langston Hughes, "Jamaica," *Essays*, 284.

78. Langston Hughes, "Foreword," *Poems from Black Africa* (1963), *Essays*, 508.

79. Quoted in Henry Louis Gates, Preface to *Langston Hughes: Critical Perspectives Past and Present*, ed. H. L. Gates and K. A. Appiah (New York: Amistad, 1993), x.

80. Louis Aragon, "Car c'est de l'homme qu'il s'agit," *Les lettres françaises*, November 3, 1960, rpt. *Honneur à Saint-John Perse*, 576–577.

81. Senghor and Damas first discovered Hughes in the *Revue du Monde Noir* during the early 1930s. Hughes translated three poems by Damas that were published in his 1949 anthology, *The Poetry of the Negro*, as well as Senghor's "To the American Negro Troops," which appeared in *An African Treasury*; and Senghor reciprocated by translating a number of Hughes's poems into French.

82. Léopold Sédar Senghor, "Saint-John Perse ou Poésie du Royaume d'Enfance," *La Table ronde* (mai 1962), *Liberté*, vol. 1 (Paris: Éditions du Seuil, 1964), 352–353; Michel Fabre, "Du mouvement nouveau noir à la négritude césairienne," *Soleil éclaté*, ed. Jacqueline Leiner (Tubingen: Gunther Grass Verlag, 1984), 149–159; Lilyan Kesteloot, *Black Writers in French*, trans. Ellen Kennedy (rpt., Washington, DC: Howard University Press, 1991), 56–74.

83. Aimé Césaire, "Introduction to Negro American Poetry," *Tropiques* 3 (October 1941), 42; Fabre, *From Harlem to Paris*, 157; Thomas Hale, "From Afro-America to Afro-France: The Literary Triangle Trade," *French Review* 49.6 (May 1976), 1094; Charles Rowell, "It is Through Poetry that one Copes with Solitude: An Interview with Aimé Césaire," *Callaloo* 388 (Winter 1989), 51.

84. Langston Hughes, "Draft Ideas" (December 3, 1964), *Essays*, 408.

85. Yves Bonnefoy, 'L'Illumination et l'éloge," *Le Nuage rouge* (Paris: Mercure de France, 1977), 221; Ostrovsky, *Under the Sign of Ambiguity*, 53–54, 116; Rigolot, *Forged Genealogies*, 27–28.

86. Arnold, *Modernism and Negritude*, 54, 66.

87. Derek Walcott, "The Muse of History," *What the Twilight Says*, 51–52.

88. Aimé Césaire, "Cérémonie vaudou pour Saint John Perse . . . ," *The Collected Poetry*, trans. Clayton Eshleman and Annette Smith (Berkeley: University of California Press, 1983), 374.

89. Césaire, "Cérémonie vaudou pour Saint John Perse . . . ," *The Collected Poetry*, 374.

90. Jacques Roumain, *Oeuvres complètes*, ed. Léon-François Hoffmann (Paris: Collection Archivos, 2003), 722–723.

91. D'Henock Trouillot, *Dimension et limites de Jacques Roumain*, (2nd edn., Port au Prince, Haiti: Éditions Faradin, 1981), 19, 53; Carolyn Fowler, *A Knot in the Thread: The Life and Work of Jacques Roumain* (Washington, DC: Howard University Press, 1980), 20, 22.

92. Roger Dorsinville, *Jacques Roumain* (Paris: Présence Africaine, 1981), 31.

93. Dorsinville, *Jacques Roumain*, 64.

94. Jacques Roumain, "Le Buvard: le chant de l'homme," *Oeuvres complètes*, 22; Fowler, *A Knot in the Thread*, 19.

95. Léon-François Hoffmann, "Introduction," in Roumain, *Oeuvres complètes*, xxxvi.

96. Hoffmann, "Introduction," in Roumain, *Oeuvres complètes*, xli; Jacques Roumain, "Le sacrifice du Tambour-Assôtô," *Oeuvres complètes*, 1076.

97. Jacques Roumain, "Le Buvard: orage" and "À jouer aux billes," *Oeuvres complètes*, 21, 29.

98. Jacques Roumain, *When the Tom-Tom Beats: Selected Prose and Poems*, trans. Joanne Fungaroli and Ronald Sauer (Washington, DC: Azul, 1995), 22.

99. Jacques Roumain, "Discours de Jacques Roumain," *Oeuvres complètes*, 693–694.

100. Michel Fabre, "Hughes's Literary Reputation in France," *Langston Hughes Review* 6.1 (Spring 1987), 25.

101. Hughes's translations of Roumain 's "Quand Bat le tam-tam" and "Guinée" were published in *Anthology of Contemporary Latin-American Poetry*, ed. Dudley Fitts (Connecticut: New Directions, 1942), and in *The Poetry of the Negro, 1746–1949*, ed. Langston Hughes and Arna Bontemps (Garden City, NY: Doubleday, 1949). His translation of *Gouverneurs de la rosée*, done in collaboration with Mercer Cook, was completed in 1945 and published two years later.

102. Langston Hughes, "An Appeal for Jacques Roumain" [Letter to the Editor], *Essays*, 554–555; Hughes, "An Appeal for Jacques Roumain," *New Masses* (January 1935), 34.

103. Langston Hughes, Address to the Second International Writers' Congress, Paris, July 1937, *Good Morning, Revolution: Uncollected Writings of Social Protest*, ed. Faith Berry (New York: Lawrence Hill, 1973), 99.

104. Naomi Garrett, *The Renaissance of Haitian Poetry* (Paris: Présence Africaine, [1963]), 116; Martha Cobb, *Harlem, Haiti, and Havana: A Comparative Critical Study of Langston Hughes, Jacques Roumain, Nicolás Guillén* (Washington, DC: Three Continents Press, 1979), 88–89; Carolyn Fowler, "The Shared Vision of Langston Hughes and Jacques Roumain," *Black American Literature Forum* 15.3 (Autumn 1981), 84–88; Trouillot, *Dimension et limites*, 22.

105. Maurice Lubine, "Langston Hughes and Haiti," trans. Faith Berry, *Langston Hughes Review* 6.1 (Spring 1987), 6.

106. Jean Price-Mars, "À Propos de la 'Renaissance nègre' aux États-Unis," *La Relève* (July, Aug., Sept., 1932) [Nendeln: Kraus Reprint, 1970], 10.

107. Hughes, *I Wonder as I Wander*, 29–32, 319; "Dinner Reception to be Given Haitian by Writers and Artists," *New York Age*, November 11, 1939, 7.

108. Hughes, *I Wonder as I Wander*, 3.

109. Langston Hughes, "A Letter from Haiti" [letter to the editor], *New Masses* 7 (July 1931–1932), 9; Langston Hughes, "People without Shoes," *New Masses* 12 (October 1931), 12; "Un Nègre américain nous abîme," *Haiti-Journal* (July 26, 1934).

110. Langston Hughes, "White Shadows in a Black Land," *Crisis* 41 (May 1932), 157; Langston Hughes, "An Impression of Haiti," *New Republic* (September 25, 1960), 22; Langston Hughes, "Haiti: Mood for Maracas," *New Republic* 145 (September 25, 1961), 22.

111. Fowler, "The Shared Vision," 85.

112. Hughes, *I Wonder as I Wander*, 31.

113. Jacques Roumain, "Présentation de Langston Hughes," *Oeuvres complètes*, 635–636.

114. Émile Ollivier, "L'internationalisme de Jacques Roumain et ses zones d'ombre," in Roumain, *Oeuvres complètes*, 1301.

115. Antonio Vieux, "Entre nous: Jacques Roumain," *La Revue indigène* (September 1927), 103–104; Garrett, *The Renaissance of Haitian Poetry*, 109.

116. Jacques Roumain, "Comment on traite les nègres aux États-Unis," *Le Petit Impartial* (29 February 1928).

117. Jacques Roumain, "Lettre à Tristan Rémy," *Oeuvres complètes*, 639.

118. Jacques Roumain, "Le Buvard: insomnie," *La Revue indigéne* (September 1927).

119. Langston Hughes, "Summer Night," *Collected Poems*, 59.

120. Fowler, *A Knot in the Thread*, 101; Mercer Cook, "Introduction," *Masters of the Dew*, trans. Langston Hughes and Mercer Cook (New York: Collier Books, 1971), 19; Jacques Roumain, "Midi" and "Le Buvard: calme," *Oeuvres complètes*, 13, 24.

121. Jacques Roumain, "Art poétique," *Oeuvres complètes*, 581.

122. Marc Roland Thadal, *Jacques Roumain: l'unité d'une oeuvre* (Port-au-Prince, Haiti: Collection Quisqueye, 1997), 11.

123. Jacques Roumain, "Créole," *Haiti-Journal* (July 6, 1931), *When the Tom-Tom Beats*, 22.

124. Jacques Roumain, "La Danse du poète-clown," *Oeuvres complètes*, 17; Pradel Pompilus, "De l'élégie à la poésie entraînante," in Roumain, *Oeuvres complètes*, 1499.
125. Jacques Roumain, "S'échapper," *Oeuvres complètes*, 83.
126. Fowler, *A Knot in the Thread*, 134.
127. Langston Hughes, "Danse africaine," *Collected Poems*, 28; Jacques Roumain, "Quand bat le tam-tam," *Oeuvres complètes*, 44.
128. Langston Hughes, "When The Tom-Tom Beats," *The Poetry of the Negro*, ed. Hughes and Bontemps, 365.
129. Jacques Roumain, "Langston Hughes," *Oeuvres complètes*, 47.
130. Michael Dash, "Engagement, Exile, and Errance: Some Trends in Haitian Poetry, 1946–1986," *Callaloo* 15.3 (Summer 1992), 747.
131. Langston Hughes, "A Poem for Jacques Roumain (Late Poet of Haiti)" (ms.), March 25, 1945, quoted in Berry, *Langston Hughes*, 311–313.
132. Langston Hughes, "Black Writers in a Troubled World" (March 26, 1966), *Essays*, 476–477.

4 SIGNIFYING MODERNISM IN WILSON HARRIS'S *ETERNITY TO SEASON*

1. Wilson Harris, *Tradition, the Writer, and Society: Critical Essays* (London: New Beacon, 1967), 46.
2. Eva Searl, "T. S. Eliot's *Four Quartets* and Wilson Harris' *The Waiting Room*," *Commonwealth Literature and the Modern World*, ed. H. Maes-Jelinek (Brussels: Didier, 1976), 51–59.
3. Bruce King, *New English Literatures: Cultural Nationalism[s] in a Changing World* (New York: St. Martin's Press, 1980), 109–110.
4. King, *New English Literatures*, 109–110.
5. Pollard, *New World Modernisms*, 3.
6. Gikandi, *Writing in Limbo*, 4.
7. Hena Maes-Jelinek, "'Numinous Proportions'; Wilson Harris's Alternative to All 'Posts,'" *Past the Last Post: Theorizing Post-Colonialism and Post-Modernism*, ed. Ian Adam and Helen Tiffin (Calgary, Alberta, Canada: University of Calgary Press, 1990), 47–64.
8. Wilson Harris, "Originality and Tradition," *The Radical Imagination: Lectures and Talks by Wilson Harris*, ed. Alan Riach and Mark Williams (Liège: University of Liège, 1992), 124.
9. Ashis Nandy, *The Intimate Enemy: Loss and Recovery of Self under Colonialism* (Delhi: Oxford University Press, 1983), xiv; Benita Parry, "The Postcolonial: Conceptual Category or Chimera?" *Yearbook of English Studies* 27 (1997), 3–21.
10. Eliot, *Notes Towards the Definition of Culture*, 114.
11. Gates, *Figures in Black*, xxxi.
12. Wilson Harris, "Artifice and Root," *The Womb of Space: The Cross-Cultural Imagination* (Westport, CT: Greenwood Press, 1983), 124.

13. Stuart Murray, "Postcoloniality/Modernity: Wilson Harris and Postcolonial Theory," *Review of Contemporary Fiction* 17.2 (Summer 1997), 55.

14. Sandra Drake, *Wilson Harris and the Modern Tradition* (New York: Greenwood Press); Michael Gilkes, *Wilson Harris and the Caribbean Novel* (London: Longman, 1975), 1–21; Rolstan Adams, "Wilson Harris: The Pre-novel Poet," *Journal of Commonwealth Literature* 13.3 (April 1979), 71–85; Rhonda Cobham, "The Texts of Wilson Harris' *Eternity to Season*," *World Literature Written in English* 22 (Spring 1983), 27–38; W. J. Howard, "Shaping a New Voice: The Poetry of Wilson Harris," *Commonwealth Newsletter* 9 (January 1976), 26–31.

15. Joyce Adler, "Melville and Harris: Poetic Imaginations Related in Their Response to the Modern World," *Commonwealth Literature and the Modern World*, ed. Hena Maes-Jelinek (Brussels: Didier, 1976), 33–41.

16. Kenneth Ramchand, *The West Indian Novel and its Background* (New York: Barnes and Noble, 1970), 8; Hena Maes-Jelinek, "Natural and Psychological Landscapes," *Journal of Commonwealth Literature* 7.1 (1971), 117–120; Nick Wilkinson, "The Novel and a Vision of the Land," *Awakened Conscience: Studies in Commonwealth Literature*, ed. C. D. Narasimhaiah (New Delhi: Sterling, 1978), 185–194.

17. Wilson Harris, "The Music of Living Landscapes," *The Unfinished Genesis of the Imagination: Selected Essays of Wilson Harris*, ed. A. Bundy (London: Routledge Press, 1999), 40.

18. Wilson Harris, "Books – A Long View," *Tradition, The Writer, and Society*, 21.

19. Wilson Harris, "Trail," *Eternity to Season* (London: New Beacon, 1978), 43.

20. Kenneth Andrews, *Trade, Plunder, and Settlement: Maritime Enterprise and the Genesis of the British Empire, 1480–1630* (Cambridge: Cambridge University Press, 1984), 303; Vere Daly, *The Making of Guyana* (London: Macmillan, 1974), 35, 19.

21. T. S. Eliot, "Tradition and the Individual Talent," *The Sacred Wood* (New York: Barnes and Noble, 1960), 51.

22. Eliot, "Tradition and the Individual Talent," 51.

23. Ronald Bush, "The Presence of the Past: Ethnographic Thinking / Literary Politics," *Prehistories of the Future*, ed. Bush and Barkan, 40–41.

24. Eliot, "War-paint and Feathers."

25. Maes-Jelinek, "Numinous Proportions," 54–55.

26. Wilson Harris, "The Phenomenal Legacy," *Explorations*, ed. H. Maes-Jelinek (Aarhus: Dangaroo Press, 1981), 47.

27. Pratt, *Imperial Eyes*, 6.

28. Wilson Harris, "A Talk on the Subjective Imagination," *Explorations*, 63.

29. Wilson Harris, "Adversarial Contexts and Creativity," *New Left Review* 154 (November/December 1985), 126–127.

30. Wilson Harris, "Profiles of Myth in the New World," *Selected Essays of Wilson Harris*, 202; Wilson Harris, "Oedipus and the Middle Passage," *Crisis and Creativity in the New Literatures in English*, ed. Geoffrey V. Davis and Hena Maes-Jelinek (Atlanta, GA: Rodopi, 1999), 10.

31. Wilson Harris, "Comedy and Modern Allegory: A Personal View," *A Shaping of Connections: Commonwealth Literature Studies – Then and Now*, ed. Hena Maes-Jelinek, Kirsten Holst Petersen and Anna Rutherford (Aarhus: Dangaroo Press, 1989), 137.

32. F. R. Leavis, *For Continuity* (Cambridge: The Minority Press, 1933).

33. Wilson Harris, "The Frontier on Which *Heart of Darkness* Stands," *Explorations*, 139.

34. Wilson Harris, "Continuity and Discontinuity," *Selected Essays of Wilson Harris*, 183.

35. Eliot, "Tradition and the Individual Talent," *The Sacred Wood*, 49.

36. Wilson Harris, "Art and Criticism," *Tradition, the Writer, and Society*, 7; Harris, "Literacy and Imagination," *The Literate Imagination: Essays on the Novels of Wilson Harris*, ed. Michael Gilkes (London: Macmillan, 1989), 27.

37. Eliot, "Tradition and the Individual Talent," *The Sacred Wood*, 50, 59.

38. Harris, "A Talk on the Subjective Imagination," *Explorations*, 63; Wilson Harris, "The Native Phenomenon," *Explorations*, 51.

39. Monica Pozzi, "A Conversation with Wilson Harris," *Journal of Caribbean Literatures* 2.1–3 (Spring 2000), 266.

40. Wilson Harris, "Preface: Cross Cultural Community and the Womb of Space," *Selected Essays of Wilson Harris*, 177.

41. Gikandi, *Writing in Limbo*, 24.

42. Wilson Harris, "Tradition and the West Indian Novel," *Tradition, the Writer, and Society*, 30–31.

43. Wilson Harris, "Trail," *Eternity to Season*, 43.

44. William Empson, *Some Versions of Pastoral* (London: Chatto and Windus, 1935), 188.

45. William Wordsworth, *The Fourteen-Book Prelude*, ed. W. J. B. Owen (Ithaca: Cornell University Press), 131, VI, lines 620–622, 625–641.

46. William Wordsworth, "Elegiac Verses," *Poems, In Two Volumes, and Other Poems, 1800–1807*, ed. Jared Curtis (Ithaca: Cornell University Press, 1983), 616, VI, lines 56–57.

47. See, for example, "Bad Talk and Sweet Speaking," *CRNLE Reviews Journal* (May 1979), 45.

48. Wilson Harris, "Across the Editor's Desk," *Kyk-over-al* 35 (October 1986), 3.

49. Wilson Harris, "Laocoon," *Eternity to Season*, 45.

50. Wilson Harris, "The Fabric of the Imagination," *The Radical Imagination*, 74.

51. Harris, "Laocoon," *Eternity to Season*, 45.

52. Paula Burnett, "Opening New Doors: Harris and Walcott," *Theatre of the Arts*, ed. Hena Maes-Jelinek and Bénédicte Ledent (Amsterdam: Rodopi, 1992), 68–69.

53. Thomas Hardy, "The Discovery," *The Complete Poems of Thomas Hardy*, ed. James Gibson (London: Macmillan London Ltd., 1976), 332.

54. Harris, "The Fabric of the Imagination," *The Radical Imagination*, 75.

55. Harris, "Laocoon," *Eternity to Season*, lines 10–12, 18–22.

56. Wilson Harris, "Originality and Tradition," *The Radical Imagination*, 123.

57. T. S. Eliot, "Unity and Diversity: the Region," *Notes Towards the Definition of Culture*, 62; Wilson Harris interviewed by Alan Riach, *The Radical Imagination*, 41.
58. Wilson Harris, "Creation," *Eternity to Season*, 49.
59. Harris, "Creation," *Eternity to Season*, 49–50.
60. Harold Bloom, *A Map of Misreading* (Oxford: Oxford University Press, 1975), 180; Richard Adams, "Whitman's 'Lilacs' and the Tradition of Pastoral Elegy," *PMLA* 72.3 (June 1957), 479–487.
61. Quoted in Rolstan Adams, "Wilson Harris: The Pre-novel Poet," 71.
62. Bloom, *A Map of Misreading*, 181–182; Walt Whitman, *As I Ebb'd with the Ocean of Life* (II), *Complete Poetry and Collected Prose*, 394–395.
63. Wilson Harris, "The Amerindian Legacy," *Selected Essays of Wilson Harris*, 174.
64. Wilson Harris, "In the Name of Liberty," *Selected Essays of Wilson Harris*, 213.
65. Wilson Harris, "Home," *Eternity to Season*, 35.
66. "Canje" was omitted from the 1978 New Beacon edition of *Eternity to Season*.
67. Harris, "Canje," *Eternity to Season*, 72.
68. Wilson Harris, "The Golden Age," *Eternity to Season*, 47.
69. Harris, "Creation," *Eternity to Season*, 49.
70. Gilroy, *The Black Atlantic*, 34.
71. Harris, "Artifice and Root," *The Womb of Space*, 119, 120; Wilson Harris, "History, Fable and Myth in the Caribbean and Guianas," *Explorations*, 26.
72. Harris, "The Music of Living Landscapes," *Selected Essays of Wilson Harris*, 41.
73. Wilson Harris, "Behring Straits," *Eternity to Season*, 13–14.
74. Paula Burnett, "Opening New Doors: A Glimpse of Wilson Harris and Derek Walcott," *Theatre of the Arts: Wilson Harris and the Caribbean*, ed. Hena Maes-Jelinek and Bénédicte Ledent (Amsterdam: Rodopi, 2002), 72.
75. Gilkes, *Wilson Harris and the Caribbean Novel*, 12.
76. Harris, "History, Fable and Myth," *Explorations*, 156.
77. Wilson Harris, "Some Aspects of Myth and the Intuitive Imagination," *Explorations*, 100.
78. Derek Walcott, *Another Life*, in *Collected Poems, 1948–1984* (New York: Farrar, Straus and Giroux, 1986), Chapter 22, section 1, 285.
79. T. S. Eliot, "The Dry Salvages" (II), *Complete Poems*, 133.
80. Eliot, "The Dry Salvages" (III), *Complete Poems*, 135.
81. T. S. Eliot, "'Ulysses,' Order, and Myth," *Selected Prose of T. S. Eliot*, 175, 177; Richard Ellmann, *James Joyce* (New York: Oxford University Pres, 1969), 514, 526, 536–539.
82. Wilson Harris, "Carnival of Psyche: Jean Rhys's Wide Sargasso Sea," *Explorations*, 125–126.
83. Harris, "History, Fable and Myth," *Explorations*, 156.
84. Michael Bell, *Literature, Modernism and Myth: Belief and Responsibility in the Twentieth Century* (Cambridge: Cambridge University Press, 1997).
85. Harris, "History, Fable, and Myth," *Explorations*, 166.
86. Harris, "Continuity and Discontinuity," *Selected Essays of Wilson Harris*, 177.

87. Wilson Harris, "The Absent Presence: The Caribbean, Central and South America," *The Radical Imagination*, 91–92.

88. Wilson Harris, "Cumberland," *Eternity to Season*, 65.

89. Harris, "Profiles of Myth," *Selected Essays of Wilson Harris*, 201.

90. Harris, "Profiles of Myth," *Selected Essays of Wilson Harris*, 201.

91. Wilson Harris, "Tiresias," *Eternity to Season*, 31.

92. T. S. Eliot, *The Waste Land, Complete Poems*, 52 n.218.

93. Walter Rodney, *A History of the Guyanese Working People, 1881–1905* (Baltimore: Johns Hopkins University Press, 1981), 1.

94. Bonham Richardson, *The Caribbean in the Wider World 1492–1992* (Cambridge: Cambridge University Press, 1992), 136.

95. Orlando Patterson, "Migration in Caribbean Societies: Socioeconomic and Symbolic Resource," *Human Migration: Patterns and Policies*, ed. W. McNeill (Bloomington: Indiana University Press, 1978), 115.

96. Wilson Harris, "Creative and Re-creative Balance Between Diverse Cultures," *The Radical Imagination*, 112–113.

5 BEYOND APPRENTICESHIP: DEREK WALCOTT'S PASSAGE TO THE AMERICAS

1. Derek Walcott, interview with Edward Hirsch (1985), *Conversations with Derek Walcott*, ed. William Baer (Jackson: University of Mississippi Press, 1996), 103.

2. Derek Walcott, Interview, *South Bank Show*, ITV, London, January 15, 1989.

3. Keith Alleyne, review of *Epitaph for the Young, Critical Perspectives on Derek Walcott*, ed. Robert Hamner (Boulder, CO: Three Continents Press, 1997), 100; Stewart Brown, "The Apprentice: *25 Poems, Epitaph for the Young, Poems* and *In a Green Night*," *The Art of Derek Walcott*, ed. Stuart Brown (Chester Springs, PA: Dufour, 1991), 16; Robert Hamner, *Derek Walcott* (New York: Twayne, 1993), 23; A. Alvarez, "Visions of Light," *New York Review of Books*, May 11, 2000, 27.

4. Rei Terada, *Derek Walcott's Poetry: American Mimicry* (Boston: Northeastern University Press, 1992), 14; John Thieme, *Derek Walcott* (Manchester: Manchester University Press, 1999), 15–16; Laurence Breiner, *An Introduction to West Indian Poetry* (Cambridge: Cambridge University Press, 1998), 201–208; Paula Burnett, *Derek Walcott: Politics and Poetics* (Gainesville: University Press of Florida, 2000), 98; Pollard, *New World Modernisms*.

5. Derek Walcott, "The Muse of History," *What the Twilight Says*, 54.

6. Edward Baugh, "The Arkansas Testament," *The Art of Derek Walcott*, ed. Brown, 124–125; Mervyn Morris, "Walcott and the Audience for Poetry," *Critical Perspectives*, ed. Hamner, 189.

7. Derek Walcott, interview with Edward Hirsch (1985), *Conversations*, 101–102.

8. Derek Walcott, "Leaving School," *Critical Perspectives*, ed. Hammer, 26–27.

9. Allison Blakely, "Historical Ties Among Suriname, The Netherlands Antilles, Aruba, and the Netherlands," *Callaloo* 21.3 (Summer 1998), 472–478.

10. Derek Walcott, interview with J. P. White (1990), *Conversations*, 152.

11. Walcott, "The Muse of History," *What the Twilight Says*, 62.
12. Mervyn Allyne, "A Linguistic Perspective on the Caribbean," *Caribbean Contours*, ed. S. Mintz and S. Price (Baltimore: Johns Hopkins University Press, 1985), 155–179.
13. Derek Walcott, "Cul de Sac Valley," *The Arkansas Testament* (New York: Farrar, Straus and Giroux, 1987), 9–10.
14. Derek Walcott, "The Antilles," *What the Twilight Says*, 74, 81.
15. T. S. Eliot, "Milton I," *Selected Prose of T. S. Eliot*, 261–262.
16. Eliot, "Milton I," 262.
17. Ezra Pound, "I Gather the Limbs of Osiris," *Selected Prose 1909–1965*, ed. W. Cookson (London: Faber and Faber, 1973), 33.
18. Pound, "I Gather the Limbs of Osiris," 35.
19. Pound, "I Gather the Limbs of Osiris," 35.
20. John Unterecker, *Voyager: A Life of Hart Crane* (New York: Farrar, Straus and Giroux, 1969), 439–457.
21. Derek Walcott, "Hart Crane," *Poems* (Jamaica: Kingston City Printery, [1951]), 14.
22. Walcott, "Hart Crane," 14.
23. Derek Walcott, interview with Edward Hirsch (1977), *Conversations*, 57.
24. Walcott, interview with Edward Hirsch (1985), *Conversations*, 104.
25. Walcott, interview with Edward Hirsch (1977), *Conversations*, 62.
26. R. P. Blackmur, *Form and Value in Modern Poetry* (Garden City, NY: Doubleday, 1957), 275.
27. Walcott, "Hart Crane," *Poems*, 14.
28. Derek Walcott, "Tales of the Islands," *Bim* 26 (1958).
29. Walt Whitman, "Preface" (1855), *Leaves of Grass*, in *Complete Poetry and Collected Prose*, 13.
30. Walt Whitman, "Democratic Vistas," *Complete Poetry and Collected Prose*, 970.
31. Derek Walcott, *Trinidad Express*, March 14, 1982.
32. Walcott, "The Muse of History," *What the Twilight Says*, 37.
33. Derek Walcott, "Crocodile Dandy: Les Murray," *What the Twilight Says*, 189–190.
34. Derek Walcott, "Elegy," *Collected Poems*, 109–110.
35. Bruce King, *Derek Walcott: A Caribbean Life* (Oxford: Oxford University Press, 2000), 255.
36. Walcott, interview with Edward Hirsch (1977), *Conversations*, 63.
37. Derek Walcott, "Over Colorado," *Sea Grapes* (London: J. Cape, 1976), 56.
38. Walcott, "Leaving School," *Critical Perspectives*, ed. Hamner, 26; interview with the author, Boston University, November 23, 1999.
39. Walcott, "The Muse of History," *What the Twilight Says*, 55, 37.
40. Derek Walcott, "The Yellow Cemetery," *Caribbean Quarterly* 5.3 (April 1958), 216.
41. Ezra Pound, *The Letters of Ezra Pound, 1907–1941*, ed. D. Paige (London: Faber and Faber, 1951), 21.
42. Walcott, *Another Life*, in *Collected Poems*, chapter 12, section 1, 216.

43. Derek Walcott, *Another Life*, in *Collected Poems*, chapter 12, section 1, 216.
44. Derek Walcott, Canto 10, *Epitaph for the Young* (Barbados: Advocate, 1949), 30–31.
45. Ezra Pound, *Selected Poems of Ezra Pound* (New York: New Directions, 1957), 35.
46. Ezra Pound, *Lustra of Ezra Pound* (1916) (New York: Haskell House, 1973), 57.
47. Derek Walcott, Canto 7, *Epitaph for the Young*, 19.
48. Hugh Kenner, "Mauberley," *The Poetry of Ezra Pound* (New York: New Directions, 1951), 166.
49. Pound, "I Gather the Limbs of Osiris," *Selected Prose 1909–1965*, 34.
50. Ezra Pound, *The Spirit of Romance* (rpt. New York: New Directions, 2005), 88; Alison Burford, *Craftsmen in Greek and Roman Society* (Ithaca: Cornell University Press, 1972), 102–103.
51. Walcott, "Leaving School," *Critical Perspectives*, ed. Hamner, 40.
52. Derek Walcott, "The Caribbean: Culture or Mimicry?," *Journal of Interamerican Studies and World Affairs* 16.1 (February 1974), 13.
53. Derek Walcott, *Desert Island Discs*, BBC Radio 4, London, June 14, 1991.
54. Derek Walcott, "For All Craftsmen," *Bim* 5.19 (December 1953), 166.
55. Kenner, *The Poetry of Ezra Pound*, 123; Donald Davie, *Ezra Pound: Poet as Sculptor* (New York: Oxford University Press, 1964); Michael North, *The Final Sculpture: Public Monuments and Modern Poets* (Ithaca: Cornell University Press, 1985), 103–104; Ezra Pound, "The Serious Artist" (1913), *Literary Essays*, ed. Eliot, 54.
56. Pound, "I Gather the Limbs of Osiris," *Selected Prose 1909–1965*, 41–42; Pound, "The Serious Artist," *Literary Essays*, 50.
57. Ezra Pound, *Homage to Sextus Propertius* (III), *Diptych Rome–London* (New York: New Directions, 1994), 14.
58. Gustave Flaubert, *Oeuvres complètes*, vol. II (nouvelle édition augmentée, Paris: Louis Conard, 1926), 399.
59. Derek Walcott, interview with J. P. White (1990), *Conversations*, 158–159.
60. Hannah Arendt, *The Human Condition* (Chicago: University of Chicago Press, 1958), 166.
61. Walcott, "For All Craftsmen," 166.
62. Pound, "The Serious Artist," *Literary Essays*, 54.
63. For a discussion of how shame figures in the historical emergence of women's poetry in Jamaica, see Anita Patterson, "Contingencies of Pleasure and Shame: Jamaican Women's Poetry," *Feminist Consequences: Theory for the New Century*, ed. E. Bronfen and M. Kavka (New York: Columbia University Press, 2001), 254–282.
64. Ezra Pound, *The Cantos of Ezra Pound* (New York: New Directions, 1948), 98–99.
65. Jahan Ramazani, "The Wound of History: Walcott's *Omeros* and the Postcolonial Poetics of Affliction," *PMLA* 112.3 (May 1997), 405–417.
66. Walcott, "For All Craftsmen," 166.
67. Walcott, *Another Life*, in *Collected Poems*, chapter 2, section 2, 153.

68. Edward Baugh, "Painters and Painting in Another Life," *Critical Perspectives*, ed. Hamner, 240.

69. Walcott, "Leaving School," *Critical Perspectives*, ed. Hamner, 28.

70. Derek Walcott, *Omeros* (New York: Farrar, Straus, Giroux, 1990), chapter 11, section 1, 68.

71. Walcott, "The Caribbean: Culture or Mimicry?" 4; Walcott, "The Muse of History," *What the Twilight Says*, 41.

72. Phoebe Pittingell, review of *The Bounty*, in *New Leader*, September 8, 1997.

73. Derek Walcott, "Steersman, My Brother" (1), *In a Green Night* (London: Jonathan Cape, 1962), 39.

74. Derek Walcott, "Robert Frost," *What the Twilight Says*, 209.

75. C. L. R. James, *Mariners, Renegades and Castaways: The Story of Herman Melville and the World We Live In*, published privately in New York, 1953 (London: Allison & Busby, 1984); Derek Walcott, "C. L. R. James," *What the Twilight Says*, 117.

76. C. L. R. James, *American Civilization* (Cambridge: Blackwell, 1993), 69.

77. Paul Giles, *Hart Crane: The Contexts of "The Bridge"* (Cambridge: Cambridge University Press, 1986), 199–200.

78. Walcott, "Steersman, My Brother" (1), *In A Green Night*, 39.

79. Donald Pease, "C. L. R. James, *Moby-Dick*, and the Emergence of Transnational American Studies," *Arizona Quarterly* 56.3 (Autumn 2000), 114.

80. Walcott, "Steersman, My Brother" (11), *In A Green Night*, 40.

81. Walcott, "Steersman, My Brother" (111), *In A Green Night*, 40.

82. Eliot, *Notes Towards the Definition of Culture*, 111.

83. Derek Walcott, *Tiepolo's Hound* (New York: Farrar, Straus, and Giroux, 2000), book 1, section 2, 11.

84. T. S. Eliot, *Notes Towards the Definition of Culture*, 43.

85. Walcott, *Tiepolo's Hound*, book 14, section 1, 87.

EPILOGUE

1. See, for example, Ramazani, *The Hybrid Muse: Postcolonial Poetry in English*, and Charles Pollard, "Traveling with Joyce: Derek Walcott's Discrepant Cosmopolitan Modernism," *Twentieth Century Literature* 47.2 (2001), 197–216.

Bibliography

Abel, Richard. "The Influence of St.-John Perse on T. S. Eliot." *Contemporary Literature* 14.2 (Spring 1973): 213–239.

Adam, Ian, and Helen Tiffin, eds. *Past the Last Post: Theorizing Post-Colonialism and Post-Modernism*. Calgary: University of Calgary Press, 1990.

Adams, Henry. *The Education of Henry Adams*. New York: Oxford University Press, 1999.
 Novels, Mont St. Michel, The Education. Ed. E. Samuels. New York: Library of America, 1983.

Adams, Rolstan. "Wilson Harris: The Pre-novel Poet." *Journal of Commonwealth Literature* 13.3 (April 1979): 71–85.

Adler, Joyce. "Melville and Harris: Poetic Imaginations Related in Their Response to the Modern World." In *Commonwealth Literature and the Modern World*, ed. Hena Maes-Jelinek. Brussels: Didier, 1976: 33–41.

Aiken, Conrad. "Prefatory Note" to "Anatomy of Melancholy." 1958. In *T. S. Eliot: The Man and His Work*, ed. Allen Tate. New York: Dell, 1966: 196.

Allen, Gay Wilson. *American Prosody*. New York: Farrar, Straus and Giroux, 1978.

Allyne, Mervyn. "A Linguistic Perspective on the Caribbean." In *Caribbean Contours*, ed. S. Mintz and S. Price. Baltimore: Johns Hopkins University Press, 1985: 155–179.

Alvarez, A. "Visions of Light." *New York Review of Books* (May 11, 2000): 27.

Andrews, Kenneth. *Trade, Plunder, and Settlement: Maritime Enterprise and the Genesis of the British Empire, 1480–1630*. Cambridge: Cambridge University Press, 1984.

Antoine, Régis. *Les écrivains français et les Antilles*. Paris: Maisonneuve et Larose, 1978.

Anzaldua, Gloria. *Borderlands / La Frontera*. 2nd edn. San Francisco: Aunt Lute Books, 1999.

Appadurai, Arjun. *Modernity at Large: Cultural Dimensions of Globalization*. Minneapolis: University of Minnesota Press, 1996.

Aragon, Louis. "Magnitogorsk." Trans. Langston Hughes. *Littérature internationale* 4 (1933–1934): 82–83.

Arendt, Hannah. *The Human Condition*. Chicago: University of Chicago Press, 1958.

Arkell, David. *Looking for Laforgue: An Informal Biography*. Manchester: Carcanet Press, 1979.

Arnold, James A. *Modernism and Negritude: The Poetry and Poetics of Aimé Césaire*. Cambridge, MA: Harvard University Press, 1981.

Ashcroft, Bill, Gareth Griffiths and Helen Tiffin, eds. *The Empire Writes Back: Theory and Practice in Post-Colonial Literatures*. New York: Routledge Press, 1989.

Asher, Kenneth. *T. S. Eliot and Ideology*. Cambridge: Cambridge University Press, 1995.

Bailyn, Bernard, and Philip Morgan, eds. *Strangers Within the Realism: Cultural Margins of the First British Empire*. Chapel Hill: University of North Carolina Press, 1991.

Barksdale, Richard. *Langston Hughes: The Poet and His Critics*. Chicago, IL: American Library Association, 1977.

Basch, Linda, Nina Glick Schiller and Cristina Szanton Blanc, eds. *Nations Unbound: Transnational Projects, Postcolonial Predicaments, and Deterritorialized Nation-states*. New York: Gordon and Breach, 1994.

Baudelaire, Charles. *Baudelaire on Poe: Critical Papers*. Trans. and ed. L. Hyslop and F. Hyslop. State College, PA: Bald Eagle Press, 1952.

Correspondance. Paris: Gallimard, 1973.

Les Fleurs du mal. Paris: Gallinard, 1999.

The Flowers of Evil. Trans. James McGowan. Oxford: Oxford University Press, 1993.

Bell, Michael. *Literature, Modernism and Myth: Belief and Responsibility in the Twentieth Century*. Cambridge: Cambridge University Press, 1997.

Benjamin, Walter. *Charles Baudelaire: A Lyric Poet in the Era of High Capitalism*. Trans. Harry Zohn. London: Verso, 1985.

Selected Writings. 2 vols. Ed. M. Jennings. Cambridge, MA: Harvard University Press, 1999.

Berry, Faith. *Langston Hughes: Before and Beyond Harlem*. Westport, CT: Lawrence Hill, 1983.

Bhabha, Homi. *The Location of Culture*. London: Routledge, 1994.

"Unsatisfied: Notes on Vernacular Cosmopolitanism." In *Text and Nation: Cross-Disciplinary Essays on Cultural and National Identities*, ed. Laura Garcia-Moreno and Peter Pfeiffer. Columbia, SC: Camden House, 1996: 191–207.

Blackmur, R. P. *Form and Value in Modern Poetry*. New York: Doubleday, 1957.

Blakely, Allison. "Historical Ties Among Suriname, The Netherlands Antilles, Aruba, and the Netherlands." *Callaloo* 21.3 (Summer 1998): 472–478.

Bloom, Harold. *A Map of Misreading*. Oxford: Oxford University Press, 1975.

Poetry and Repression: Revisionism from Blake to Stevens. New Haven: Yale University Press, 1976.

ed. *T. S. Eliot's The Waste Land*. New York: Chelsea House, 1986.

Breiner, Laurence. *An Introduction to West Indian Poetry*. Cambridge: Cambridge University Press, 1998.

Brickhouse, Anna. *Transamerican Literary Relations and the Nineteenth-Century Public Sphere.* Cambridge: Cambridge University Press, 2004.

Brooks, Cleanth. *Modern Poetry and the Tradition.* 1939. Reprint, New York: Oxford University Press, 1965.

Brown, Stewart, ed. *The Art of Derek Walcott.* Chester Springs, PA: Dufour, 1991.

Buell, Lawrence. "Circling the Spheres: A Dialogue." *American Literature* 70 (1998): 465–490.

——. ed. *Henry Wadsworth Longfellow, Selected Poems.* New York: Penguin, 1988.

Burnett, Paula. *Derek Walcott: Politics and Poetics.* Gainesville: University Press of Florida Press, 2000.

——. "Opening New Doors: A Glimpse of Wilson Harris and Derek Walcott." In *Theatre of the Arts: Wilson Harris and the Caribbean,* ed. Hena Maes-Jelinek and Bénédicte Ledent. Amsterdam: Rodopi, 2002.

Bush, Ronald. "Nathaniel Hawthorne and T. S. Eliot's American Connection." *Southern Review* 21 (October 1985): 924–933.

——. *T. S. Eliot: A Study in Character and Style.* New York: Oxford University Press, 1984.

——. "T. S. Eliot: Singing the Emerson Blues." In *Emerson: Prospect and Retrospect,* ed. J. Porte. Cambridge, MA: Harvard University Press, 1982: 179–197.

——. ed. *T. S. Eliot: The Modernist in History.* Cambridge: Cambridge University Press, 1991.

Bush, Ronald, and Elazar Barkan, eds. *Prehistories of the Future: The Primitivist Project and the Culture of Modernism.* Stanford: Stanford University Press, 1995.

Cameron, Elizabeth. "Alexis Saint-Léger Léger" [*sic*]. In *The Diplomats, 1919–1939,* ed. Gordon Craig and Felix Gilbert. Princeton: Princeton University Press, 1953.

Césaire, Aimé. *The Collected Poetry.* Trans. Clayton Eshleman and Annette Smith. Berkeley: University of California Press, 1983.

——. "Introduction to Negro American Poetry." *Tropiques* 3 (October 1941).

Chace, William. *The Political Identities of Ezra Pound and T. S. Eliot.* Stanford: Stanford University Press, 1973.

Chinitz, David. *T. S. Eliot and the Cultural Divide.* Chicago: University of Chicago Press, 2003.

Clark, T. J. *Farewell to an Idea: Episodes from a History of Modernism.* New Haven: Yale University Press, 1999.

Clarke, Graham, ed. *Edgar Allan Poe: Critical Assessments.* 2 vols. Mountfield, East Sussex: Helm Information, 1991.

Clayton, Douglas. *Pierrot in Petrograd: The Commedia dell'Arte/Balagan in Twentieth Century Russian Theatre and Drama.* Montreal: McGill-Queen's University Press, 1993.

Clifford, James. *Routes: Travel and Translation in the Late Twentieth Century.* Cambridge, MA: Harvard University Press, 1997.

Cobb, Martha. *Harlem, Haiti, and Havana: A Comparative Critical Study of Langston Hughes, Jacques Roumain, Nicolás Guillén.* Washington, DC: Three Continents Press, 1979.

Cobham, Rhonda. "The Texts of Wilson Harris' *Eternity to Season.*" *World Literature Written in English* 22 (Spring 1983): 27–38.

Collie, Michael. *Jules Laforgue.* London: Athlone Press, 1977.

Cowley, Malcolm. *Exile's Return: A Literary Odyssey of the 1920s.* New York: Viking, 1956.

Coyle, Michael, ed. *Ezra Pound and African American Modernism.* Orono, ME: National Poetry Foundation, 2001.

Culler, Jonathan. "Baudelaire and Poe." *Zeitschrift für Französische Sprache* 100 (1990): 61–73.

Cutler, Edward. *Recovering the New: Transatlantic Roots of Modernism.* Hanover, NH: University Press of New England, 2003.

Daly, Vere. *The Making of Guyana.* London: Macmillan, 1974.

Dash, J. Michael. "Engagement, Exile, and Errance: Some Trends in Haitian Poetry, 1946–1986." *Callaloo* 15.3 (Summer 1992): 474–760.

  The Other America: Caribbean Literature in a New World Context. Charlottesville: University Press of Virginia, 1998.

  "The World and The Word: French Caribbean Writing in The Twentieth Century." *Callaloo* 34 (Winter 1988): 112–130.

Davie, Donald. *Ezra Pound: Poet as Sculptor.* New York: Oxford University Press, 1964.

de Man, Paul. *Blindness and Insight: Essays in the Rhetoric of Contemporary Criticism.* 2nd edn., Minneapolis: University of Minnesota Press, 1983.

de Oliveira, Celso. "A Note on Eliot and Baudelaire." *American Literature* 55.1 (March 1983): 81–82.

Deshmukh, Madhuri. "Langston Hughes as Black Pierrot: A Transatlantic Game of Masks." *Langston Hughes Review* 18 (Fall 2004).

Dimock, Wai-Chee. *Empire for Liberty: Melville and the Poetics of Individualism.* Princeton: Princeton University Press, 1989.

Donoghue, Denis. *Being Modern Together.* Atlanta, GA: Scholars Press, 1991.

Dorsinville, Roger. *Jacques Roumain.* Paris: Présence Africaine, 1981.

Douglas, Ann. *Terrible Honesty: Mongrel Manhattan in the 1920s.* New York: Noonday Press, 1995.

Drake, Sandra. *Wilson Harris and the Modern Tradition.* New York: Greenwood Press, 1986.

Drew, Elizabeth. *T. S. Eliot: The Design of His Poetry.* New York: Charles Scribner's Sons, 1949.

During, Simon. "Waiting for the Post: Some Relations between Modernity, Colonization, and Writing." *Ariel* 20.4 (October 1989): 31–61.

Eagleton, Terry. *Criticism and Ideology.* 1976. Reprint, London: Verso, 1985.

Edwards, Brent. *The Practice of Diaspora: Literature, Translation, and the Rise of Black Internationalism.* Cambridge, MA: Harvard University Press, 2003.

Eliot, T. S. "American Literature." *Athenaeum* 4643 (April 25, 1919): 236–237.

"A Brief Introduction to the Method of Paul Valéry." In *Le Serpent* by Paul Valéry. Trans. Mark Wardle. London: R. Cobden-Sanderson, 1924: 7–15.

Collected Poems, 1909–1962. New York: Harcourt Brace Jovanovich, 1988.

"A Commentary." *Criterion* (April 1931): 484.

"A Commentary: That Poetry is Made with Words." *New English Weekly* 15.2 (27 April 1939): 27–28.

The Complete Poems and Plays, 1909–1950. New York: Harcourt Brace, 1952.

"'A Dream within a Dream': T. S. Eliot on Edgar Allan Poe." *Listener* 29 (February 25, 1943): 243–244.

"Un feuillet unique." *Saint-John Perse: Hommage international des "Cahiers de la Pléiade."* Paris: Boivin, 1950: 18–19.

Foreword to *Symbolisme from Poe to Mallarmé: The Growth of a Myth*, by Joseph Chiari. London: Rockliff, 1956: v–vi.

The Idea of a Christian Society. 1939. Reprint, with *Notes Towards the Definition of Culture*, in *Christianity and Culture*. San Diego: Harcourt Brace Jovanovich, 1977.

"The Influence of Landscape upon the Poet." *Daedalus* 89.2 (Spring, 1960): 421–422.

Interview with T. S. Eliot. In George Plimpton, ed., *Writers at Work*. New York: Penguin, 1977: 91–110.

Introduction to *Ezra Pound: Selected Poems*. London: Faber and Faber, 1928.

Inventions of the March Hare: Poems, 1909–1917. Ed. Christopher Ricks. New York: Harcourt Brace, 1996.

"Note sur Mallarmé et Poe." Trans. Ramón Fernandez. *La Nouvelle Revue Française* (November 1, 1926): 524–526.

Notes Towards the Definition of Culture. 1948. Reprint, London: Faber and Faber Ltd., 1962.

On Poetry and Poets. London: Faber and Faber, 1957.

Preface to *This American World* by Edgar Ansel Mowrer. London: Faber and Gwyer, 1928: ix–xv.

Preface to *Transit of Venus: Poems by Harry Crosby*. Paris: Black Sun Press, 1931: i–ix.

"Prose and Verse." In *Poetry and Prose: Three Essays by T. S. Eliot, Frederic Manning [and] Richard Aldington*. London: The Poetry Bookshop, 1921.

Review of *Israfel*, by Hervey Allen. *Nation and Athenaeum* 41 (May 21, 1927): 219.

The Sacred Wood. 2nd edn. London: Methuen, 1928. Reprint, New York: Barnes and Noble, 1960.

"A Sceptical Patrician." Review of *The Education of Henry Adams*. *Athenaeum* 4647 (May 23, 1919): 361–362.

Selected Essays. New York: Harcourt, Brace and World, 1950.

Selected Prose of T. S. Eliot. Ed. F. Kermode. New York: Harvest, 1975.

"The Three Provincialities." 1922. Reprint, *Essays in Criticism* 1.1 (January 1951): 39–40.

To Criticize the Critic and Other Writings. 1965. Reprint, Lincoln: University of Nebraska Press, 1991.

The Use of Poetry and the Use of Criticism. 1933. Reprint, Cambridge, MA: Harvard University Press, 1964.

The Varieties of Metaphysical Poetry. Ed. Ronald Schuchard. New York: Harcourt Brace, 1993.

"War-paint and Feathers." Review of *An Anthology of Songs and Chants from the Indians of North America*. *Athenaeum* 4668 (October 17, 1919): 1036.

The Waste Land: A Facsimile and Transcript of the Original Drafts. Ed. Valerie Eliot. New York: Harcourt Brace Jovanovich, 1971.

"Whitman and Tennyson." *Nation and Athenaeum* (December 18, 1926).

Ellmann, Richard. *James Joyce*. New York: Oxford University Press, 1969.

Elmer, Jonathan. *Reading at the Social Limit: Affect, Mass Culture, and Edgar Allan Poe*. Stanford: Stanford University Press, 1995.

Emanuel, James. *Langston Hughes*. New York: Twayne, 1967.

Empson, William. *Some Versions of Pastoral*. London: Chatto and Windus, 1935.

Erkkila, Betsy. "The Poetics of Whiteness: Poe and the Racial Imaginary." In *Romancing the Shadow: Poe and Race*, ed. J. Kennedy and L. Weissberg. New York: Oxford University Press, 2001: 41–74.

Walt Whitman Among the French: Poet and Myth. Princeton: Princeton University Press, 1980.

Whitman: The Political Poet. New York: Oxford University Press, 1989.

Erkkila, Betsy, and Jay Grossman, eds. *Breaking Bounds: Whitman and American Cultural Studies*. New York: Oxford University Press, 1996.

Fabre, Michel. "Du mouvement nouveau noir à la négritude césairienne." In *Soleil éclaté*, ed. Jacqueline Leiner. Tubingen: Gunther Grass Verlag, 1984: 149–159.

From Harlem to Paris: Black American Writers in France, 1840–1980. Urbana: University of Illinois Press, 1993.

"Hughes's Literary Reputation in France." *Langston Hughes Review* 6.1 (Spring 1987).

Farnsworth, Robert. *Melvin Tolson, 1898–1966: Plain Talk and Poetic Prophecy*. Columbia: University of Missouri Press, 1984.

Farrell, Walter, and Patricia Johnson . "Poetic Interpretations of Urban Black Folk Culture: Langston Hughes and the 'Bebop' Era." *MELUS* 8.3 (1981): 57–72.

Feidelson, Charles. *Symbolism and American Literature*. Chicago: University of Chicago Press, 1953.

Fowler, Carolyn. *A Knot in the Thread: The Life and Work of Jacques Roumain*. Washington, DC: Howard University Press, 1980.

"The Shared Vision of Langston Hughes and Jacques Roumain." *Black American Literature Forum* 15.3 (Autumn 1981): 84–88.

Fowlie, Wallace. "Baudelaire and Eliot: Interpreters of Their Age." *Sewannee Review*, ed. Allan Tate, 74.1 (January–March 1966): 293–309.

Gallup, Donald. "Mr. Eliot at the Churchill Club." *Southern Review* 21.4 (October, 1985): 969–973.

Gardner, Helen. *The Art of T. S. Eliot*. New York; E. P. Dutton, 1950.

The Composition of "Four Quartets." London: Faber and Faber, 1978.

Garrett, Naomi. *The Renaissance of Haitian Poetry*. Paris: Présence Africaine, 1963.

Gates, Henry Louis. *Figures in Black: Words, Signs, and the "Racial" Self*. New York: Oxford University Press, 1987.

Preface to *Langston Hughes: Critical Perspectives Past and Present*. Ed. H. L. Gates and K. A. Appiah. New York: Amistad, 1993.

Gelpi, Albert. *A Coherent Splendor: The American Poetic Renaissance, 1910–1950*. New York: Cambridge University Press, 1987.

Giddens, Anthony. *The Consequences of Modernity*. Stanford: Stanford University Press, 1990.

Gikandi, Simon. *Writing in Limbo: Modernism and Caribbean Literature*. Ithaca: Cornell University Press, 1992.

Giles, Paul. *Hart Crane: The Contexts of "The Bridge."* Cambridge: Cambridge University Press, 1986.

Transatlantic Insurrections: British Culture and the Formation of American Literature. Philadelphia: University of Pennsylvania Press, 2001.

Virtual Americas: Transnational Fiction and the Transatlantic Imaginary. Durham, NC: Duke University Press, 2002.

Gilkes, Michael. *Wilson Harris and the Caribbean Novel*. London: Longman, 1975.

Gilroy, Paul. *The Black Atlantic: Modernity and Double Consciousness*. Cambridge, MA: Harvard University Press, 1993.

Glissant, Edouard. *Caribbean Discourse: Selected Essays*. Trans. J. Michael Dash. Charlottesville: University Press of Virginia, 1989.

Faulkner, Mississippi. Chicago: University of Chicago Press, 1996.

Goldin, Liliana, ed. *Identities on the Move: Transnational Processes in North America and the Caribbean Basin*. Albany, NY: Institute for Mesoamerican Studies, 1999.

Gordon, Lyndall. "The American Eliot and 'The Dry Salvages.'" In *Words in Time: New Essays on Eliot's Four Quartets*, ed. Edward Lobb. Ann Arbor: University of Michigan Press, 1993: 38–51.

Eliot's Early Years. London: Oxford University Press, 1977.

T. S. Eliot: An Imperfect Life. New York: Norton, 1998.

Green, Martin, and John Swan. *The Triumph of Pierrot: The Commedia dell'Arte and the Modern Imagination*. University Park: Pennsylvania State University Press, 1986.

Greene, Edward. *T. S. Eliot et la France*. Paris: Boivin, 1951.

Greenspan, E., ed. *The Cambridge Companion to Whitman*. New York: Cambridge University Press, 1995.

Griffin, Farrah. *Who Set You Flowing?* New York: Oxford University Press, 1995.

Grossman, James. *Land of Hope*. Chicago: University of Chicago Press, 1989.

Guillaume, Alfred J. "And Bid Him Translate: Langston Hughes's Translations of Poetry from French." *Langston Hughes Review*, 4.2 (Fall 1985): 1–23.

Hale, Thomas. "From Afro-America to Afro-France: The Literary Triangle Trade." *French Review* 49.6 (May 1976): 1089–1096.

Hamner, Robert *Derek Walcott*. New York: Twayne, 1993.

ed. *Critical Perspectives on Derek Walcott*. Boulder, CO: Three Continents Press, 1997.

Handley, George. *New World Poetics: Nature and the Adamic Imagination in Whitman, Neruda, and Walcott*. Athens: University of Georgia Press, 2007.

Handlin, Oscar, *The Uprooted*. Boston, MA: Little, Brown, 1952.

Hardy, Thomas. *The Complete Poems of Thomas Hardy*. Ed. James Gibson. London: Macmillan London Ltd., 1976.

Hargrove, Nancy Duvall. *Landscape as Symbol in the Poetry of T. S. Eliot*. Jackson: University Press of Mississippi, 1978.

Harris, Wilson. "Across the Editor's Desk." *Kyk-over-al* 35 (October 1986): 3.

"Adversarial Contexts and Creativity." *New Left Review* 154 (November/December 1985): 124–128.

"Comedy and Modern Allegory: A Personal View." In *A Shaping of Connections: Commonwealth Literature Studies – Then and Now*, ed. Hena Maes-Jelinek, Kirsten Holst Petersen and Anna Rutherford. Aarhus: Dangaroo Press, 1989: 127–140.

Eternity to Season. London: New Beacon, 1978.

Explorations. Ed. Hena Maes-Jelinek. Aarhus: Dangaroo Press, 1981.

"Literacy and Imagination." In *The Literate Imagination: Essays on the Novels of Wilson Harris*, ed. Michael Gilkes. London: Macmillan, 1989.

"Oedipus and the Middle Passage." In *Crisis and Creativity in the New Literatures in English*, ed. Geoffrey V. Davis and Hena Maes-Jelinek. Atlanta, GA: Rodopi, 1999: 9–21.

The Radical Imagination: Lectures and Talks by Wilson Harris. Ed. Alan Riach and Marte Williams. Liège: University of Liège, 1992.

Tradition, the Writer, and Society: Critical Essays. London: New Beacon, 1967.

The Unfinished Genesis of the Imagination: Selected Essays of Wilson Harris. Ed. Andrew Bundy. London: Routledge, 1999.

The Womb of Space: The Cross-Cultural Imagination. Westport, CT: Greenwood Press, 1983.

Hay, Eloise Knapp. *T. S. Eliot's Negative Way*. Cambridge, MA: Harvard University Press, 1982.

Hayes, Kevin, ed. *The Cambridge Companion to Edgar Allan Poe*. Cambridge: Cambridge University Press, 2002.

Henry, Albert. *Anabase de Saint-John Perse*. Paris: Gallimard, 1983.

Hobsbaum, Philip. "Eliot, Whitman, and the American Tradition." *Journal of American Studies* 3 (1969): 239–264.

Hokanson, Robert O'Brien. "Jazzing It Up: The Be-bop Modernism of Langston Hughes." *Mosaic* 31.4 (December 1998): 61–82.

Holmes, Anne. *Jules Laforgue and Poetic Innovation*. Oxford: Clarendon Press, 1993.

Howard, W. J. "Shaping a New Voice: The Poetry of Wilson Harris." *Commonwealth Newsletter* 9 (January 1976): 26–31.

Hughes, Langston. *The American Negro Reference Book*. Ed. John P. Davis. Englewood Cliffs, NJ: Prentice-Hall, 1966.

The Big Sea. Reprint, New York: Hill and Wang, 1993.

The Collected Poems of Langston Hughes. Ed. A. Rampersad. New York: Knopf, 1994.

The Collected Works of Langston Hughes. Vol. IX: *Essays on Art, Race, Politics, and World Affairs*. Ed. Christopher de Santis. Columbia: University of Missouri Press, 2002.

Good Morning, Revolution: Uncollected Writings of Social Protest. Ed. Faith Berry. New York: Lawrence Hill, 1973.

I Wonder as I Wander. 1956. Reprint, New York: Hill and Wang, 1964.

Hughes, Langston, and Arna Bontemps, eds. *The Poetry of the Negro, 1746–1949*. Garden City, NY: Doubleday, 1949.

Hutchinson, George. *The Harlem Renaissance in Black and White*. Cambridge, MA: Harvard University Press, 1995.

James, C. L. R. *American Civilization*. Cambridge: Blackwell, 1993.

Mariners, Renegades and Castaways: The Story of Herman Melville and the World We Live In. Reprint, London: Allison and Busby, 1984.

James, Henry. *Collected Travel Writings: Great Britain and America*. New York: Library of America, 1993.

"Paris Revisited." *Galaxy* 24.1 (January 1878).

Jay, Gregory. *T. S. Eliot and the Poetics of Literary History*. Baton Rouge: Louisiana State University Press, 1983.

Jehlen, Myra, and Michael Warner, eds. *The English Literatures of America, 1500–1800*. New York: Routledge, 1997.

Jemie, Onwuchekwa. *Langston Hughes: An Introduction to the Poetry*. New York: Columbia University Press, 1976.

Johnson, James Weldon. *Along This Way*. New York: Viking Press, 1933.

Julius, Anthony. *T. S. Eliot, Anti-Semitism, and Literary Form*. Cambridge: Cambridge University Press, 1995.

Kaplan, Amy. *The Anarchy of Empire in the Making of U.S. Culture*. Cambridge, MA: Harvard University Press, 2005.

Kenner, Hugh. *The Invisible Poet: T. S. Eliot*. New York: McDowell, Obolensky, 1959.

The Poetry of Ezra Pound. New York: New Directions, 1951.

Kesteloot, Lilyan. *Black Writers in French*. Trans. Ellen Kennedy. Reprint, Washington, DC: Howard University Press, 1991.

King, Bruce. *Derek Walcott: A Caribbean Life*. Oxford: Oxford University Press, 2000.

New English Literatures: Cultural Nationalism[s] in a Changing World. New York: St. Martin's Press, 1980.

Klein, Herbert, ed. *The Middle Passage: Comparative Studies in the Atlantic Slave Trade*. Princeton: Princeton University Press, 1978.

Knodel, Arthur. *Saint-John Perse: A Study of His Poetry*. George Square: University Press Edinburgh, 1966.

"Towards an Understanding of *Anabase*." *PMLA* 79.3 (June 1964): 329–343.

Laforgue, Jules. *Lettres à un ami (1880–6)*. Ed. G. Jean-Aubry. Paris: Mercure de France, 1941.

Mélanges posthumes. Reprint, Paris: Ressources, 1979.

Moralités légendaires. Paris: La Collection POL, 1992.

Poems. Trans. Peter Dale. London: Anvil Press, 2007.

Poésies complètes. 2 vols. Ed. Pascal Pia. Paris: Gallimard, 1979.

Laraque, Maurice. "La rosée de l'espoir." *Rencontre* 4.1 (Port-au-Prince, Haiti) (1993).

Lawler, James. "Demons of the Intellect: The Symbolists and Poe." *Critical Inquiry* 14.1 (Autumn 1987): 109–110.

Lawrence, D. H. *Studies in Classic American Literature*. New York: Thomas Seltzer, 1923.

Leavis, F. R. *For Continuity*. Cambridge: The Minority Press, 1933.

Lemann, Nicolas. *The Promised Land: The Great Black Migration and How It Changed America*. New York: Knopf, 1991.

Lentricchia, Frank. *Modernist Quartet*. Cambridge: Cambridge University Press, 1994.

Levenson, Michael. *A Genealogy of Modernism*. Cambridge: Cambridge University Press, 1984.

Levie, Sophie. *Commerce, 1924–1932: une revue internationale moderniste*. Rome: Fondazione Camillo Caetani, 1989.

Levillain, H., and M. Sacotte, eds. *Saint-John Perse: Antillanité et universalité*. Paris: Éditions Caribéennes, 1988.

Little, Roger. "T. S. Eliot and Saint-John Perse." *Arlington Quarterly* 2.2 (Autumn 1969): 5–17.

Longenbach, James. *Modernist Poetics of History: Pound, Eliot, and the Sense of the Past*. Princeton: Princeton University Press, 1987.

Look-Lai, Walton. *Indentured Labor, Caribbean Sugar: Chinese and Indian Migrants to the British West Indies, 1838–1918*. Baltimore, MD: Johns Hopkins University Press, 2004.

Lubine, Maurice. "Langston Hughes and Haiti." Trans. Faith Berry. *Langston Hughes Review* 6.1 (Spring 1987).

MacLeish, Archibald. Preface to *Éloges and Other Poems by St.-John Perse*. Trans. Louis Varèse. New York: Norton, 1944.

Maes-Jelinek, Hena. "Natural and Psychological Landscapes." *Journal of Commonwealth Literature* 7.1 (1971): 117–120.

"'Numinous Proportions': Wilson Harris's Alternative to All 'Posts.'" In *Past the Last Post: Theorizing Post-Colonialism and Post-Modernism*, ed. Ian Adam and Helen Tiffin. Calgary: University of Calgary Press, 1990: 47–64.

Mallarmé, Stéphane. *Oeuvres complètes*. Paris: Gallimard, 1945.

Poésies. Paris: Flammarion, 1989.

Marks, Carol. *Farewell, We're Good and Gone*. Bloomington: Indiana University Press, 1989.

Martin, Robert. *The Homosexual Tradition in American Poetry*. Iowa City: University of Iowa Press, 1998.

Matthiessen, F. O. *The Achievement of T. S. Eliot*. Boston, MA: Houghton Mifflin, 1935.

American Renaissance: Art and Expression in the Age of Emerson and Whitman. London: Oxford University Press, 1941.

"The 'Quartets.'" In *Four Quartets: A Casebook*, ed. Bernard Bergonzi. London: Macmilllan, 1969.

McGill, Meredith. "Poe, Literary Nationalism, and Authorial Identity." In *The American Face of Edgar Allan Poe*, ed. S. Rosenheim and S. Rachman. Baltimore, MD: Johns Hopkins University Press, 1995.

McLuhan, Marshall. "The Aesthetic Moment in Landscape Poetry." In *English Institute Essays*, ed. Alan Downer. New York: Columbia University Press, 1952.

"Tennyson and Picturesque Poetry." *Essays in Criticism* 1 (July 1951): 262–282.

Mehlman, Jeffrey. *Émigré New York: French Intellectuals in Wartime Manhattan, 1940–1944.* Baltimore, MD: Johns Hopkins University Press, 2000.

Menand, Louis. *American Studies.* New York: Farrar, Straus and Giroux, 2002.

Michaels, Walter Benn. *Our America: Nativism, Modernism, and Pluralism.* Durham, NC: Duke University Press, 1995.

Miller, James. *The American Quest for a Supreme Fiction.* Chicago: University of Chicago Press, 1979.

A Critical Guide to Leaves of Grass. Chicago: University of Chicago Press, 1957.

Miller, R. Baxter. *The Art and Imagination of Langston Hughes.* Lexington: University Press of Kentucky, 1989.

Moody, A. David. "The American Strain." In *The Placing of T. S. Eliot*, ed. Jewel Spears Brooker. Columbia: University of Missouri Press, 1991: 77–89.

Thomas Stearns Eliot: Poet. 2nd edn. Cambridge: Cambridge University Press, 1994.

ed. *The Cambridge Companion to T. S. Eliot.* Cambridge: Cambridge University Press, 1994.

Motherwell, Robert, ed. *Dada Painters and Poets.* Cambridge, MA: Belknap Press, 2005.

Mullen, Edward J. *Langston Hughes in the Hispanic World and Haiti.* Hamden, CT: Arcon, 1977.

Murray, Stuart. "Postcoloniality/Modernity: Wilson Harris and Postcolonial Theory." *Review of Contemporary Fiction* 17.2 (Summer 1997): 53–58.

Musgrove, Sydney. *T. S. Eliot and Walt Whitman.* Wellington: New Zealand University Press, 1952.

Nandy, Ashis. *The Intimate Enemy: Loss and Recovery of Self under Colonialism.* Delhi: Oxford University Press, 1983.

Nelson, C. E. "Saint-John Perse and T. S. Eliot." *Western Humanities Review* 17.2 (Spring 1963): 163–171.

Nielsen, Aldon Lynn. *Reading Race: White American Poets and Racial Discourse in the Twentieth Century.* Athens: University of Georgia Press, 1988.

North, Michael. *The Dialect of Modernism: Race, Language, and Twentieth-Century Literature.* New York: Oxford University Press, 1994.

The Final Sculpture: Public Monuments and Modern Poets. Ithaca: Cornell University Press, 1985.

Oliver, Paul, ed. *Black Music in Britain*. Philadelphia: Open University Press, 1990.

Oser, Lee. *T. S. Eliot and American Poetry*. Columbia: University of Missouri Press, 1998.

Ostrovsky, Erika. *Under the Sign of Ambiguity: Saint-John Perse / Alexis Leger*. New York: New York University Press, 1985.

Parry, Benita. "The Postcolonial: Conceptual Category or Chimera?" *Yearbook of English Studies* 27 (1997): 3–21.

Patterson, Anita. "Contingencies of Pleasure and Shame: Jamaican Women's Poetry." In *Feminist Consequences: Theory for the New Century*, ed. E. Bronfen and M. Kavka. New York: Columbia University Press, 2001: 254–282.

From Emerson to King: Democracy, Race, and the Politics of Protest. New York: Oxford University Press, 1997.

"Jazz, Realism, and the Modernist Lyric: The Poetry of Langston Hughes." *Modern Language Quarterly* 61.4 (December 2000): 651–682.

"Pastoral Poetry and Transculturation: The Contexts of Wilson Harris's 'Trail'." *Journal of Commonwealth Literature* 37.2 (2002): 107–138.

Patterson, Orlando. "Migration in Caribbean Societies: Socioeconomic and Symbolic Resource." In *Human Migration: Patterns and Policies*, ed. W. McNeill. Bloomington: Indiana University Press, 1978.

Peach, Ceri. *West Indian Migration to Britain: A Social Geography*. London: Oxford University Press, 1968.

Pearce, Roy Harvey. *The Continuity of American Poetry*. Middletown, CT: Wesleyan University Press, 1987.

Pease, Donald. "Blake, Crane, Whitman, and Modernism: A Poetics of Pure Possibility." *PMLA* 96.1 (January 1981): 64–65.

"C. L. R. James, *Moby-Dick*, and the Emergence of Transnational American Studies." *Arizona Quarterly* 56.3 (Autumn 2000): 93–123.

Perse, St.-John. *Anabasis*. Trans. T. S. Eliot. New York: Harcourt Brace, 1938.

Anabasis: A Poem by St.-J. Perse. Trans. T. S. Eliot. London: Faber and Faber, 1930.

Anabasis: A Poem by St.-J. Perse. Trans. T. S. Eliot. 2nd edn. London: Faber and Faber, 1949.

Anabasis: A Poem by St.-J. Perse. Trans. T. S. Eliot. 3rd edn. London: Faber and Faber, 1959.

Collected Poems. Trans. W. H Auden, Hugh Chisholm, Denis Devlin, T. S. Eliot, Robert Fitzgerald, Wallace Fowlie, Richard Howard and Louis Varèse. Princeton: Princeton University Press, 1971.

Honneur à Saint-John Perse. Paris: Gallimard, 1965.

Interview. *Le Figaro littéraire* (November 5, 1960).

Letters. Trans. and ed. Arthur Knodel. Princeton: Princeton University Press, 1979.

Lettres d'Alexis Leger à Gabriel Frizeau. Ed. Albert Henry. Brussels: Académie Royale de Belgique, 1993.

Oeuvres complètes. Paris: Gallinard, 1982.

Pinsky, Robert. *Democracy, Culture and the Voice of Poetry*. Princeton: Princeton University Press, 2002.

Poe, Edgar Allan. *Complete Poems*. Ed. T. O. Mabbott. Urbana: University of Illinois Press, 2000.

Essays and Reviews. Ed. G. R. Thompson. New York: Library of America, 1984.

Poirier, Richard. *The Renewal of Literature: Emersonian Reflections*. New York: Random House, 1987.

Pollard, Charles. *New World Modernisms: T. S. Eliot, Derek Walcott, and Kamau Brathwaite*. Charlottesville: University Press of Virginia, 2004.

"Traveling with Joyce: Derek Walcott's Discrepant Cosmopolitan Modernism." *Twentieth Century Literature* 47.2 (2001): 197–216.

Posnock, Ross. *Color and Culture: Black Writers and the Making of the Modern Intellectual*. Cambridge, MA: Harvard University Press, 1998.

Pound, Ezra. *The Letters of Ezra Pound, 1907–1941*. Ed. D. Paige. London: Faber and Faber, 1951.

Literary Essays of Ezra Pound. Ed. T. S. Eliot. Norfolk, CT: New Directions, 1954.

Polite Essays. Norfolk, CT: New Directions, 1939.

Selected Poems of Ezra Pound. New York: New Directions, 1957.

Selected Prose 1909–1965. Ed. W. Cookson. London: Faber and Faber, 1973.

The Spirit of Romance. Reprint, New York: New Directions, 2005.

Pozzi, Monica. "A Conversation with Wilson Harris." *Journal of Caribbean Literatures* 2.1–3 (Spring 2000): 260–270.

Pratt, Mary Louise. *Imperial Eyes: Travel Writing and Transculturation*. London: Routledge, 1992.

Proudfoot, M. J. *Population Movements in the Caribbean*. Port of Spain, Trinidad: Kent House, 1950.

Ramazani, Jahan. *The Hybrid Muse: Postcolonial Poetry in English*. Chicago: University of Chicago Press, 2001.

Poetry of Mourning: The Modern Elegy from Hardy to Heaney. Chicago: University of Chicago Press, 1994.

"A Transnational Poetics." *American Literary History* 18.2 (Summer 2006): 332–359.

"The Wound of History: Walcott's *Omeros* and the Postcolonial Poetics of Affliction." *PMLA* 112.3 (May 1997): 405–417.

Ramchand, Kenneth. *The West Indian Novel and its Background*. New York: Barnes and Noble, 1970.

Rampersad, Arnold. "Future Scholarly Projects on Langston Hughes." *Black American Literature Forum* 21.3 (Autumn 1987): 305–316.

"Langston Hughes and Approaches to Modernism in the Harlem Renaissance." In *The Harlem Renaissance: Revaluations*, ed. A. Singh, W. Shiver and S. Brodwin. New York: Garland, 1989: 49–72.

The Life of Langston Hughes. 2 vols. New York: Oxford University Press, 1986.

Ramsey, Warren. *Jules Laforgue and the Ironic Inheritance*. New York: Oxford University Press, 1953.

Rhodes, S. A. *The Cult of Beauty in Charles Baudelaire.* New York: Institute of French Studies at Columbia University, 1929.

Richardson, Bonham. *The Caribbean in the Wider World 1492–1992.* Cambridge: Cambridge University Press, 1992.

Ricks, Christopher. "À l'envers ou à Anvers?" *Times Literary Supplement* (March 14, 1997).

T. S. Eliot and Prejudice. Berkeley: University of California Press, 1988.

Rigolot, Carol. *Forged Genealogies: Saint-John Perse's Conversations with Culture.* Chapel Hill: University of North Carolina Press, 2001.

Riquelme, John Paul. *Harmony of Dissonances: T. S. Eliot, Romanticism, and Imagination.* Baltimore, MD: Johns Hopkins University Press, 1991.

Rodney, Walter. *A History of the Guyanese Working People, 1881–1905.* Baltimore, MD: Johns Hopkins University Press, 1981.

Roumain, Jacques. *Oeuvres complètes.* Ed. Léon-François Hoffmann. Paris: Collection Archivos, 2003.

When the Tom-Tom Beats: Selected Prose & Poems. Trans. Joanne Fungaroli and Ronald Sauer. Washington, DC: Azul, 1995.

Rowe, John Carlos. "Edgar Allan Poe's Imperial Fantasy and the American Frontier." In *Romancing the Shadow: Poe and Race*, ed. J. Kennedy and L. Weissberg. New York: Oxford University Press, 2001: 75–105.

Literary Culture and U.S. Imperialism: From the Revolution to World War II. Oxford: Oxford University Press, 2000.

"Nineteenth-Century United States Literary Culture and Transnationality." *PMLA* 118.1 (January 2003): 78–89.

ed. *Post-Nationalist American Studies.* Berkeley: University of California Press, 2000.

Said, Edward. *Culture and Imperialism.* New York: Knopf, 1993.

"Representing the Colonized: Anthropology's Interlocutors." *Critical Inquiry* 15.2 (1989): 205–225.

Salmon, André. *Créances: 1905–1910.* Paris: Gallimard, 1926.

Sassen, Saskia. *The Mobility of Labor and Capital.* Cambridge: Cambridge University Press, 1988.

Sayre, Robert. *Thoreau and the American Indians.* Princeton: Princeton University Press, 1977.

Schiller, Nina Glick. "Transmigrants and Nation-States: Something Old and Something New in the Immigrant Experience." In *The Handbook of International Migration: The American Experience*, ed. Charles Hirshman, Josh Dewind and Philip Kasinitz. New York: Russell Sage Foundation, 1999.

Schuchard, Ronald. "Burbank with a Baedecker, Eliot with a Cigar: American Intellectuals, Anti-Semitism, and the Idea of Culture." *Modernism/Modernity* 10.1 (January 2003): 1–56.

Eliot's Dark Angel: Intersections of Life and Art. New York: Oxford University Press, 1999.

Schwartz, Sanford. *The Matrix of Modernism: Pound, Eliot, and Early Twentieth-Century Thought.* Princeton: Princeton University Press, 1985.

Scruggs, Charles, *Sweet Home: Invisible Cities in the Afro-American Novel*. Baltimore, MD: Johns Hopkins University Press, 1993.

Searl, Eva. "T. S. Eliot's *Four Quartets* and Wilson Harris' *The Waiting Room*." In *Commonwealth Literature and the Modern World*, ed. H. Maes-Jelinek. Brussels: Didier, 1976: 51–59.

Senghor, Léopold Sédar. *Liberté*. 5 vols. Paris: Éditions du Seuil, 1964.

Sharpe, William Chapman. *Unreal Cities: Urban Figuration in Wordsworth, Baudelaire, Whitman, Eliot, and Williams*. Baltimore, MD: Johns Hopkins University Press, 1990.

Sigg, Eric. *The American T. S. Eliot: A Study of the Early Writings*. Cambridge: Cambridge University Press, 1989.

Singh, Amritjit, and Peter Schmidt, eds. *Postcolonial Theory and the United States: Race, Ethnicity, and Literature*. Jackson: University Press of Mississippi, 2000.

Slotkin, Richard. *Regeneration Through Violence: The Mythology of the American Frontier, 1600–1860*. Middletown, CT: Wesleyan University Press, 1973.

Smith, Grover. *T. S. Eliot and the Use of Memory*. Lewisburg: Bucknell University Press, 1996.

 T. S. Eliot's Poetry and Plays: A Study in Sources and Meaning. Chicago: University of Chicago Press, 1956.

Smith, Stan. *The Origins of Modernism: Eliot, Pound, Yeats and the Rhetorics of Renewal*. New York: Harvester, 1994.

Soldo, John. *The Tempering of T. S. Eliot*. Ann Arbor: UMI Research Press, 1983.

Sollors, Werner. *Beyond Ethnicity: Consent and Descent in American Culture*. New York: Oxford University Press, 1986.

 Neither Black Nor White Yet Both: Thematic Explorations of Interracial Literature. Cambridge, MA: Harvard University Press, 1997.

 ed. *The Invention of Ethnicity*. New York: Oxford University Press, 1989.

Spender, Stephen. *The Struggle of the Modern*. London: Hamish Hamilton, 1963.

Symons, Arthur. *The Symbolist Movement in Literature*. 1908. Revised and enlarged edn. New York: Haskell House, 1971.

Tate, Allen, ed. *T. S. Eliot: The Man and His Work*. London: Chatto and Windus, 1967.

Terada, Rei. *Derek Walcott's Poetry: American Mimicry*. Boston: Northeastern University Press, 1992.

Thadal, Marc Roland. *Jacques Roumain: l'unité d'une oeuvre*. Port-au-Prince, Haiti: Collection Quisqueye, 1997.

Thieme, John. *Derek Walcott*. Manchester: Manchester University Press, 1999.

Torres-Saillant, Silvio. *Caribbean Poetics: Toward an Aesthetic of West Indian Literature*. Cambridge: Cambridge University Press, 1997.

Tracy, Steven. *Langston Hughes and the Blues*. Urbana: University of Illinois Press, 1988.

Trouillot, D'Henock. *Dimension et limites de Jacques Roumain.* 2nd edn. Port-au-Prince, Haiti: Éditions Faradin, 1981.

Unterecker, John. *Voyager: A Life of Hart Crane.* New York: Farrar, Straus and Giroux, 1969.

Valéry, Paul. *Variété.* Vol. II. Paris: Librairie Gallinard, 1930.

Vendler, Helen. *Coming of Age as a Poet.* Cambridge, MA: Harvard University Press, 2003.

   The Given and the Made: Strategies of Poetic Redefinition. Cambridge, MA: Harvard University Press, 1995.

Walcott, Derek. *The Arkansas Testament.* New York: Farrar, Straus and Giroux, 1987.

   "The Caribbean: Culture or Mimicry?" *Journal of Interamerican Studies and World Affairs* 16.1 (February 1974).

   Collected Poems, 1948–1984. New York: Farrar, Straus and Giroux, 1986.

   Conversations with Derek Walcott. Ed. William Baer. Jackson: University of Mississippi Press, 1996.

   Epitaph for the Young: XII Cantos. Barbados: Advocate, 1949.

   "For All Craftsmen." *Bim* 5.19 (December 1953): 166.

   In a Green Night. London: Jonathan Cape, 1962.

   Interview. *South Bank Show,* ITV. London: January 15, 1989.

   Interview. *Trinidad Express* (March 14, 1982).

   Poems. Kingston, Jamaica: Kingston City Printery, [1951].

   "Reflections on *Omeros.*" *South Atlantic Quarterly* 29.2 (Spring 1997): 229–246.

   Sea Grapes. London: J. Cape, 1976.

   Tiepolo's Hound. New York: Farrar, Straus, and Giroux, 2000.

   What the Twilight Says. New York: Farrar, Straus and Giroux, 1998.

Watts, Edward. *Writing and Postcolonialism in the Early Republic.* Charlottesville: University Press of Viriginia, 1998.

Weisbuch, Robert. *Atlantic Double-Cross: American Literature and British Influence in the Age of Emerson.* Chicago: University of Chicago Press, 1986.

Werner, Craig. "Blues for T. S. Eliot and Langston Hughes: The Afro-Modernist Aesthetic of Harlem Gallery." *Black American Literature Forum* 24.3 (Fall 1990): 453–472.

Wetherill, Peter Michael. *Charles Baudelaire et la poésie d'Edgar Allan Poe.* Paris: A. G. Nizet, 1962.

Wetzel, Andreas. "Poe/Baudelaire: Poetics in Translation." *Cincinnati Romance Review* 6 (1987).

Whalen, Terence. *Edgar Allan Poe and the Masses: The Political Economy of Literature in Antebellum America.* Princeton: Princeton University Press, 1999.

Whitman, Walt. *Complete Poetry and Collected Prose.* Ed. J. Kaplan. New York: Library of America, 1982.

   Leaves of Grass: Comprehensive Reader's Edition. Ed. H. Blodgett and S. Bradley. New York: New York University Press, 1965.

Williams, Raymond. *The Politics of Modernism: Against the New Conformists.* London: Verso, 1989.

Wilson, Edmund. *Axel's Castle: A Study in the Imaginative Literature of 1870–1930.* New York: Scribner's, 1931.

Winters, Ivor. *In Defense of Reason.* New York: The Swallows Press, 1947.

Wordsworth, William. *The Fourteen-Book Prelude.* Ed. W. J. B. Owen. Ithaca: Cornell University Press.

   Poems, In Two Volumes, and Other Poems, 1800–1807. Ed. Jared Curtis. Ithaca: Cornell University Press, 1983.

Young, Howard, ed. *T. S. Eliot and Hispanic Modernity, 1924–1993.* Denver: Society of Spanish and Spanish-American Studies, 1994.

Index